Analyzing Literary Works

ANALYZING
LITERARY
WORKS

a guide for college students

edited by

Lee Steinmetz
Eastern Illinois University

═══════

ROW, PETERSON AND COMPANY
Evanston, Illinois   Elmsford, New York

Published for sale in the United States and Canada

Copyright © 1962

ROW, PETERSON AND COMPANY

6384

ACKNOWLEDGMENTS

The editor wishes to express his thanks to the following publishers and individuals for granting permission to reprint the following selections:

Excerpts from Quentin Anderson's "George Eliot in *Middlemarch*," from *From Dickens to Hardy*, Copyright 1958. Edited by Boris Ford. Reprinted by permission of Penguin Books, Limited.

Virginia Ogden Birdsall's "Hawthorne's Fair-Haired Maidens: The Fading Light," from *PMLA*, LXXV (June, 1960), 250–56. Reprinted by permission of The Modern Language Association of America.

Carl Bode's review of Henry Beetle Hough's *Thoreau of Walden: The Man and His Eventful Life*, from *American Literature*, XXVIII (January, 1957), 534. Reprinted by permission of the Duke University Press.

E. K. Brown's analysis of *The Professor's House*. Reprinted from *Willa Cather: A Critical Biography* by E. K. Brown, by permission of Alfred A. Knopf, Inc. Copyright 1953 by Margaret Brown.

I. B. Cauthen, Jr.'s "Fielding's Digressions in *Joseph Andrews*," from *College English*, XVII (April, 1956), 379–81. Reprinted by permission of the National Council of Teachers of English.

Excerpts from Clifton Fadiman's "My Life Is an Open Book: Confessions and Digressions of an Incurable," from *Reading I've Liked*, Copyright 1941 by Simon and Schuster, Inc. Edited by Clifton Fadiman.

Norman Foerster's "Thoreau as Artist," from *Sewanee Review*, XXIX (January, 1921), 2–13. Reprinted by permission of Norman Foerster and *The Sewanee Review*.

Graham Greene's "The Lost Childhood," from *The Lost Childhood* by Graham Greene. Copyright 1951 by Graham Greene. Reprinted by permission of The Viking Press, Inc. (for United States) and Laurence Pollinger, Limited (other rights).

Alfred Kazin's Introduction to *The Stature of Theodore Dreiser*, Copyright 1955. Edited by Alfred Kazin and Charles Shapiro. Reprinted by permission of the Indiana University Press.

Arnold Kettle's analysis of *Tess of the D'Urbervilles*, from *An Introduction to the English Novel* by Arnold Kettle, Copyright 1951. Reprinted by permission of The Hutchinson Group.

Murray Krieger's "Conrad's *Youth*: A Naive Opening to Art and Life," from *College English*, XX (March, 1959), 275–80. Reprinted by permission of the National Council of Teachers of English.

Lauriat Lane, Jr.'s "Why *Huckleberry Finn* Is a Great World Novel," from *College English*, XVII (October, 1955), 1–5. Reprinted by permission of the National Council of Teachers of English.

Marion Lee's "Irony in Chapter XXII of *Huckleberry Finn*," from *Quivera*, III (March, 1958), 43–47. Reprinted by permission of *Quivera*.

Excerpts from W. Somerset Maugham's *The Summing Up*, from *The Summing Up*. Copyright 1938 by W. Somerset Maugham. Reprinted by permission of Doubleday & Company, Inc. (for United States) and A. P. Watt & Son (other rights).

USING THE MANUAL

This manual is designed, among other things, to aid students in the preparation of a literary research paper. A student using the manual for this purpose will choose some reputable author for study, read books by and about him, and, as he reads, select some subject with which his author deals as the basis for his study. The notes he takes on this subject will help him formulate a thesis, which he may ultimately work into a final research paper. (I have always required students to study novelists as the basis for their research, although there is no reason why some classes, or some students within a given class, could not study short story writers, essayists, or even literary historians.)

Instructors using the manual in this way will face the question of how to provide a student with a subject that will be congenial to him, and how soon to provide the subject. This question, which will be given immediacy by the time limitations of the course, is one which various instructors will no doubt choose to answer differently. It would be quite possible simply to provide a student with a subject relating to his writer—to assign him, during the first week of class, the task of studying "The Negro in the Works of William Faulkner" or "The Conflict between Generations in the Works of Willa Cather." My practice has consistently been to let students find their own subjects. This may be less efficient, but it strikes me as more realistic, and possibly more valuable, ultimately, to the student. In practice, students vary considerably in the time it takes them to hit upon a workable subject. One student will read Thomas Wolfe's *Look Homeward, Angel* and immediately decide that the subject of "The Search in the Novels of Thomas Wolfe" is the subject he wishes to pursue. Another student, equally knowledgeable, will read several novels by Robert Penn Warren before deciding upon "The Use of Literary Allusion in the Novels of Robert Penn Warren." A third student, following his initial reading, will find himself interested in, say, his writer's treatment of conflicts between various racial groups, but may discover, to his dismay, that his writer has had the audacity completely to ignore this subject in other works, and that he will consequently be obliged to change, or at least modify, his original intention. And so on. All of this seems to me healthy, since it corresponds to the situation that any research scholar faces: that of allowing a subject to define itself as study progresses.

The choice of a writer, in the case of the individual student, may likewise be arrived at variously. Each student within a given class may select a writer of his own choosing, presumably from a list of writers provided by the instructor, or all students within a given class may be asked to study the same writer. Both practices are rewarding, although in slightly different ways. Having students choose different authors allows for more flexibility within a course, and, as an interesting by-product of this approach, some students will become interested in a writer other than the one they are studying, because of the work of one of their classmates. Having students read the same writer allows, quite naturally, for more class discussion concerning the writer's works.

The manual assumes that students will write weekly essays as their research progresses, and that this work will culminate in a final critical research paper. The pattern suggested is threefold: first, the students will read, and discuss in class, one or more examples of good critical writing which does the sort of thing they will be asked to do; second, they will write papers of their own; third, they will discuss and criticize what they have written. The space given in this manual to critical essays about literature reflects the importance I attach to step one of this threefold process. Whatever may be the past history of a student's reading, he is not likely to bring to his work a large backlog of reading in literary criticism. I have become increasingly skeptical about asking students to perform a type of writing with which they have had no reading acquaintance. This is not to suggest that students be asked to indulge in slavish imitation. The critical essays in this manual are here, not to provide models, but to create in students a greater awareness than they may possess of the possibilities open to them in the area of critical writing.

An important feature of the manual is the opportunity it affords the student to practice systematically and over a period of time the various expository techniques used in critical writing. If an instructor chooses to center his entire course, both in and out of the classroom, around the research his students are doing, he will discover that his more able students will produce research papers that are better than he would have supposed likely, largely because mistakes they would have made, had they worked on their papers independently, have already been made, and corrected, in the weekly essays they have written as their study progressed. These weekly essays will not only give students training in expository techniques, but will also serve as a sort of continual sounding board for their ideas as they evolve.

I have resisted the temptation to give formal treatment in the manual to specific exercises which I have found useful in conducting classes, on the assumption that each instructor will discover what works best and is most helpful with his own classes. I might indicate in passing a single *modus operandi* which students seem to find particularly helpful and enjoyable. In keeping with the critical attitude which a course predicated on this manual attempts to foster, I make considerable use in class of essays that students themselves have written. Following each writing assignment, up to several class periods may be spent discussing some of their writing with the class. At the beginning of the term, the majority of students may be rather limited in their ability to criticize constructively the writing of their classmates, largely because they need to be supplied with a critical vocabulary and a critical point of view; but with training they can become remarkably acute commentators on the work of their peers. (Class sessions, by the way, are livelier and comments more acute when the essay to be discussed, instead of simply being read to the students, is duplicated and a copy given to each student.)

A word about the organization of the manual. Chapters 1–9, concerned with various types of critical writing, provide examples of critical writing for study as well as suggestions for the students' weekly essays. Within this section of the manual, the first six chapters are centered around primary source material, while the seventh, eighth, and ninth chapters concern themselves with writing based on secondary sources. The arrangement of these chapters indicates a workable order of use, although the order in which they are used may understandably vary somewhat among users of the manual, depending upon their approach. I have consciously included more areas of study and more writing assignments within this section of the manual than I find time to use in a single course, in order to provide some choice within a given course, or from term to term.

Since Chapter 10 concerns techniques of research and critical writing, the material in this chapter is applicable to the writing that students do throughout the entire term. The material is arranged in what seems to be the most usable order, although the exact point at which a given part of the chapter will be introduced may well vary from one instructor to another.

Chapter 11 provides several examples of critical writing of the sort toward which students will ultimately be directing their efforts, and hence furnishes examples for study.

Although this manual provides material for an entire course in the writing of a literary research paper, it should be useful in at least two other ways. While working toward a final research paper gives a course a certain unity and direction, and students a concrete goal, the writing of such a final paper should not, it seems to me, be looked upon as a requisite to using the manual. Each writing assignment suggested in the manual possesses a validity of its own, and the manual may consequently be used in any course in expository writing where the instructor wishes the writing to be critical and to possess a literary frame of reference. (As a matter of fact, the final paper need not be radically different from the previous essays the students will have written throughout the course. A good plan, I have found, is to limit final papers to a maximum of around two thousand words, in order to encourage succinctness and conciseness.)

The manual should also prove useful as a supplementary text in literature courses where students are asked to write about the literature they are studying, since it provides help in answering questions such as students in literature courses frequently ask when faced with the task of writing critical papers.

Lee Steinmetz

Eastern Illinois University

TABLE OF CONTENTS

3 A Comparison of Two Works

4 An Analysis of the Form of a Work

5 The Evolution of a Writer's Thought

6 An Analysis of Point of View

7 The Writing of a Book Review

8 The Study of a Writer's Reputation

9 The Writing of Self-evaluations

10   Techniques of Research and Critical Writing

11   The Critical Essay

THE CHOICE OF A WRITER

Introduction

The first step in any literary study must be the selection of a subject. When this subject happens to be a writer, the choice, and one's attitude toward it, will presumably grow out of past interests and past experiences with literature.

Interest in past reading experiences has prompted more than one writer to comment. Below are two essays whose authors write about their interest in literature. In "The Lost Childhood," Graham Greene indicates the steps leading up to his interest in Marjorie Bowen's *The Viper of Milan,* and the effect of this interest upon him; the excerpts from Clifton Fadiman's "My Life Is an Open Book" recount Fadiman's childhood reading habits and explain his interest in particular books.

GRAHAM GREENE

The Lost Childhood

*P*erhaps it is only in childhood that books have any deep influence on our lives. In later life we admire, we are entertained, we may modify some views we already hold, but we are more likely to find in books merely a confirmation of what is in our minds already: as in a love affair it is our own features that we see reflected flatteringly back.

But in childhood all books are books of divination, telling us about the future, and like the fortune teller who sees a long journey in the cards or death by water they influence the future. I suppose that is why books excited us so much. What do we ever get nowadays from reading to equal the excitement and the revelation in those first fourteen years? Of course I should be interested to hear that a new novel by Mr. E. M. Forster was going to appear this spring, but I could never compare that mild expectation of civilized pleasure with the missed heartbeat, the appalled glee I felt when I found on a library shelf a novel by Rider Haggard, Percy Westerman, Captain Brereton or Stanley Weyman which I had not read before. No, it is in those early years that I would look for the crisis, the moment when life took a new slant in its journey towards death.

I remember distinctly the suddenness with which a key turned in a lock and I found I could read—not just the sentences in a reading book with the syllables coupled like railway carriages, but a real book. It was paper-covered with the picture of a boy, bound and gagged, dangling at the end of a rope inside a well with the water rising above his waist— an adventure of Dixon Brett, detective. All a long summer holiday I kept my secret, as I believed: I did not want anybody to know that I could read. I suppose I half consciously realized even then that this was the dangerous moment. I was safe so long as I could not read—the wheels had not begun to turn, but now the future stood around on bookshelves everywhere waiting for the child to choose—the life of a chartered accountant perhaps, a colonial civil servant, a planter in China, a steady job in a bank, happiness and misery, eventually one particular form of death, for surely we choose our death much as we choose our job. It grows out of our acts and our evasions, out of our fears and out of our moments of courage. I suppose my mother must have discovered my secret, for on the journey home I was presented for the train with another real book, a copy of Ballantyne's *Coral Island* with only a single picture to look at, a coloured frontispiece. But I would admit nothing. All the long journey I stared at the one picture and never opened the book.

But there on the shelves at home (so many shelves for we were a large family) the books waited—one book in particular, but before I reach that one down let me take a few others at random from the shelf. Each was a crystal in which the child dreamed that he saw life moving. Here in a cover stamped dramatically in several colours was Captain Gilson's *The Pirate Aeroplane*. I must have read that book six times at least—the story of a lost civilization in the Sahara and of a villainous Yankee pirate with an aeroplane like a box kite and bombs the size of tennis balls who held the golden city to ransom. It was saved by the hero, a young subaltern who crept up to the pirate camp to put the aeroplane out of action. He was captured and watched his enemies dig his grave. He was to be shot at dawn, and to pass the time and keep his mind from uncomfortable thoughts the amiable Yankee pirate played cards with him—the mild nursery game of Kuhn Kan. The memory of that nocturnal game on the edge of life haunted me for years, until I set it to rest at last in one of my own novels with a game of poker played in remotely similar circumstances.

And here is *Sophy of Kravonia* by Anthony Hope—the story of a kitchen-maid who became a queen. One of the first films I ever saw, about 1911, was made from that book, and I can hear still the rumble of the Queen's guns crossing the high Kravonian pass beaten hollowly out of a single piano. Then there was Stanley Weyman's *The Story of Francis Cludde,* and above all other books at that time of my life, *King Solomon's Mines.*

This book did not perhaps provide the crisis, but it certainly influenced the future. If it had not been for that romantic tale of Allan Quatermain, Sir Henry Curtis, Captain Good, and, above all, the ancient witch Gagool, would I at nineteen have studied the appointments list of the Colonial Office and very nearly picked on the Nigerian Navy for a career? And later, when surely I ought to have known better, the odd African fixation remained. In 1935 I found myself sick with fever on a camp bed in a Liberian native's hut with a candle going out in an empty whisky bottle and a rat moving in the shadows. Wasn't it the incurable fascination of Gagool with her bare yellow skull, the wrinkled scalp that moved and contracted like the hood of a cobra, that led me to work all through 1942 in a little stuffy office in Freetown, Sierra Leone? There is not much in common between the land of the Kukuanas, behind the desert and the mountain range of Sheba's Breast, and a tin-roofed house on a bit of swamp where the vultures moved like domestic turkeys and the pi-dogs kept me awake on moonlight nights with their wailing, and the white women yellowed by atebrin drove by to the club; but the two belonged at any rate to the same continent, and, however distantly, to the same region of the imagination—the region of uncertainty, of not knowing the way about. Once I came a little nearer to Gagool and her witch-hunters, one night in Zigita on the Liberian side of the French Guinea border, when my servants sat in their shuttered hut with their hands over their eyes and someone beat a drum and a whole town stayed behind closed doors while the big bush devil—whom it would mean blindness to see—moved between the huts.

But *King Solomon's Mines* could not finally satisfy. It was not the right answer. The key did not quite fit. Gagool I could recognize—didn't she wait for me in dreams every night in the passage by the linen cupboard, near the nursery door? and she continues to wait, when the mind is sick or tired, though now she is dressed in the theological garments of Despair and speaks in Spenser's accents:

> The longer life, I wote the greater sin,
> The greater sin, the greater punishment.

Yes, Gagool has remained a permanent part of the imagination, but

Quatermain and Curtis—weren't they, even when I was only ten years old, a little too good to be true? They were men of such unyielding integrity (they would only admit to a fault in order to show how it might be overcome) that the wavering personality of a child could not rest for long against those monumental shoulders. A child, after all, knows most of the game—it is only an attitude to it that he lacks. He is quite well aware of cowardice, shame, deception, disappointment. Sir Henry Curtis perched upon a rock bleeding from a dozen wounds but fighting on with the remnant of the Greys against the hordes of Twala was too heroic. These men were like Platonic ideas: they were not life as one had already begun to know it.

But when—perhaps I was fourteen by that time—I took Miss Marjorie Bowen's *The Viper of Milan* from the library shelf, the future for better or worse really struck. From that moment I began to write. All the other possible futures slid away: the potential civil servant, the don, the clerk had to look for other incarnations. Imitation after imitation of Miss Bowen's magnificent novel went into exercise books—stories of sixteenth-century Italy or twelfth-century England marked with enormous brutality and a despairing romanticism. It was as if I had been supplied once and for all with a subject.

Why? On the surface *The Viper of Milan* is only the story of a war between Gian Galeazzo Visconti, Duke of Milan, and Mastino della Scala, Duke of Verona, told with zest and cunning and an amazing pictorial sense. Why did it creep in and colour and explain the terrible living world of the stone stairs and the never quiet dormitory? It was no good in that real world to dream that one would ever be a Sir Henry Curtis, but della Scala who at last turned from an honesty that never paid and betrayed his friends and died dishonoured and a failure even at treachery—it was easier for a child to escape behind his mask. As for Visconti, with his beauty, his patience and his genius for evil, I had watched him pass by many a time in his black Sunday suit smelling of mothballs. His name was Carter. He exercised terror from a distance like a snowcloud over the young fields. Goodness has only once found a perfect incarnation in the human body and never will again, but evil can always find a home there. Human nature is not black and white but black and grey. I read all that in *The Viper of Milan* and I looked round and I saw that it was so.

There was another theme I found there. At the end of *The Viper of Milan*—you will remember if you have once read it—comes the great scene of complete success—della Scala is dead, Ferrara, Verona, Novara, Mantua have all fallen, the messengers pour in with news of fresh victories, the whole outside is cracking up, and Visconti sits and jokes in the wine light. I was not on the classical side or I would have discovered, I suppose, in Greek literature instead of in Miss Bowen's novel the sense of doom that lies over success—the feeling that the pendulum is about to swing. That too made sense; one looked around and saw the doomed everywhere—the champion runner who one day would sag over the tape; the head of the school who would atone, poor devil, during forty dreary undistinguished years; the scholar . . . and when success began to touch oneself too, however mildly, one could only pray that failure would not be held off for too long.

One had lived for fourteen years in a wild jungle country without a map, but now the paths had been traced and naturally one had to follow them. But I think it was Miss Bowen's apparent zest that made me want to write. One could not read her without believing that to write was to live and to enjoy, and before one had discovered one's mistake it was too late—the first book one does enjoy. Anyway she had given me my pattern—religion might later explain it to me in other terms, but the pattern was already there—perfect evil walking the world where perfect good can never walk again, and only the pendulum ensures that after all in the end justice is done. Man is never satisfied, and often I have wished that my hand had not moved further than *King Solomon's Mines,* and that the future I had taken down from the nursery shelf had been a district office in Sierra Leone and twelve tours of malarial duty and a finishing dose of blackwater fever when the danger of retirement approached. What is the good of wishing? The books are always there, the moment of crisis waits, and now our children in their turn are taking down the future and opening the pages. In his poem "Germinal" A. E. wrote:

> In ancient shadows and twilights
>   Where childhood had strayed,
> The world's great sorrows were born
>   And its heroes were made.
> In the lost boyhood of Judas
>   Christ was betrayed.

Comments and Questions

1. Graham Greene says that, as adults, "we are more likely to find in books merely a confirmation of what is in our minds already." Think of some serious work you have read lately, in the light of this statement.

2. Throughout his essay Greene mentions death a number of times. Study his development of this subject and its relationship to what he says about books and reading.

3. What, exactly, differentiates *The Viper of Milan* from Greene's previous reading?

4. Did the knowledge which came to Greene from reading *The Viper of Milan* make him happy? Sad? What, as nearly as you can define it, is Greene's attitude toward this new knowledge?

5. Since he is writing an informal essay, Greene is concerned with giving a certain impression of himself, with reflecting himself as a distinct personality. What impression of Greene does the essay provide?

6. Note Greene's constant use of metaphorical expression ("a key turned in a lock"; "the wheels had not begun to turn"; "each was a crystal"; "that nocturnal game on the edge of life"; "a child . . . knows most of the game"; "in a wild jungle country without a map"). What do these metaphors contribute to the meaning of the essay?

7. Is the poem, "Germinal," a fitting close for the essay? What meaning does Greene give the poem as a result of what he has written; and, conversely, what added dimension does the poem give the essay?

CLIFTON FADIMAN

from

My Life Is an Open Book: Confessions and Digressions of an Incurable

*T*hose to whom reading is fated to become important generally shake hands with books early. But this is not always true. Many distinguished writers were blockheads at their letters until a comparatively advanced age. I think, however, of an undistinguished one who was a busy reader at four: me. My first book was entitled *The Overall Boys*. *The Overall Boys* was and doubtless still is a rousing tale of two devoted brothers, aged five and seven, and their monosyllabic adventures on a farm. The style was of transparent lucidity. I found *The Overall Boys* a perfect job then, and looking back, I haven't yet been able to detect any flaws in it. I remember it in greater detail and certainly with greater pleasure than I do the 576-page novel I finished yesterday. At four I was convinced that *The Overall Boys* represented the peak of the art of narrative and sternly rejected all attempts to make me continue my reading adventures. This resistance endured for a lengthy period—about a week, I should say. Then I broke down, tried another book, and have been doing the same sort of thing ever since. But all devout readers will agree that my first literary judgment was correct. Everything after *The Overall Boys* has been anticlimax. The same new world can never be discovered twice. One's first book, kiss, home run, is always the best.

Between the ages of four and ten I read but moderately and with absolute catholicity. We had in our household the usual meaningless miscellany that accumulates if the parents are not specifically literary. Thus I read whatever lay behind the glassed-in shelves of two dreary-looking black-walnut bookcases. I devoured the standard "boys' books" scornfully discarded by my elder brother. I bored my way through at least ten volumes of an unreadable set of historical novels by some worthy named Mühlbach, I think, and got absolutely nothing from them; the same result would be achieved were I to read them now. I read an adventure story about the Belgian Congo that made an anti-imperialist out of me when I was eight; I have seen no reason to change my views since then. Something called *Buck Jones at Annapolis* similarly made me permanently skeptical of the warrior virtues.

I read an odd collection of "daring" books that many families of the period kept around the house, often hidden under lock and key: Reginal Wright Kaufman's *The House of Bondage;* something called *The Yoke,* which was on the same order; Maupassant complete, though this may not have been until I had reached the mature estate of twelve or thirteen; and similar luridnesses. These had no effect of any sort on me, as far as I can recollect, though I suppose a psychoanalyst could, at a price, make me tell a different story.

The child reader is an automatic selecting mechanism. What he is not emotionally ready to absorb, his mental system quietly rejects. When in later years I became a teacher of literature I could never see the point in censoring my young charges' extracurricular reading. Very often the mothers (never the fathers) of my high-school students would ask me to explain my refusal to forbid Mary or John to read James Joyce's *Ulysses.* I never offered any satisfactory explanation except to say that if John or Mary were ready to understand *Ulysses* then they were ready to understand *Ulysses,* which was a Good Thing. If they were not ready to understand it, which was apt to be the case, then *Ulysses* would at most waste their time, on which I was not prepared to set any exaggerated value. Often an anxious mother would inquire whether I didn't agree that the last chapter (Mrs. Leopold Bloom's uncorseted memories of an exuberant life) was shocking. My reply may have been frivolous, but it seems to me it contained the germ of the truth: that she found it shocking mainly because she had not had the chance to read *Ulysses* when she was seventeen, wherein Mary or John had an advantage over her. This generally closed, without settling, the controversy.

As you can see, part of my four-to-ten reading was unorthodox for a small child (I forgot to tell you that I also toddled through a volume of Ibsen, and found him impenetrable) but the unorthodoxies had no effect whatsoever. What I really liked was what any small boy or girl would like—what I was ready for. This included, of course, a moderate amount of what is called trash—the Rover Boys, Horatio Alger, Wild West yarns, Jack Harkaway, the whole conventional canon of those days.

I say trash. Actually such books are "trash" only by standards which should not be applied to children's reading. They have the incalculable value that listening to perfectly inane adult conversation holds for children: they increase the child's general awareness. They provide admittedly rough paradigms of character, motivation, life experiences. That is why it seems to me that the trash of my generation was superior to the trash of today. I submit that *The Rover Boys in the Everglades* and *Frank on a Gunboat* are preferable to Superman and his kind on two counts: they were cleanly and clearly written, and their characters were credible and not entirely unrelated to the child's experience. When I was nine I could learn something interesting about life from even such highly colored affairs as the Frank Merriwell series, but I know that my son can learn nothing whatsoever of genuine interest (that is, which he can check against the expanding universe within himself) from the comics. I believe firmly that the current juvenile literature of the impossible is meretricious compared with the honest hackwork my own generation enjoyed. I also think that the kids are about ready to kick over this thriller fare in favor of something saner and more natural.

During my younger years, mainly between the ages of eight and ten, I, like my contemporaries, read a few "good" books, though they were not recommended to me as good. Such recommendations are hardly necessary. The child, if reasonably intelligent, has almost infallible good taste. Probably his good taste reaches its peak at that time. We all felt, when we encountered *Tom Sawyer* or, to hit a lower level, Thomas Bailey Aldrich's *Story of a Bad Boy* or, on a still lower level, that fine New England classic *Lem* (is it still read?) that these books had something not possessed by *The Pony Rider Boys in the Ozarks*. It wasn't that they were more exciting, for sometimes they weren't, but that they were more "real." The other books were read eagerly and with joy, and then forgotten—indeed, they were read to be forgotten, to be "finished." But *Tom Sawyer* was something you caught yourself remembering a week later, and a year later. I know now, of course, the reason the child feels these books is that the authors felt them. It is as simple as that. That is why the so-called "better" juveniles that flood the bookdealers' shelves every year—the skillfully constructed, highly educational, carefully suited-to-age, morally sanitary, psychologically impeccable children's books—don't really make much of a dent on the child's consciousness. They are constructed for "the market." I don't mean the commercial market, but the market that is supposed to be the child's brain, as if that brain were a kind of transaction center in which each transaction was expressible in definite educational quanta.

The trouble with these juveniles is that their authors are greatly interested in children and not at all interested in themselves. Now, when Mark Twain wrote *Tom Sawyer* and *Huckleberry Finn* he never stopped to figure out whether his "boy psychology" was correct, or whether his story was properly adapted to a given age level. He wrote because he was passionately interested in himself, and the Mississippi River in himself, and the boy still alive in himself. Children ever since have unconsciously felt this intense reality, and that's what they've loved.

They've loved *Huckleberry Finn* even though it is over their heads, or written in old-fashioned English or dialect, or concerned with events that happened a long time ago. The machine-turned juveniles of our own day are "carefully adapted to the child's understanding," and that isn't what the child really wants. The child wants to be puzzled—not too much, but just enough. He doesn't want the characters' motivations to be automatically clear to him. He wants the satisfaction of figuring them out. As a matter of fact, the child delights as much in ambiguity as he does in clarity. *Alice in Wonderland* is still an overwhelming favorite, not because it's so funny but because it's so strange; it's a wonderful, gorgeous puzzle.

In this connection I always think of a comment my great and good friend Hendrik van Loon made to me one day. Going over, for editorial purposes, one of his manuscripts intended primarily for children, I pointed out to him the large number of long, difficult words which, as I thought, youngsters would never understand. He merely said, "I put them in on purpose." I learned later what he meant: that long words tickle the fancy of children, that they like the slight atmosphere of mystery distilled by a really bang-up polysyllable.

I think also that children—just ordinary, wholesome children, not bookworms—are more sensitive to beautiful writing than is generally supposed. They'll read reams of careless prose with great enjoyment, but when they come across the real thing, they know it. I don't know how they know it, but they do. My own son is not overfond of books. Rather than forgo an airplane flight he would willingly see the Forty-second Street library vanish in flames. Two years ago I tried the young barbarian—he was about seven—on *The Wind in the Willows,* and he could make nothing of it. I tried him again some few months ago. He finished it with absorbed calm, clapped the book to, and said with finality, "Now, that's what I call well written!" He has never said this about any other book he's read, many of which he has "enjoyed" more. The fact is that *The Wind in the Willows* is the best-written book he has read so far, and he somehow knew it, though he had never been given any hint to affect his judgment.

The smooth confections the publishers turn out today are not well written in the sense that *The Wind in the Willows* is. They are merely correctly written. The authors in most cases have unconsciously curbed any impulse toward style, because style would express themselves, whereas they are supposed to be writing for the sake of the children. If they would forget all about the children and set down freely and lovingly the child in themselves, they might by some glorious accident produce masterpieces. *Little Women* was not written for little women or little men or little anybodies; it was the expression of a passionate memory. When Louisa May Alcott set herself to produce "juveniles," the result was often unsatisfactory, except when her native genius outwitted her conscious resolutions.

I am a firm believer in the newer methods of understanding and handling children. But it is arguable that they have made difficult the creation of a twentieth-century *Little Women* or *Alice in Wonderland*. Such books are the product not of knowledge, or even of wisdom, but of a kind of dream life, a dreaming-back to childhood on the part of the writer. That dream life and "child psychology" do not mix. That perhaps is why the modern child classics are not to be found in books at all, but in the cartoons of Walt Disney, master of an art newer, naïver, less touched by "science" than is the art of literature.

This has been a long and prosy digression, and while I'm at it, I'd like to make it a trifle longer. One of the games bibliomaniacs play in their weaker moments is the game of Century-Hencery, or literary prophecy. It's a harmless sport, the best part of it being that there can never be a loser. Here's how it works. You list the ten books you believe will be most widely read and generally admired a hundred or five hundred or a thousand years from now. Then you defend your choices. Making the unwarrantable assumption that in 2441 our civilization will still be recognizably related to that of 1941, I will now set down the ten works of literary imagination produced by the English-speaking race that I believe will be most universally alive (not merely admired in the schoolroom) five hundred years from now. Here they are, in no special order:

> The Plays of William Shakespeare
> *Moby Dick*
> *Gulliver's Travels*
> *Robinson Crusoe*
> *Alice in Wonderland*
> *Huckleberry Finn*
> *Little Women*
> Some novel of Charles Dickens, probably *David Copperfield*
>   or *Pickwick Papers*
> *Treasure Island*
> The Mother Goose Rhymes

It is possible that in constructing this list I have been ingenious rather than ingenuous. Whether by accident or design it reflects one of my favorite theories—that the gods tend to grant immortality to those books which, in addition to being great, are loved by children. For mark well that only two books out of the ten—Shakespeare and *Moby Dick*—cannot, generally speaking, be enjoyed by youngsters. Of the remaining eight, seven are usually ranked as children's favorites. My point is simple: as the generations pass, children's tastes change more slowly than do those of grownups. They are not affected by the ukases of critics or the whims of literary fashion. Thus Shakespeare was not universally admired by the eighteenth century and again may not be (though I'd place a small bet against that possibility) by the twenty-third. But the rhymes of Mother Goose—to my mind literature, even if of a simple order—have suffered no diminution of popularity and, being unmoved by the winds of literary doctrine, are not likely to suffer any.

This is what happens. All children who read at all are introduced at a fairly early age to, let us say, *Robinson Crusoe*. Most of them like it. Later on they meet it again in school. They are told it is literature, and its hold on their minds is re-enforced. Still later, in adult life, they may encounter it again, when they are ripe to see in it qualities not apparent to them as children. Any possible resistance to accepting *Robinson Crusoe* as a great book had been broken down years ago during their childhood. Thus *Robinson Crusoe*'s prestige remains undimmed. But a classic of greater artistic weight, such as *Paradise Lost*, does not enjoy the advantage of having been liked by readers as children. It is read by a small, select group of adults (college students) and so never passes into the consciousness of the generality. I do not mean that Milton will not be read five hundred years from now. I mean he will not be a casually accepted, generally enjoyed classic as I think *Little Women* or even *Treasure Island* (the most uncertain item, by the way, on my list) is apt to be. But remember, the book must be literature to begin with. Defoe's *Robinson Crusoe* will live, but A. R. Wyss' *The Swiss Family Robinson* is already dying.

We talk a great deal about the Greek classics. Yet what Greek classic has really penetrated among us? Not Plato surely, or any of the dramatists, but Homer and more particularly the simple, beautiful Greek myths that are read with pleasure by each generation of children. Similarly, I think Perrault and *The Three Musketeers* will outlast Proust and Stendhal, and Grimm's fairy tales still be widely read when Goethe is forgotten. If you wish to live long in the memory of men, perhaps you should not write for them at all. You should write what their children will enjoy. Or, to put it in another way and use a phrase that I think belongs to Lewis Mumford, a book already has one leg on immortality's trophy when "the words are for children and the meanings are for men."

May I make one or two further random comments on this list? Note that three titles—*Moby Dick, Robinson Crusoe,* and *Treasure Island*—have no women characters to speak of, and several of the others depend hardly at all on romantic interest. I do not believe that love, commonly considered one of the great staples of literature, tends as a subject to have any supreme preservative value. It is Dickens' sentiment and humor, not his lovers, that attract us. It is hardly the most romantic of Shakespeare's plays that stand highest in popular esteem. And Melville, in providing his masterpiece with an all-male cast, knew what he was doing.

Finally, if I were asked to make a wild stab at the one book likely to outlast the nine others, I would name *Alice in Wonderland*. This does not mean it is the "best" book on the list, for obviously it is not. In the end the best survives but the best of the best does not necessarily survive longest. Mankind will cling to what it admires, but even more fiercely will it cling to what it loves. And what we love perhaps above all else (as Dr. Freud pointed out in other and more dismaying connections) is ourselves as children. That is why I think it quite conceivable that Lewis Carroll will be read at some remote future time when Shakespeare is no more remembered than, let us say, Plautus and Terence are today. Twenty centuries from now Shakespeare may be entirely owned and operated by scholars. But I do not see why people should not still be laughing and exclaiming over *Alice in Wonderland*. Among the few things resistant to the tooth of time, great fantasy is one, and great fantasy is always the special possession of children. . . .

One comment I must add about my life as a reviewer. It is directly responsible for the making of this book [*Reading I've Liked*]. This is a book of rereadings. In fact, I had originally intended to call it *A Reviewer's Rereader*. It is the result of a re-examination or reconsideration of a great many of the thousands of books I have read and reviewed or just read. I wanted for my own satisfaction to discover how much of what I had read (or characteristic excerpts from it) would stand the entirely personal acid test of at least three reperusals.

In this business of reperusal I spent many interesting months. I got a great deal of fun out of it, and many disappointments, too. As I read I thought of some of my friends who never reread and of others who don't like any book unless, like game, it is just a trifle moldy. I must admit that I could never exercise any Christian charity on that old gander who said with lardy self-satisfaction that whenever a new book appeared he reread an old one. What did he do in 1849 when *David Copperfield* was a new book? I don't suppose he paid any attention in 1605 when a grizzled Spanish veteran came out with a tale called *Don Quixote de la Mancha*. And the first time Homer smote 'is bloomin' lyre I imagine our friend was busy scrutinizing the cave drawings of Altamira.

That most of the best books were written some time ago we may freely admit. But when you consider how much more Was than Now there has always been (with every passing moment busily increasing the odds in Was' favor) the circumstance is not surprising. But what of it? Can we May-fly mortals afford to spend all our brief allotment reading only the best? So much is missed that way. Transients and second-raters ourselves, why should we deny ourselves the warm and homely feeling of kinship that comes of reading the pages of other transients and second-raters?

"Old wine, old friends, old books are best," said Hug-the-Hearth, wrapping the mantle of conservatism about the trembling bones of his timidity. This may be so, in a measure, but that is no reason for not testing our palate against new wine, our personality against new friends, our mental pliancy against new books. How many males in full possession of their faculties have been put off the quest of novelty by the reflection that to know one woman is to know all? The rut of "the best that has been thought and said in the world" is nonetheless a rut, if a noble one.

How often have you not fled the biblio-hobbyists who sport a favorite author as they would a favorite flower? The whimsical bores who "know their Alice"—and little else. The Jane-ites, so proud and prejudiced, for whom nothing has happened to the English novel since Miss Austen turned up her genteel toes. The Thackerayans, for whom rereading *The Newcomes* semiannually is a religious rite. The W. S. Gilbert-quoters, the Moby Dickensians—but why go on? Somerset Maugham puts it mildly but well: "I know people who read the same book over and over again. It can only be that they read with their eyes and not with their sensibility. It is a mechanical exercise like the Tibetan turning of a prayer wheel. It is doubtless a harmless occupation but they are wrong if they think it is an intelligent one."

On the other hand—these matters are always conveniently ambidextrous—he is no less tiresome who "keeps up with the new books" as though current literature were a motor-paced bicycle race. I should say they are well worth shunning, those earnest souls to whom reading is a form of competition, who, on finishing a new publication, feel they have beaten someone or something. Such worship of the book-of-the-day is infantile.

My venerated Columbia professor, Raymond Weaver, whose knowledge and personality are alike classical, is credited with an apposite legend. At a dinner party one evening a bright young thing queried, in her most buffed and polished finishing-school voice, "Mr. Weaver, have you read So-and-so's book?" (naming a modish best seller of the moment).

Mr. Weaver confessed he had not.

"Oh, you'd better hurry up—it's been out over three months!"

Mr. Weaver, an impressive gentleman with a voice like a Greek herald, turned to her, and said, "My dear young lady, have you read Dante's *Divine Comedy*?"

"No."

"Then you'd better hurry up—it's been out over six hundred years."

To the average male there is something a little ridiculous in the aspect of a woman wearing a hat which he has just seen advertised as the very latest thing. More, to him she is provincial. Lacking the independence that would permit her to choose a hat of yesterday, of tomorrow, or even a timeless hat, if timeless hats there be, she is, in his eyes, the prisoner of the moment, her hat-horizon bounded by the confines of a split second. The stylish (repulsive word) hat has no true style.

As with millinery, so with literature. There is no reader so parochial as the one who reads none but this morning's books. Books are not rolls, to be devoured only when they are hot and fresh. A good book retains its interior heat and will warm a generation yet unborn. He who confines himself only to today's books is more narrowly circumscribed by time than he who reads only yesteryear's. You can be inexorably old-fashioned or perennially up to the minute. In either case you are dated.

We are driven, then, to the dull, sane conclusion that the proper diet is a mixed one. No special magic virtue inheres in either old or new books.

But let us return to our muttonhead who, whenever a new book appeared, reread an old one. He must have owned one of Mr. Lindbergh's mechanical hearts, incapable of mutation, for rereading is one of the barometers by which we note the changes in our mental and emotional climate. Rarely do we reread a book once greatly loved and receive from it exactly our original pleasure. Note that I say receive; this is not to assert that we cannot recall our original pleasure, but that is not the same thing.

Of this recall value William Hazlitt says: "In reading a book which is an old favourite with me (say the first novel I ever read) I not only have the pleasure of imagination and of a critical relish of the work, but the pleasures of memory added to it. It recalls the same feelings and associations which I had in first reading it, and which I can never have again in any other way. Standard productions of this kind are links in the chain of our conscious being. They bind together the different scattered divisions of our personal identity. They are landmarks and guides in our journey through life. They are pegs and loops on which we can hang up, or from which we can take down, at pleasure, the wardrobe of a moral imagination, the relics of our best affections, the tokens and records of our happiest hours. They are 'for thoughts and for remembrance!' They are like Fortunatus's Wishing-Cap—they give us the best riches—those of Fancy; and transport us, not over half the globe, but (which is better) over half our lives, at a word's notice!"

There you have the sunny side of rereading. In the course of preparing this collection, however, I have constantly been confronted by a shady side also. For the "pleasures of memory" are not all Hazlitt cracked them up to be. Most of the time rereading is a melancholy experience. Turning pages out of which a decade or two ago surprise and excitement fairly leaped at us, we find surprise and excitement no longer summonable. A breath of autumn invades the heart—vacancy, almost a kind of paralysis. Surely this is not the book we once read, but a faded photograph of it, with all its original lights and shadows smoked over into a dim, pathetic grayness. We close the book ruefully. It is, we say, dated.

Dated? But perhaps it is we who are dated. The book may have died, but just as frequently we have died ourselves, or changed our temperament just as the physiologists tell us we replace our bodies completely every seven years or so. The other day, for example, I reread Knut Hamsun's *Pan*. A score of years ago it moved me greatly; today I cannot stomach it. Who has changed, Hamsun or I? Like the unfortunate little old woman in the rhyme, the one whose petticoats were half shot from under her, I found myself wondering if this could be I.

And it was not I, or not the same I. I tried to figure it out. Perhaps my taste had decayed. Or perhaps the book had been bad all along, and my original judgment was faulty. My pride (one of the elements of the human personality which apparently remains constant) prevented me from accepting either solution with pleasure. I introspected busily for a half-hour or so, and came up with an odd tangle of theoretical explanations.

Pan deals in part with romantic love, a subject in which I had a more burning interest at seventeen than I now have at thirty-seven. There is a kind of emotional mistiness about *Pan* which corresponded, it may be, to the Schwärmerei of youth. Today, quite possibly overvaluing it, I look for clarity above all in what I read. Finally, today I dislike Hamsun because he is a Nazi. Who am I to say that my subconscious (never a sound literary critic) does not rise up to prevent me from enjoying anything at all by a man whose political opinions I now detest?

What I am struggling to indicate is that a book may be a "good" book at one stage of your life and a "bad" book at another—and to tell absolutely how "bad" or "good" it is is impossible. The factors that make it good or bad may be nonliterary, matters of accident.

There is the whole question of "mood"—a question so involved that neither psychologists nor literary critics can say anything about it at all convincing. You just "happen" to pick up a book on Wednesday evening, and it reads well. On Tuesday evening it might have seemed a bore. What factors enter here? Who knows—metabolic rate, what you did at the office during the day, the presence or absence of fatigue, worry. . . . The fact is that a book, if it has blood in it and is not merely some standard confection, is a vital thing. To read a book is to enter into contact with something alive. It is more like talking to a friend than like driving a car. Reading is not an operation performed on something inert but a relationship entered into with another being.

At certain times you just "can't stand" anybody—your best friend, your wife or husband; it makes no difference. You don't really know why your mind refuses to touch that of another person, but you know that it does refuse. So is it with books—and that is one reason rereading even the best of books is often a disillusioning procedure.

Are there any books that the "intelligent reader" (a phrase invented by critics to circumvent immodesty) can always profitably reread? People like Mortimer Adler are certain that there are. He calls them classics, and would base education on them. To a degree he is right. There is a quality of inexhaustibility about some of the great Greeks, for example, that makes them always rereadable in that there are always new insights to be drawn from them. They have also the quality of difficulty (not to be confused with obscurity)—a quality which often helps to keep alive a book that would perish were it simpler. But even these great classics can on occasion be unrereadable. I do not contest the greatness of Plato, and yet there are certain moods in which I cannot read him, moods in which he (or his mouthpiece Socrates) seems to me to be a clever, self-satisfied, quibbling, hair-splitting, intellectual snob. And when I feel this way, the page of Plato turns to dust and ashes, and even the Phaedo (which I know to be one of the greatest things ever written) seems contrived. No matter how superior the author may be to the reader, there must be a certain harmony between them, or they cannot mate. This harmony is elusive, unattainable by mere wishing, a function of mood, whim, perhaps even temperature. I should not be surprised if our reading reactions were in part influenced by the sunspots.

There are certain books that you attempt again and again, and which continue to resist you because you are not ripe for them. During the last twenty years, for instance, I have tried perhaps ten times to read *The Brothers Karamazov* and each time given up in a rage directed equally at Dostoevsky and myself. Only recently I tried it once more and found its reputation thoroughly deserved. Reading it now with the greatest absorption, I am convinced it is the sort of book that requires the reader (that is, most readers) to be of a certain age. Until now I was simply too young for it, and that's why it seemed to me dull and farfetched. It is a book you (I mean myself) have to grow up to. One of these days I am going to reread Turgenev's *Fathers and Sons,* which I raced through at fifteen, getting, I am sure, precisely nothing from it. I have the feeling that I am now about ready for it. But I may be mistaken; I may still be too young for it.

I often think of that quiet story of the Franciscan monk who was found reading Willa Cather's *Death Comes for the Archbishop.* Asked his opinion of it, he replied, "Well, I have read it five times, but, you see, I have not finished it yet." All of us have read books that we have not finished yet, books perhaps unfinishable, books so subtle and multi-leveled as to reveal themselves newly with each rereading. I have, for example, reread Thomas Mann's *The Magic Mountain* five times (there is an extract from it in this book) and I know I have still to give it a final reading. Such books do not surrender themselves at once but are like the most desirable of women, difficult in the beginning but, once won, durable in their appeal.

What makes a book rereadable? The answer depends on the reader as well as on the book. To Mr. Adler a rereadable book is an "original communication," one marking a milestone in the history of Western thought and imagination. To the sentimentalist (that takes in a lot of us) it may be a book read in childhood; he rereads and reloves not only the book, but himself as a child. (This explains why so many people to whom their childhood is an obsession cannot bear to throw away their nursery classics.) To another a book may be rereadable if it echoes his own unalterable prejudices. It is a gauge by which he may complacently measure his lack of mental progress. People who believe in The Truth often read one book or group of books all their lives. For them the last word has been uttered by, say, Thomas Aquinas or Adolph Hitler or Friedrich Nietzsche. Hence they stick to their particular Bible and wear it to shreds. Such readers are almost always psychopaths. A one-book man is a dangerous man and should be taken in hand and taught how to diversify his literary investments.

I have been trying for some time to determine what kind of book I myself reread with pleasure. This is an exercise of no particular importance to anyone. Still, inasmuch as this entire volume consists of material that I have enjoyed, its purchaser is perhaps entitled to some explanation of my choices.

All of us are familiar with the dismaying fact that an attractive personality often has little to do with a person's moral qualities or even his physical appearance. It is quite possible to be extremely fond of a man who neglects his mother. Even his mother is often fond of him. Similarly, what I call the "magical" quality of a book—the quality which for me makes it rereadable—is not necessarily dependent on the book's importance, its intellectual weight, its position in the critics' hierarchy of values.

For example, serious students of literature would doubtless rank *Madame Bovary* as a more significant work of fiction than *Great Expectations*. Probably it is. There is no question but that it has influenced the course of literature, whereas *Great Expectations* happens to be merely a Dickens novel that millions of plain readers have enjoyed. But for me *Madame Bovary* has no virtues except those of perfection. It is without magic, without personality, it is not rereadable. It is about as interesting as Sir Galahad. *Great Expectations*, on the other hand, is magical, and its magic works every time. For me the scene on the deserted moor in which Pip meets the convict beats anything in *Madame Bovary*. I don't quite understand why this should be so, but so it is. A lycée-trained Frenchman might have the opposite reaction and be equally unable to defend it.

Now this magic is a very elusive thing. It may have any of a hundred shapes and forms. It may be a comic magic, as in the "swarry" scene from *Pickwick*. It may be a fearsome magic, as in the cave episode from *Tom Sawyer*. It may be deeply tragical—Lear on the heath. In all these

cases the writing has a penumbra, a "thickness" which the most intellectually precise notation of a Flaubert does not have. This penumbra does
not necessarily have anything to do with remoteness from reality, with
"romanticism." Nothing could be more "romantic" than the tales of Poe.
Yet, to my taste, admirable as they are, they lack magic. They are mathe-
matical, their romance is calculated. Indeed, most tales of the supernatural have this planned quality and that is why so few of them are
great literature. It is when the supernatural is accepted by the author
as related to the human that literature results. There is nothing artificial
about the *Iliad* or the *Odyssey*, though they are full of miracles and
divinities.

Penumbral literature, to use a horrible phrase, is not necessarily fanciful, then. Cabell is full of fancy but he has no magic. His words cast
no shadow. Huck Finn and Jim on the river are about as unfanciful
as you can imagine. But what they say has nonterminating reverbera-
tions.

Magic is not confined to "imaginative" literature. For me there is
magic in Russell's "A Free Man's Worship," which you will find in this
book. There is magic in Gibbon's explanation of how he came to write
the *Decline and Fall*. There is magic in the scientific popularizations of
Sir Arthur Eddington. All of these works set a bell ringing in the brain.
They do not become merely additions to your mental store but inhabitants
of your mind. There are certain clear and precise ideas that are as
haunting as Heathcliff. Descartes' system of analytical geometry can be
as stimulating to the imagination as the soliloquies of Ahab, though on a
different level.

A few pages back I said that everything in this book has been read by
the compiler at least three times with pleasure. By this I do not mean that
everything in this book is forever rereadable or that all of it is great
literature. Some of it I am sure is, but many things are included that
are not of permanent value. For example, the included stories of Somerset
Maugham have no immortal qualities. They set no bells ringing in the
mind. But they are so admirably composed, they do so perfectly the
minor thing the author set out to do, they are so exact an expression of a
particular attitude toward life, that they give me a rare and special
pleasure. I have found this pleasure, I say, repeatable three times.
Three times should be enough for any man. . . .

Comments and Questions

1. Implicit in Clifton Fadiman's essay are a number of criteria for
judging the worth of a literary work. What are these criteria? How satis-

factory and valid, when examined in the light of your own reading experience, do you find them?

2. Have you had the experience Fadiman describes of reading a book as a youngster, and again, at a more appreciative level, later on? If so, compare your reaction with Fadiman's, analyzing similarities and differences between your and Fadiman's responses to this experience.

3. Compare Fadiman's method of recounting his childhood reading experiences with that of Graham Greene in "The Lost Childhood." What similarities and differences are there between the approaches of these writers?

4. Play your own game of Century-Hencery. How nearly does your list correspond to Fadiman's? Does Fadiman, in your opinion, overly stress the immortality a book is able to achieve by appealing to children? Or does the critic make out a convincing case at this point?

5. What criteria, if any, does Fadiman give for choosing a writer for study? Obviously, one cannot go through life merely rereading books to which he has been introduced as a youngster. Does Fadiman indicate any relationship between childhood reading and the quality of reading one is able to enjoy as an adult?

Suggestions for an Essay

1. Since the first step in literary study is the selection of a subject, an initial essay might well concern reasons for your choice of a writer, as well as your past experience with literature. In developing the essay, trace the course of your reading from early childhood to the present, as Graham Greene and Clifton Fadiman have traced theirs. Try, by examining the stages through which your reading has progressed, to account for the course of events leading to the point where you now find yourself: ready to read whatever writer you have chosen.

One way to help develop a paper interestingly is to ask what questions a reader might like to have answered. For example:

What are the reasons for choosing this author in preference to others?

What works by this author have I read?

Do I like to read?

What results do I expect from my study?

What reservations, if any, do I have at present in connection with this study?

Do I expect to enjoy and appreciate the writer I have chosen as much as, more than, or less than, the reading I did as a youngster?

2. After reading a work by the author you have selected for study, write an essay in which you discuss your reaction to this work against the background of your previous reading, just as Graham Greene discusses his early reading in relation to *The Viper of Milan*.

2

AN ANALYSIS OF THE CONTENTS OF A WORK

Introduction

Much critical writing is devoted to analyzing the contents of literary works. Essentially, an analysis of this sort represents an *interpretation* of the work, and hence may aid a reader in his appreciation of it. Such an essay not only provides practice in the technique of analysis, but also, when written during the beginning stages of a research project, helps toward the definition of a subject around which the research may be centered.

Below are three essays whose authors analyze the contents of well-known works.

LAURIAT LANE, JR.

Why HUCKLEBERRY FINN Is a Great World Novel

*O*f all forms of literature, the novel is in many ways the hardest to describe with any precision. Its relative newness as a form and its varied and complex nature combine to make this so. Whenever we try to view such a full and living book as *The Adventures of Huckleberry Finn*, some of it always escapes our gaze. In fact, apart from its mere physical presence, paper, ink, glue, covers, and so forth, it is often easiest to assume that the novel does not exist at all, but only the experience of reading it. Each time we read *Huckleberry Finn* we read a certain book, and each time we read it we read a different book. No one of these books is the real *Huckleberry Finn;* in a sense, they all are.

At the heart of *Huckleberry Finn* lies a story about real human figures with genuine moral and ethical problems and decisions, figures placed in a society which we recognize as having everywhere in it the flavor of authenticity—the whole combination treated, for the most part, as directly and realistically as possible. I would like to move beyond this primary description or definition of *Huckleberry Finn,* however, and suggest that the novel may contain other elements equally important to a full appreciation. I would like to extend the novel in three directions, in space, in time, and in degree: in space, by considering some of the ways in which the book extends beyond its position as one of the masterworks of American fiction and becomes, if the term be allowed, a world novel; in time, by considering how much *Huckleberry Finn* resembles a literary form much older than the novel, the epic poem; and in degree, by considering just how much *Huckleberry Finn* transcends its position as a realistic novel and takes on the forms and qualities of allegory.

I

A world novel may be defined as that kind of novel whose importance in its own literature is so great, and whose impact on its readers is so profound and far-reaching, that it has achieved world-wide distinction. In the total picture of world literature, such a novel stands out as a work always to be reckoned with. The world novel, however, achieves its position not only through its importance but also because of its essential nature. And in discussing *Huckleberry Finn* as a world novel I shall deal not so much with this importance, as measured by permanent popularity and influence, as with the special qualities *Huckleberry Finn* has in common with certain other world novels.

The first real novel and the first world novel is, by almost universal consent, Cervantes' *The Adventures of Don Quixote.* The most important thing which *Don Quixote* has bequeathed to the novels after it (apart of course from the all-important fact of there being such a thing as a novel at all) is the theme which is central to *Don Quixote* and to almost every great novel since, the theme of appearance versus reality. This theme is also central to *Huckleberry Finn.*

Even on the simplest plot level the world of *Huckleberry Finn* is one of deception. The very existence of Huck at all is a continual deception— he is supposed to be dead. This falseness in his relations with the world at large merely reflects the difference between his standards and those of the outside world. Huck's truth and the truth of the world are diametrically opposed. Throughout the novel his truth is always cutting through the surfaces of the world's appearance and learning the contrary reality beneath. At the climax Huck tells himself, "You can't pray a lie—I found that out." That is to say, the lie of appearance is always far different from the truth of reality, and to the truly heroic and individual conscience no amount of self-delusion can ever bridge the gap lying between.

In the final section of the book, the theme of appearance versus reality reaches almost philosophical proportions. Both because of the way in which Jim's escape is carried out and because of the underlying fact of there being no need for him to escape at all, the situation is one of total dramatic and moral irony. At the end, however, Twain relaxes the tone, straightens out the plot complications, and lets the moral issue fade away. He avoids, in fact, the logical conclusion to the kind of disorder he has introduced into his world-in-fiction, a world in which the distinction between appearance and reality has, from the reader's point of view, been lost forever. For if we cannot tell appearance from reality, if the two do become totally confused and impossible to distinguish, the only answer can be the one Twain eventually came to in his most pessimistic work, *The Mysterious Stranger;* that all is illusion, and nothing really exists. In *Huckleberry Finn,* Twain does not yet reach this point of despair. By centering his action within the essentially balanced mind of the boy, Huck, he keeps his hold on reality and manages to convey this hold to the reader. But the main issue of the novel, between the way things seem and the way they are, is nevertheless one that trembles in the balance almost up to the final page.

Huckleberry Finn also gains its place as a world novel by its treatment of one of the most important events of life, the passage from youth into maturity. The novel is a novel of education. Its school is the school of life rather than of books, but Huck's education is all the more complete for that reason. Huck, like so many other great heroes of fiction—Candide, Tom Jones, Stephen Dedalus, to mention only a few—goes forth into life that he may learn. One of the central patterns of the novel is the progress of his learning.

Yet another theme which *Huckleberry Finn* shares with most of the world's great novels is that of man's obsession with the symbols of material wealth. The book opens with an account of the six thousand dollars Huck got from the robbers' hoard and ends on the same note. Throughout the intervening pages gold is shown to be not only the mainspring of most human action, but usually the only remedy mankind can offer to atone for the many hurts they are forever inflicting on one another. And as Mr. Lionel Trilling has remarked, in a certain sense all fiction is ultimately about money.

The world novel may also convey a total vision of the nation or people from which it takes its origin. It not only addresses the world in a language which is uniquely the language of that nation or people, but it brings before the view of the world at large many character types which are especially national. In *Huckleberry Finn* we recognize in Jim, in the Duke and the Dauphin, in Aunt Sally, and in Huck himself, typically

American figures whom Twain has presented for inspection by the world's eye. *Huckleberry Finn* gains much of its justification as a world novel from the fact that it is an intensely American novel as well.

II

In his essay on "The Poetic Principle" Poe remarks that "no very long poem will ever be popular again." In part, no doubt, Poe bases this remark on his own special definition of poetry. But he is also recognizing that during the eighteenth and nineteenth centuries the epic poem was gradually dying out as a literary form. Or, to be more precise, it was gradually merging with another form, the novel. Much of the poetic form of the epic came from the requirements of oral rendition; with the invention of printing, these requirements vanished. More and more writers gradually turned to prose fiction as the appropriate form to accomplish what had once been accomplished in the epic poem. Some novelists, such as Fielding or Scott, drew quite consciously on epic tradition; other novelists and novels, by a more indirect drawing on tradition, took over some of the qualities originally associated with epic poetry.

One quality of the epic poem is simply scope. Some novels confine themselves to treating exhaustively and analytically a limited segment of life. But others seem to be constantly trying to gather all life into their pages and to say, within a single story, all the important things that need to be said. Such novels derive much of their strength from the epic tradition, and *Huckleberry Finn* is such a novel. It has geographical scope. It ranges down the length of the great river and cuts through the center of a whole nation. As it does so, it gains further scope by embracing all levels of society, from the lowest to the highest. And it has the added scope of its own varying qualities, ranging from high comedy to low farce, from the poetic tranquility of life on the raft to the mob violence and human depravity always waiting on the shore.

Epic poetry gives literary form to the national destiny of the people for whom it is written. *Huckleberry Finn* gives literary form to many aspects of the national destiny of the American people. The theme of travel and adventure is characteristically American, and in Twain's day it was still a reality of everyday life. The country was still very much on the move, and during the novel Huck is moving with it. Huck's movements also embody a desire to escape from the constrictions of civilized society. Such a desire is of course not uniquely American, but during the nineteenth century Americans took it and made it their own. The American of that time could always say, as did Huck at the very end of the story, "I reckon I got to light out for the territory ahead of the rest, because Aunt Sally she's going to adopt me and sivilize me, and I can't stand it. I been there before." Another specially American theme is that of the Negro, and Huck is faced with this problem throughout the story. Starting with the typically American prejudices and easy generalizations about Jim, he is gradually shocked into an increasingly complex awareness of Jim as a human being. And although Huck's relations with Jim do not so much embody a national attitude as suggest how the nation may purge itself of one, the theme of the Negro is still one which achieves epic stature in *Huckleberry Finn*.

The epic hero is usually an embodiment of some virtue or virtues valued highly by the society from which he has sprung. Huck has many such virtues. He holds a vast store of practical knowledge which makes itself felt everywhere in the story. He knows the river and how to deal with it; and he knows mankind and how to deal with it. And he has the supreme American virtue of never being at a loss for words. In fact Huck, though he still keeps some of the innocence and naïveté of youth, has much in common with one of the greatest epic heroes, Odysseus, the practical man. Jim also has some of the qualities of an epic hero. He has strength and courage, and he possesses the supreme virtue of epic poetry, loyalty. It is part of Twain's irony that in Huck and Jim we have, in one sense, the two halves of an epic hero. In Huck, the skill and canniness; in Jim, the strength and simple loyalty.

In the society along the shore we see traces of other epic values, values which have survived from a more primitive world. The Grangerford-Shepherdson feud strikes the modern reader as a senseless mess, but as Buck says, "There ain't a coward amongst them Sheperdsons—not a one. And there ain't no cowards amongst the Grangerfords either." Huck sees the essential folly behind this courage, but the reader, one degree further removed from the harsh reality, is allowed the luxury of a double vision. Similarly, Colonel Sherburn, destroying a lynching mob merely by the courage of his presence, illustrates another epic theme, the bravery of one against many.

One final quality which *Huckleberry Finn* derives from its epic ancestry is its poetry. The novel is full of poetry. Not just the passages of lyric description, which mark a pause between the main actions and give a heightened and more literary tone just as they often did in the traditional epic, but also the many similes and turns of speech Huck uses, which, if they are not quite Homeric, are certainly unforgettable. And much of the exaggerated language of the frontier world, one not far removed in kind from that of the primitive migrations, is also a natural part of the epic style.

III

Allegory may be defined simply as the representation of one thing in the form of another. A second definition, more germane to literature, is that allegory is a process by which the spiritual is embodied in the physical. To go one step further, the main purpose of allegory is somehow to embody a spiritual action in a physical action. By making a suitable physical object stand for some metaphysical one, or at least for one which cannot be contained in the terms of normal, everyday life, the writer carries out one of the main purposes of all art, which is to bring to its audience, through the representation of real objects, an awareness and knowledge which transcend the limitations of such reality. Allegory, that is, deals primarily with matters of the spirit.

This assumption helps to explain why the great allegories deal either with a physical journey or a physical conflict or both. For a spiritual change, when embodied allegorically, will take the form of a meaningful physical journey through symbolic space. And a spiritual conflict, when embodied allegorically, will take the form of a real physical conflict between significant forces, each of them representing some metaphysical quality.

Although all novels are in a certain sense descended from *Don Quixote,* it is also true that in another sense all novels, and especially English ones, are descended from Bunyan's *Pilgrim's Progress.* The main difference between the allegorical novel as we know it today and Bunyan's narrative of the human soul is that whereas in *Pilgrim's Progress* we have an allegory that tends to turn into a novel, in most modern instances we have a novel that tends to turn into an allegory. As the author, whether he be Melville or Mann or Twain, develops and elaborates his original materials, he may become aware of certain meaningful connections which are tending to establish themselves between the physical objects and the physical narrative he is describing and the related spiritual values and conflicts. Drawing on a tradition which has existed for a long time in literature and which is a natural part of the artistic process in any form, the author finds himself writing allegory. And this is what happened to Mark Twain. Writing as he was a great novel, his masterpiece in fact, he organized and related certain physical materials to certain metaphysical conditions so that their relationship became meaningful in a special way—became, in short, allegory.

Huckleberry Finn is the story of a journey, a real journey. If we are to find any meaning in Huck's journey beyond the literal level, we must seek it first in the medium through which Huck journeys, in the great river down which he drifts during much of the story. And Huck's movements take on at least the external form of a basic symbolic pattern, one seen in such poems as Shelley's *Alastor,* Arnold's *The Future,* and Rimbaud's *Bateau Ivre,* a pattern stated most directly in *Prometheus Unbound,* "My soul is an enchanted boat." Implicit in this pattern is the suggestion that the river journey can have a distinctly metaphysical quality, that it can be, in fact, a journey of the soul as well as of the body. This suggestion is not at all arbitrary. Of all forms of physical progression, that of drifting downstream in a boat, or on a raft, is the most passive one possible. The mind under such conditions is lulled, as Huck's mind is, into the illusion that it has lost all contact with reality and is drifting bodilessly through a world of sleep and of dreams. Thus the nakedness of Huck and Jim when they are alone on the raft becomes a symbol of how they have shucked off the excrescences of the real world, their clothes, and have come as close as possible to the world of the spirit.

All journeys, even allegorical ones, must have a goal. What is the goal of Huck's journey? We find the answer in what happens while Huck and Jim float down the river. The pattern is, very simply, one of an ever-increasing engagement of the world of the raft, of the spirit, with the world of the shore, of reality. As the book progresses, more and more Huck tells about events that take place on the banks, and less and less he tells about those that take place out on the river. No matter how hard Huck and Jim try to escape, the real world is always drawing them back into it. Finally, in the Duke and the Dauphin, themselves fleeing for the moment from the harsh reality of the river's shores, the real world invades the world of the raft, and the latter loses forever the dream-like and idyllic quality it has often had for the two voyagers. The climax of Huck's lyric praise of the river comes significantly just before this mood is shattered forever by the arrival of the Duke and the Dauphin.

Parallel to this pattern of the ever-increasing engagement of the world of the shore with that of the raft is a pattern which begins with Huck's pretended death, a death which is actual to all the world but Huck and Jim. The symbolic fact of his death accomplished, Huck must find an identity with which he can face the real world. His assumption of various such identities forms a significant pattern. The various masks he assumes, starting with that of a girl, as far removed from the reality as possible, gradually draw back nearer the truth. Huck's final disguise, as Tom Sawyer, is only slightly removed from his real self. When he is about to reveal this real self and is instead taken for Tom, Huck almost recognizes the meaning of his journey. For he says to himself, "But if they was joyful, it warn't nothing to what I was; for it was like being born again, I was so glad to find out who I was."

This, then, is the allegory of *Huckleberry Finn.* Dying symbolically almost at the opening of the novel, Huck journeys through the world of the spirit, ever working out a pattern of increasing involvement with the world of reality and with his own self, both cast aside at the beginning of the journey. Only when he is finally forced to assume this real self in the eyes of the world, through the sudden arrival of Aunt Polly, is he allowed to learn the all-important truth Jim has kept from him throughout the novel, that his Pap "ain't comin back no mo." We cannot say that Huck has undergone a total initiation and is now fully prepared to take on adulthood, but neither can we doubt that he has undergone a knowledgeful and maturing experience. And at the end of the story he is about to undertake another journey, this time to the west, in search of further experience and further knowledge.

Comments and Questions

1. Throughout his essay, Lauriat Lane, Jr. refers to various literary works (*Don Quixote, The Mysterious Stranger*, "The Poetic Principle," *Pilgrim's Progress, Alastor, The Future, Bateau Ivre*); to various writers in addition to Twain (Cervantes, Trilling, Poe, Bunyan, Shelley, Arnold, Rimbaud, Fielding, Scott, Melville, Mann); to several literary characters (Candide, Tom Jones, Stephen Dedalus). Using literary allusions is a common practice of literary critics. Decide what use Lane makes of each allusion, and whether, in each instance, the use is successful. Do Lane's literary allusions increase confidence in what he says?

2. Lane's essay attempts to accomplish two purposes: to analyze the contents of *Huckleberry Finn*, and to evaluate the worth of the book. Comment on the relationship between these two aims, the extent to which Lane fuses them into an organic whole, and the degree to which he succeeds in accomplishing his aims. Is either of these aims more important than the other, or do the two complement one another?

3. Lane works with a concept which he calls the "world novel." Study his definition of a "world novel," and decide how important to his evaluation of the book this phrase is. Could he have said what he had to say about the book without using this term?

4. Analyze with care Lane's introductory remarks (the first two paragraphs of the essay). What, specifically, does this introduction accomplish? Does it seek in any way to disarm possible adverse criticism of the essay?

5. If you are familiar with *Huckleberry Finn*, you will, as you read Lane's essay, naturally want to compare your own reading of the novel with his. In the light of Lane's introductory comment that "Each time we read *Huckleberry Finn* we read a certain book, and each time we read it we read a different book," do you feel that Lane himself has given only *one* reading? Are there in fact other possible readings?

6. Lane's evaluation of *Huckleberry Finn* is consistently favorable. Does this conscious one-sidedness weaken the essay? Is Lane guilty of oversimplification in finding no fault with the novel? Or does he forestall this possible criticism?

7. Evaluate the three sections of the essay. Is one particularly strong? One weaker than the others? All of approximately equal strength?

8. Compare Lane's praise of *Huckleberry Finn* with Clifton Fadiman's praise in "My Life Is an Open Book: Confessions and Digressions of an Incurable" (see Chapter 1). To what extent do these critics agree concerning Twain's book? To what extent do their interpretations diverge?

ARNOLD KETTLE

an analysis of

TESS OF THE D'URBERVILLES

*T*he subject of *Tess of the D'Urbervilles* is stated clearly by
Hardy to be the fate of a "pure woman"; in fact it is the destruction of the
English peasantry. More than any other nineteenth-century novel we have
touched on it has the quality of a social document. It has even, for all
its high-pitched emotional quality, the kind of impersonality that the
expression suggests. Its subject is all-pervasive, affecting and determining
the nature of every part. It is a novel with a thesis—a *roman à thèse*—and
the thesis is true.

The thesis is that in the course of the nineteenth century the disintegration of the peasantry—a process which had its roots deep in the
past—had reached its final and tragic stage. With the extension of
capitalist farming (farming, that is to say, in which the landowner farms
not for sustenance but for profit and in which the land-workers become
wage-earners) the old yeoman class of small-holders or peasants, with
their traditions of independence and their own native culture, was bound
to disappear. The developing forces of history were too strong for them
and their way of life. And because that way of life had been proud and
deep-rooted its destruction was necessarily painful and tragic. *Tess* is the
story and the symbol of the destruction.

Tess Durbeyfield is a peasant girl. Her parents belong to a class ranking
above the farm-labourers, a class "including the carpenter, the smith, the
shoemaker, the huckster, together with nondescript workers other than
farm-labourers; a set of people who owed a certain stability of aim and
conduct to the fact of their being life-holders, like Tess's father, or copy-
holders, or, occasionally, small freeholders." [1] Already by the opening of
the novel the Durbeyfields have fallen on hard times, a plight by no
means solely due to the lack of stability in the characters of John and
Joan. A further twist is given to their difficulty in making ends meet by
the accident in which their horse is killed.* It is her sense of guilt over
this accident that allows Tess to be persuaded by her mother into visiting
the Trantridge D'Urbervilles to "claim kin" with a more prosperous

---

*This very accident is a striking symbol of the struggles of the peasantry.
The mail-cart "with its two noiseless wheels, speeding along these lanes like
an arrow" runs into Tess's slow, unlighted wagon. Anyone who happened to
be in Italy during the last war will recall the running-down of peasant carts
by army vehicles. The army drivers were not always to blame. The peasants
as often as not had no lights and were on the wrong side of the road. But
every accident represented a clash between something more than two individual vehicles and the results in hardship or worse can well be imagined.

branch of the family. And from this visit (itself an attempt to solve the Durbeyfields' economic problems) the whole tragedy derives.

In these opening chapters of the novel there is an immediate and insistent emphasis on historical processes, so that from the start the characters are not seen merely as individuals. The discovery by John Durbeyfield of his ancestry is not just an introductory comic scene, a display of quaint 'character.' It states the basic theme of the novel—what the Durbeyfields have been and what they become. The landscape in the second chapter (it is far more effective description than the famous setpiece at the beginning of *The Return of the Native*) is described and given significance almost wholly in terms of history. The 'club-walking' scene, again, is contrasted with the May Day dances of the past and early pagan rites are recalled. Tess is revealed as one of a group, typical ("not handsomer than others" [2]), and in the comparison between her and her mother the differences brought about by historical changes are emphasized. Joan Durbeyfield lives in the peasant folk-lore of the past, Tess has been to a National school. "When they were together the Jacobean and the Victorian ages were juxtaposed." [3]

The sacrifice of Tess to D'Urberville is symbolic of the historical process at work. D'Urberville is not, of course, a D'Urberville at all, but the son of the *nouveau riche* Stoke family, capitalists who have bought their way into the gentry, and Tess's cry when she sees the D'Urberville estate: "I thought we were an old family; but this is all new!" [4] carries a world of irony. Tess herself does not want to go to D'Urberville's and when she does finally agree to go she dresses in her working clothes. But her mother insists on her dressing up for the occasion.

" 'Very well; I suppose you know,' replied Tess with calm abandonment.

And to please her parent the girl put herself quite in Joan's hands, saying serenely, 'Do what you like with me, Mother.' " [5]

Again the moment is symbolic. Tess, prepared to become, since change she must, a worker, is handed over by her mother to the life and the mercies of the ruling class.

From the moment of her seduction by D'Urberville, Tess's story becomes a hopeless struggle, against overwhelming odds, to maintain her self-respect. After the death of her child she becomes a wage-labourer at the dairy-farm at Talbothays. The social degradation is mitigated by the kindness of the dairyman and his wife, but the work is only seasonal. Here however she meets and falls in love with Angel Clare and through marriage to him thinks to escape her fate. But Angel, the intellectual, turns out to be more cruel than D'Urberville, the sensualist. Angel, with all his emancipated ideas, is not merely a prig and a hypocrite but a snob as well. He understands nothing of the meaning of the decline of the D'Urbervilles and his attitude to Tess is one of self-righteous idealization.

" 'My position—is this,' he said abruptly. 'I thought—any man would have thought—that by giving up all ambition to win a wife with social standing, with fortune, with knowledge of the world, I should secure rustic innocence as surely as I should secure pink cheeks. . . .' " [6]

And when his dream of rustic innocence is shattered he can only taunt Tess with:

" 'Don't, Tess; don't argue. Different societies, different manners. You almost make me say you are an unapprehending peasant woman, who have never been initiated into the proportions of social things. . . .' " [7]

Even at the moment of her deepest humiliation Tess is stung to the retort:

" 'Lots of families are as bad as mine in that! Retty's family were once large landowners, and so were Dairyman Billett's. And the Debbyhouses, who now are carters, were once the De Bayeux family. You find such as I everywhere; 'tis a feature of the country, and I can't help it.' " [8]

It is important (I shall return to this point) to give these passages their full weight because they emphasize the kind of novel this is. Such passages, read as 'psychological drama,' ring queer and unconvincing. Their function in the novel is to stress the social nature of Tess's destiny and its typicality.

After Angel has left her the social degradation of Tess continues. At the farm at Flintcomb Ash she and the other girls (once again it is significant that Tess's fate is shared by Marion and Izz who have not, in the same way, 'sinned' morally) become fully proletarianized, working for wages in the hardest, most degrading conditions. The scene at the threshing is here particularly important, a symbol of the dehumanized relationships of the new capitalist farms. At Talbothays there had at least been some possibility of pride and interest in the labour as well as a certain kindliness in the common kitchen at which the dairyman's wife presided. Here there is nothing kind or satisfying and the emphasis on Marion's bottle is not casual, not just a matter of the individual 'character.'

The final blow to Tess's attempts to maintain her self-respect comes with the death of her father and the consequent expulsion of the Durbeyfields from their cottage. John Durbeyfield had been a life-holder.

"But as the long holdings fell in they were seldom again let to similar tenants, and were mostly pulled down, if not absolutely required by the farmer for his hands. Cottagers who were not directly employed on the land were looked upon with disfavour, and the banishment of some starved the trade of others, who were thus obliged to follow. These families, who had formed the backbone of the village life in the past, who were the depositories of the village traditions, had to seek refuge in the large centres; the process, humorously designated by statisticians as 'the tendency of the rural population towards the large towns,' being really the tendency of water to flow uphill when forced by machinery." [9]

It is the need to support her family, thus driven off the land, that finally forces Tess back to Alec D'Urberville. And when Angel, chastened and penitent, returns, the final sacrifice is inevitable. Tess kills D'Urberville. The policemen take her from the altar at Stonehenge and the black flag is run up on Winchester jail.

It is important for a number of reasons to emphasize that *Tess of the D'Urbervilles* is a moral fable, that it is the expression of a generalized human situation in history and neither (what it is generally assumed to be) a purely personal tragedy nor (what Hardy appears to have intended) a philosophic comment on Life in general and the fate of Woman in particular. If we read the novel as a personal tragedy, the individual history of Tess Durbeyfield, a great deal strikes us as extremely unsatisfactory.

In the first place there is (as has been noted frequently enough) Hardy's flouting of normal probability in his insistence on a series of the most unlucky chances. In *Tess* the most notable of these chances are the episode in which Tess's written confession, pushed under Angel's door, goes under the carpet and the moment when Tess, having walked from Flintcomb Ash to Emminster, overhears Angel's brothers talking about her and has not the heart to visit her parents-in-law. If either of these chance happenings had not occurred, all might easily have been saved. Again, in the broader realm of probability, is there really any adequate reason why Tess, at the end, should murder D'Urberville? True, she does not know the full extent of Angel's forgiveness, but at least she knows that he has basically changed. It is not perhaps any one of these manifestations of tragic improbability that we are likely to jib at, but rather the combination of them. Mr. J. I. M. Stewart, in an interesting essay, has stated the problem.

"Always in Hardy it is certain that the incidence of fatality within the general operation of chance will be higher than we are commonly prepared to accept of its being in nature. Why does he thus so often seem to play against his characters with loaded dice; why does he darken the sky with his arrows when Elfride Swancourt and her many successors are fighting for life? The universe of his novels is one of a determinism slightly modified to meet the needs of tragedy, the individual will being conceived as having its measure of freedom during certain moments of equilibrium in the universal Will, within which it is comprised (the image is Hardy's). It is thus still a *neutral* universe. Why then does the screw turn so frequently and so disastrously as it does?" [10]

Now if we read the novel as a detailed particularized study of an individual life it is clear that this turning of the screw does constitute a serious weakness. What it amounts to in *Tess* is that we must regard the characters—Tess herself in particular—as having less than normal luck and—more important—less than normal human resilience in the situation in which they find themselves. Is not Tess, after all (admitting her superiority of sensitiveness), a good deal less shrewd and worldly-wise than a peasant girl of her age might naturally be assumed to be? Is not her very sensitiveness a little false? (Could she, for instance, have *afforded*—bearing in mind the conditions of Flintcomb Ash—to be merely hurt and unprotesting when Angel's brothers take away her boots when they find them in the ditch?) Such considerations are, if the novel is a realistic psychological study, entirely relevant. But they seem to me, in fact, no more relevant than the criticism which says of *King Lear* that Lear's conduct in the first act is unlikely or that the Gloucester sub-plot is ill-planned because the existence of two such cases of filial impiety within so small a circumference is improbable. *Tess* is not a novel of the kind of *Emma* or *Middlemarch*. It does not illuminate within a detailed framework particular problems of human conduct and feeling. Its sphere is the more generalized movement of human destiny.

Once we recognize that the subject of *Tess* is the destruction of the peasantry many of the more casual criticisms of the book are seen to be rather wide of the mark.

There is the question, for instance, of Alec D'Urberville. Many readers are antagonized by his presentation as what amounts to the stock villain of Victorian melodrama, the florid, moustache-twirling bounder who refers to the heroine (whom he is about to seduce) as "Well, my Beauty. . . ." Is this not a character who has stepped direct out of the tenth-rate theatre or "She was poor but she was honest"? It seems to me that almost the whole point about D'Urberville is that he is indeed the archetypal Victorian villain. Far from being weakened by the associations of crude melodrama he in fact illuminates the whole type and we understand better *why* the character of which he is a symbol did dominate a certain grade of Victorian entertainment and was enthusiastically hissed by the audience. It is the very typicality of D'Urberville that serves the purposes of the novel.

The treatment of Christianity in the book has a similar relevance. The conversion of D'Urberville is not in itself necessary to the plot of the novel (his rediscovery of Tess could easily have been contrived some other way). Hardy's object here is clearly to heighten the association, implicit throughout the book, of the Christian faith and Tess's downfall. The man with the paint-pot who regales Tess with the assurance that THY DAMNATION SLUMBERETH NOT at the moment of her betrayal turns up again with the converted D'Urberville. Is the comment fair to Christianity? The question is not relevant. Hardy is not attempting an estimate of the total validity of the Christian philosophy. His subject is the destruction of the peasant Tess. It is the place of religious influence in that destruction that is his concern. And in the pattern of the novel the Christian church is seen as at best a neutral observer, at worst an active abettor in the process of destruction. It is not, historically considered, an unreasonable comment.

At best a neutral observer, at worst an active abettor: the phrase

applies to a good deal more than Hardy's view of Christianity. One of
the aspects of *Tess* that we tend to find peculiarly unconvincing—if not
repulsive—is the sense of the loaded dice to which Mr. Stewart refers.
It emerges in its least palatable form in passages of the book most obviously intended as fundamental philosophical comment. There is the
famous episode, for instance, in which Tess, driving the cart to market,
speaks to her little brother of the stars:

" 'Did you say the stars were worlds, Tess?'
'Yes.'
'All like ours?'
'I don't know; but I think so. They sometimes seem to be like the
apples on our stubbard-tree. Most of them splendid and sound—a few
blighted.'
'Which do we live on—a splendid one or a blighted one?'
'A blighted one.'
'Tis very unlucky that we didn't pitch on a sound one, when there
were so many more of 'em!'
'Yes.'
'Is it like that really, Tess?' said Abraham, turning to her much im-
pressed, on reconsideration of this rare information. 'How would it have
been if we had pitched on a sound one?'
'Well, Father wouldn't have coughed and creeped about as he does, and
wouldn't have got too tipsy to go this journey; and Mother wouldn't have
been always washing, and never getting finished.'
'And you would have been a rich lady ready-made, and not have had
to be made rich by marrying a gentleman?'
'O Aby, don't—don't talk of that any more!' " [11]

We tend to reject such an episode on two grounds: in the first place
we are not convinced that any peasant girl would talk like that, in the
second the philosophy implied (and the whole organization of the book
makes us give it the weight of the author's full sympathy, if not assent)
is not calculated to win our support. The world as a blighted apple is
an image too facile to satisfy us, even though we may recognize the
force of Tess's pessimism. I think it is important, however, to emphasize
that even in this passage the pessimism is given a very explicit basis in
actual conditions. It is the kind of life her parents lead that drives Tess
to her feelings of despair and it is the sentence about her mother never
getting finished that in fact saves the scene. For here is no pretentious
philosophy of fatality but a bitterly realistic recalling of the actual fate
of millions of working women.

The scene just quoted seems to me to give a most instructive insight
into the kind of book *Tess of the D'Urbervilles* is. It is not, it has already
been emphasized, a 'psychological novel'; the presentation of Tess's actual
thoughts in this episode is not at all convincing. Nor is it a symbolic
statement on the level of *Wuthering Heights;* Hardy does not penetrate
to the profundity of Emily Brontë's understanding of the processes of life
and when he goes in for philosophical generalizations the result is often

embarrassing. And yet this novel, with its queer cramped 'literary' style* and its bogus 'Aeschylean' philosophy, gets hold of something of life and illuminates a phase of human history with an extraordinary compulsion and an insight of oddly moving delicacy.

What Hardy got hold of was not, I think, quite what his conscious mind believed. In the scene we have just discussed the *intention* (as opposed to the total effect) is to concentrate into the image of the blighted star a whole world of philosophical significance. Hardy took his philosophy of the Immanent Will very seriously and undoubtedly saw Tess as the victim of "the President of the Immortals." A pessimistic and determinist view of the world in which man (and, even more, woman) is at the mercy of an unyielding outside Fate is the conscious philosophy behind the novel. The sub-title "a pure woman" is indicative of the kind of significance Hardy gave to his story, and there is no doubt that this conscious philosophy affects the book, in general for the worse. It is responsible, for instance, for the 'literary' quality which mars the final sentence. It is responsible for our sense of loaded dice. And it is responsible ultimately for the psychological weakness such as the idealization of Tess, for the characters are made too often to respond not to life but to Hardy's philosophy.†

And yet *Tess* survives Hardy's philosophy. It survives because his imaginative understanding of the disintegration of the peasantry is more powerful than the limiting tendencies of his conscious outlook. As a matter of fact I do not think we ought to sneer too securely at Hardy's philosophy. No doubt it is, like Tolstoy's, an unsatisfactory philosophy and yet also, like Tolstoy's (the views of history expressed in *War and Peace* and *The Dynasts* are worth comparing) it emerges from a passionately honest attempt to grapple with real problems of quite overwhelming difficulty. Hardy at least did have a philosophy (which is more than can be said for most of his contemporaries) and there was more basis to his pessimism—the pessimism of the Wessex peasant who sees his world and his values being destroyed—than can be laughed away with an easy gesture of contempt.

For the odd thing about this strange and moving novel is that although so much about it has a note of falsity—the manipulation of the plot, the character-study of Tess herself, the inadequate, self-conscious, stilted writing—the total impression is not false at all. Part of the achievement is due undoubtedly to the always effective and often

---

* "When (Hardy) remarked that had he known what a stir *Tess* was going to create he would have made it a really good book he probably meant that he would have gone over the grammar, and would have inserted more of those references to mythology or painting that he believed an important means of toning up a literary style." [12] Mr. Stewart's comment seems to me fair enough.

†All three of these qualities are combined in the dreadful moment when Angel, at the very climax of the book, after Tess's confession of her 'sin,' exclaims: "My God—how can forgiveness meet such a grotesque—prestidigitation as that!" [13]

superb evocation of the natural background. This is a special triumph of Hardy's and one which—in the novels we have previously discussed— had hitherto scarcely been attempted. Such a description as that of the dawn at Talbothays may perhaps best be compared with the descriptions of London in *Oliver Twist*. In neither case is the word 'descriptive,' with its cold suggestion of an objective backcloth, adequate.

"They met continually; they could not help it. They met daily in that strange and solemn interval, the twilight of the morning, in the violet or pink dawn; for it was necessary to rise early, so very early, here. Milking was done betimes; and before the milking came the skimming, which began at a little past three. It usually fell to the lot of some one or other of them to wake the rest, the first being aroused by an alarm-clock; and, as Tess was the latest arrival, and they soon discovered that she could be depended upon not to sleep through the alarm as the others did, this task was thrust most frequently upon her. No sooner had the hour of three struck and whizzed, than she left her room and ran to the dairyman's door; then up the ladder to Angel's, calling him in a loud whisper; then woke her fellow-milkmaids. By the time that Tess was dressed Clare was downstairs and out in the humid air. The remaining maids and the dairyman usually gave themselves another turn on the pillow, and did not appear till a quarter of an hour later.

The grey half-tones of daybreak are not the grey half-tones of the day's close, though the degree of their shade may be the same. In the twilight of the morning light seems active, darkness passive; in the twilight of evening it is the darkness which is active and crescent, and light which is the drowsy reverse. . . .

At these non-human hours they could get quite close to the waterfowl. Herons came, with a great bold noise as of opening doors and shutters, out of the boughs of a plantation which they frequented at the side of the mead; or, if already on the spot, hardily maintained their standing in the water as the pair walked by, watching them by moving their heads round in a slow, horizontal, passionless wheel, like the turn of puppets by clockwork.

They could then see the faint summer fogs in layers, wholly, level, and apparently no thicker than counterpanes, spread about the meadows in detached remnants of small extent. On the grey moisture of the grass were marks where the cows had lain through the night—dark-green islands of dry herbage the size of their carcases, in the general sea of dew. From each island proceeded a serpentine trail, by which the cow had rambled away to feed after getting up, at the end of which trail they found her; the snoring puff from her nostrils, when she recognized them, making an intenser little fog of her own amid the prevailing one. Then they drove the animals back to the barton, or sat down to milk them on the spot, as the case might require.

Or perhaps the summer fog was more general, and the meadows lay like a white sea, out of which the scattered trees rose like dangerous rocks. Birds would soar through it into the upper radiance, and hang on the wing sunning themselves, or alight on the wet rails subdividing the mead, which now shone like glass rods. Minute diamonds of moisture from the mist hung, too, upon Tess's eyelashes and drops upon her hair, like seed pearls. When the day grew quite strong and commonplace these dried off her; moreover, Tess then lost her strange and ethereal beauty; her teeth, lips, and eyes scintillated in the sunbeams, and she was again the dazzlingly fair dairymaid only, who had to hold her own against the other women of the world." [14]

The atmosphere evoked in such description is not an embellishment to the book, but an integral part of it. We cannot think of Tess and Angel except in the context of such scenes any more than we can think of Sikes outside the context of the London which has made him. We believe in Tess, just as we believe in Sikes, because her relationship to her world is so successfully conveyed. When Hardy begins theorizing, discussing in abstract terms Tess's plight, we become uneasy; when he presents her to us in the misty dawn at Talbothays we feel no need to question her authenticity.* She *is* a peasant girl and she *is* splendid, heroic even, and we know what Hardy means when he talks of "a pure woman." The unconvincing moments are those when to make a 'point' Hardy allows his own, inadequate *ideas* to weaken his profound instinctive *understanding*. Such a moment arises when, just before Tess's confession to Angel, he too is made to confess a sexual lapse. Now Hardy can convince us that Angel is a prig and a hypocrite but he simply cannot convince us that the Angel he presents to us in the novel would be quite so morally obtuse as to see no affinity whatever between his confession and hers. He might well convince us that a man only slightly less morally aware would be thus blinded (heaven knows the situation is common enough). He might even convince us that Angel himself would be capable of putting a youthful indiscretion into a separate compartment of his mind and there burying it. But to ask us to believe that the Angel we know (and one is not claiming of course any very admirable qualities for him) would within a few minutes of confessing such a lapse of his own respond in quite the way he does to Tess's confession is simply asking us to stretch our credulity beyond its limit. And the reason for it all is obvious. Hardy is determined at all costs to make his point (fair enough in the abstract) about male hypocrisy on this sexual matter. He is determined to get in another blow on behalf of his pure woman. But, because the moral point is unconvincingly realized in this particular scene between these particular characters, the blow rebounds.

It is not, of course, a fatal error (there are far greater difficulties in

---

* D. H. Lawrence in his *Study of Thomas Hardy* wrote:
" . . . it is not as a metaphysician that we must consider Hardy. He makes a poor show there. For nothing in his work is so pitiable as his clumsy efforts to push events into line with his theory of being, and to make calamity fall on those who represent the principle of Love. . . .
His feeling, his instinct, his sensuous understanding is, however, apart from his metaphysic, very great and deep, deeper than that, perhaps, of any other English novelist. Putting aside his metaphysic, which must always obtrude when he thinks of people, and turning to the earth, to landscape, then he is true to himself." *Phoenix* (1936), p. 980.

the book) but I quote it to illustrate the battle going on throughout *Tess* between Hardy's ideas and his understanding. It is the inadequacy of his ideas that gives much of the book its oddly thin and stilted quality and which leads, in particular, to the unsatisfactory manipulation of chance which, more than anything in the novel, arouses our suspicions as to its validity. For the loading of the dice is an admission not so much of cunning as of impotence, a desperate gesture which attempts through artificial stimulation to achieve a consummation otherwise unobtainable. Hardy's understanding, his deep instinctive comprehension of the fate of the Wessex peasants, told him what had to be said, but his conscious philosophy did not give him adequate means always to say it. Hence the unduly long arm of coincidence, hence the half-digested classical allusions, hence the psychological weaknesses. Whereas from the social understanding emerges the strength of the novel, the superb revelation of the relation of men to nature, the haunting evocation of the Wessex landscape not as backcloth but as the living challenging material of human existence, and the profoundly moving story of the peasant Tess.

It is easy enough to list imperfections of this novel. What also needs explanation is its triumph, epitomized in that extraordinary final scene at Stonehenge. There is nothing bogus about the achievement here, no sleight of hand, no counterfeit notes of false emotion. The words of speech have not quite the ring of speech nor the integral force of poetry; the symbolism is obvious, one might almost say crude. And yet this very clumsiness, the almost amateurish manipulation of the mechanics of the scene, contributes something to its force, to its expression of the pathetic and yet heroic losing battle waged by Tess against a world she cannot successfully fight and can only dimly apprehend. The final mood evoked by *Tess of the D'Urbervilles* is not hopelessness but indignation and the indignation is none the less profound for being incompletely intellectualized. Hardy is not a Shakespeare or an Emily Brontë. His art does not quite achieve that sense of the inner movement of life which transcends abstractions. He is constantly weakening his apprehension of this movement by inadequate attitudes and judgements. But in spite of this weakening *Tess* emerges as a fine novel, a moral fable, the most moving expression in our literature—not forgetting Wordsworth—of the destruction of the peasant world.

Notes and References

[1] *Tess,* Chap. LI.
[2] Ibid., Chap. II.
[3] Ibid., Chap. III.
[4] Ibid., Chap. V.
[5] Ibid., Chap. VII.
[6] Ibid., Chap. XXXVI.

⁷ Ibid., Chap. XXXV.
⁸ Ibid.
⁹ Ibid., Chap. LI.
¹⁰ *English Studies* (1948), p. 19.
¹¹ *Tess,* Chap. IV.
¹² Op. cit., p. 6.
¹³ *Tess,* Chap. XXXV.
¹⁴ Ibid., Chap. XX.

Comments and Questions

1. In his opening sentence Arnold Kettle indicates that his interpretation of the subject of *Tess of the D'Urbervilles* differs from Hardy's professed subject. Is this a forceful way to begin an essay? Does Kettle ever resolve the apparent contradiction between his interpretation of the book and Hardy's announced intention?

2. In keeping with his thesis that *Tess* concerns historic change rather than the fortunes and misfortunes of one family, Kettle seeks to establish the symbolic basis of the novel. Study the methods he uses to convince the reader that the novel should be read symbolically. How convincing do you find the author at this point? In this connection, study the quotation from the book which shows Tess preparing to go to the Trantridge D'Urbervilles. Kettle's comment on this quote is: "Again the moment is symbolic. . . ." Do you agree that this moment is symbolic? How has Kettle made this quote work for him?

3. Unlike Lauriat Lane, Jr., who finds in *Huckleberry Finn* several significant levels of meaning, Kettle feels that *Tess* has only one subject: "the destruction of the English peasantry." Throughout his essay Kettle is concerned with showing how various elements in the book, which on the surface might appear gratuitous, do in fact contribute to the development of this subject. Find the instances in which Kettle does this, and note the methods he uses in attempting to convince the reader that these elements are a part of the structure of the book.

4. Kettle calls *Tess* a "moving novel," yet lists three elements in the book ("the manipulation of the plot, the character-study of Tess herself, the inadequate, self-conscious, stilted writing") which have "a note of falsity." The critic here indulges in a paradox: *Tess* is powerful despite evident weaknesses. How does Kettle make this paradox work for him?

5. What distinction does Kettle draw throughout his essay between Hardy's "ideas" and his "understanding"? How is this related to Kettle's point about the true contents of the novel?

6. At the close of the next to the last paragraph Kettle lists what appear to him to be successful and unsuccessful elements in *Tess*. To

what extent, and in what ways, has Kettle defined the success or lack
of it in these elements?

7. Does Kettle, in advancing arguments for his interpretation of
the novel, adequately deal with the question of what in the novel has
prompted interpretations differing from his own?

8. A strong point of Kettle's essay is the way in which, by implication, he is able to suggest the nature of the interpretations of *Tess* which
differ from his own without explicitly stating them. Make a study of
the ways Kettle uses to imply interpretations which have been given the
novel. List them.

9. On the basis of Kettle's essay, make a list of possible lines of
inquiry which suggest themselves in connection with a study of Hardy's
novels.

10. Notice that, although Kettle concerns himself with Hardy's
subject in *Tess,* what he says constitutes an evaluation of the worth of
the novel. How does Kettle integrate this re-creative and evaluative
criticism in his essay?

PAUL ELMER MORE

Henry Adams

*T*he display of a copy of *The Education of Henry Adams* has
been a kind of hall-mark of distinction for any private library, ever since
the book was printed and distributed to a few friends of the author in
1907. Even to have read its jealously guarded pages was something to
boast of, and the initiated were wont to wag their heads over its revelations
as over some exotic drink which they were expected to admire, but which
teased their palate by its strange flavour. And now the volume is published
to the world, and one wonders what the world will make of it—perhaps
nothing. Yet simply as the record of an unusual life it is certainly entertaining above the average, and would be doubly so were it half as long.
The virtue of cynicism is its point, and only the genial can afford to be
diffuse. Mr. Adams was nothing if not cynical; had he learned the rare
art of compression, he might have produced a work worthy of a place
beside the autobiographies of Gibbon and Franklin.

No other man of this country, save his brothers, one of whom, the
late Charles Francis Adams, has followed his example, had quite such
material at his disposal. Son of the elder Charles Francis Adams, grand-

son of a President, and great-grandson of the mighty John of Revolutionary fame, his conscience was a kind of historical epitome. As private secretary of his father at the British court during the Civil War, he saw the inside of that society and government towards whose public manifestation his family had lived in a state of hereditary feud. As a member of the Harvard faculty for seven years, he is said to have introduced the first historical seminary into an American college. As an author, not to mention his privately printed *Mont-Saint-Michel and Chartres* (recently republished by the authority of the American Institute of Architects) and his unacknowledged novels *Esther* and *Democracy*, he produced a history of the United States under Jefferson and Madison notable for its original and broad use of sources, for its judicious characterizations, and its sustained interest. As a citizen of Washington, where his later and some of his earlier years were spent, he saw familiarly the working of a government which he admired no more than he did that of London. As a friend, he was close to John Hay and Clarence King, great men in this field, the latter especially, though little known to the world, yet by the few idolized as the *deus praesens* of social joy and wisdom.

Not many men of the past generation enjoyed such opportunities of watching the drama of life, and perhaps none of them excelled him in the power of penetrating beneath the surface of things; and this power is none the less amazing when, as often happened with him, the lifted curtain, behind which we looked for the revelation of some well-staged scene of history, exhibited only the disarray of planless confusion. That indeed is the moral of the book—if moral it may be called—the baffled sense of mystery behind the veil of apparent design. "King and Hay and Adams could neither of them escape floundering through the corridors of chaos," he says, with an ungrammatical reminiscence of Longfellow, "that opened as they passed to the end."

But this is to anticipate. What we have to note now is the pungent interest of Adams's comments on the figures thrown up in flashes of light beside him as he journeyed through these shadowy corridors. Sometimes it is a whole society that furnished him with a discharge of epigrams. First it is the people among whom he was born, and who stamped their traits upon his own soul:

Resistance to something was the law of New England nature; the boy looked out on the world with the instinct of resistance; for numberless generations his predecessors had viewed the world chiefly as a thing to be reformed, filled with evil forces to be abolished, and they saw no reason to suppose that they had wholly succeeded in the abolition; the duty was unchanged. That duty implied not only resistance to evil, but hatred of it. Boys naturally look on all force as an enemy, and generally find it so, but the New Englander, whether boy or man, in his long struggle with a stingy or hostile universe, had learned also to love the pleasure of hating; his joys were few.

Beside this one might set his summary characterization of the opposite type as he came into contact with it as a Harvard undergraduate: "Strictly, the southerner had no mind; he had temperament. He was not a scholar; he had no intellectual training; he could not analyse an idea, and he could not even conceive of admitting two; but in life one could get along very well without ideas, if one had only the social instinct." To complete the gallery I may quote his report of a national trait which had exercised the wit of Shakespeare and Swift and Horace Walpole and a long succession of observers of human nature as minted in Great Britain.

The English themselves [he remarks while in London] hardly conceived that their mind was either economical, sharp, or direct; but the defect that most struck an American was its enormous waste in eccentricity. Americans needed and used their whole energy, and applied it with close economy; but English society was eccentric by law and for sake of the eccentricity itself. The commonest phrase overheard at an English club or dinner-table was that so-and-so "is quite mad." It was no offense to so-and-so; it hardly distinguished him from his fellows; and when applied to a public man, like Gladstone, it was qualified by epithets much more forcible. Eccentricity was so general as to become hereditary distinction. It made the chief charm of English society as well as its chief terror.

The epigrammatic flavour is sufficient to lend some freshness to a truism as old as Hamlet's clown, but Adams's further query whether this eccentricity is a sign of strength or weakness, and his remarks on its working when brought into conflict with the plainer methods of his father and Thurlow and William Evarts, add a quality of reflection that is not at all trite. Nor did his keen understanding forsake him when dealing with individuals, as might be instanced by his characterizations of the men just named, or of such other politicians as Grant and McKinley and their Cabinets. Of mere anecdote the pages contain comparatively little, although here and there a good story gets entangled in his web of comment. Those who have some knowledge of Henry Reeve, the solemn, bulky, busy, doctrinaire editor of the *Edinburgh Review*, and of the Grotes, will be amused by this rencontre. "Every one," says Adams, "had heard of Mrs. Grote as 'the origin of the word grotesque.' Every one had laughed at the story of Reeve approaching Mrs. Grote, with his usual somewhat florid manner, asking in his literary dialect how her husband the historian was:—'And how is the learned Grotius?' 'Pretty well, thank you, Puffendorf!' One winced at the word, as though it were a drawing of Forain." Best of all, best of all at least for the lover of literature who tempers his enthusiasms with a grain of hard-headed cynicism, is Adams's account of meeting with Swinburne at the home of Lord Houghton, and this pendant to it of a later date:

Ten years afterwards Adams met him [Swinburne] at the Geneva Conference, fresh from Paris, bubbling with delight at a call he had made on Hugo:—"I was shown into a large room," he said, "with women and men seated in chairs against the walls, and Hugo at one end throned. No one spoke. At last Hugo raised his voice solemnly, and uttered the words:—'Quant à moi, je crois en Dieu!' Silence followed. Then a woman responded as if in deep meditation:—'Chose sublime! un Dieu qui croit en Dieu!' "

But it is not as a gallery of character etchings or as a repertory of stories that Mr. Adams's book mainly interests us; it is always the observer more than the observed that holds our attention, the effect being much the same as if we were reading a novel of Henry James, in which we are less concerned with the narrated acts of a group of men and women than with the colour these actions will take in the mind of some outside spectator, revealed or half-revealed. With both the novelist and the biographer the impelling motive is curiosity rather than sympathy; but with a difference. In James we feel more the detachment of a mere psychological experimenter, the unconcern of one who creates a world of complex emotions and wills for the somewhat chilly pleasure of taking apart what he has so carefully put together; whereas in Adams there is always present the eager desire to discover in the drama some elusive truth which, if found, would give a meaning to its unfolding scenes. The autobiography is well named *The Education of Henry Adams,* though we surmise from the beginning that no lesson will ever be learned, and that the learner has set himself to decipher a text in a foreign tongue without grammar or lexicon in his hands.

In a way the text before him was not one of his own choice, but forced on him by birth and inheritance. This breed of New England, of whom he was so consciously a titled representative, had once come out from the world for the sake of a religious and political affirmation —the two were originally one—to confirm which they were ready to deny all the other values of life. For the liberty to follow this affirmation they would discard tradition and authority and form and symbol and all that ordinarily binds men together in the bonds of habit. But the liberty of denying may itself become a habit. The intellectual history of New England is in fact the record of the encroachment of this liberty on the very affirmation for which it was at first the bulwark. By a gradual elimination of its positive content the faith of the people had passed from Calvinism to Unitarianism, and from this to free thinking, until in the days of our Adams there was little left to the intellect but a great denial:

Of all the conditions of his youth which afterwards puzzled the grown up man, this disappearance of religion puzzled him most. The boy went to church twice every Sunday; he was taught to read his Bible, and he learned religious poetry by heart; he believed in a mild Deism; he prayed;

he went through all the forms; but neither to him nor to his brothers or sisters was religion real. Even the mild discipline of the Unitarian church was so irksome that they all threw it off at the first possible moment, and never afterwards entered a church. The religious instinct had vanished, and could not be revived, although one made in later life many efforts to recover it. That the most powerful emotion of man, next to the sexual, should disappear, might be a personal defect of his own; but that the most intelligent society, led by the most intelligent clergy, in the most moral conditions he ever knew, should have solved all the problems of the universe so thoroughly as to have quite ceased making itself anxious about past or future, and should have persuaded itself that all the problems which had convulsed human thought from earliest recorded time, were not worth discussing, seemed to him the most curious social phenomenon he had to account for in a long life.

So the original affirmation had been swallowed up in its own defences, while the negative impulse grew "to a degree that in the long run became positive and hostile." But with this intellectual negation there remained almost in full force the moral impulse which from the first had been so intimately associated with a negative separatism. This is the key we must hold in our hands if we would enter into the inner life of Henry Adams and the other New Englanders of his generation, taking the word broadly—we must, if possible, put ourselves into the state of men whose conscience was moving, so to speak, *in vacuo*, like a dispossessed ghost seeking a substantial habitation. Adams "tended towards negation on his own account, as one side of the New England mind had always done." In this vacuum various minds sought relief in various ways, connecting themselves naturally with the contemporary currents of European thought. Emerson, as the purest spirit of them all, would rest in the bare liberty of prophesying, in the security of an intuition content in itself and careless of all preceding experience as formulated in law and custom. He was *par excellence* the pure Romantic, yet withal a New Englander at heart, not a German. John Fiske, if we may extend the limits of a generation so far, looked to the new discoveries of scientific evolution to give substance to the vague cosmic deity which had swum into the place of the Christian Jehovah. Most significant of all in some respects for our present subject is the case of Charles Eliot Norton. With him New England scepticism merges into the contented agnosticism of his British friends, particularly of Leslie Stephen, while the sting of conscience takes the form of distress at the licence of an agnostic society. So he writes, in one vein to Goldwin Smith:

Possibly I regret less than you do the giving up of the old faith, and the being compelled to renounce as hopeless every attempt to solve the problems which excite our curiosity. The position toward the universe in which we find ourselves seems to me on the whole the manliest which has been attained. We are thrown back on our own resources to make the best of our lives. A new sense of responsibility is aroused in us, and, by the narrowing of the limits of our hopes and expectations, we find ourselves more capable of using our faculties for legitimate and rational ends.

But when the conscience of Norton is speaking we hear words very different from those of his reason just quoted. So, for instance, he writes to Leslie Stephen:

It looks as if the world were entering on a new stage of experience, unlike anything heretofore, in which there must be a new discipline of suffering to fit men for the new conditions. I fear that America is beginning a long course of error and of wrong, and is likely to become more and more a power for disturbance and for barbarism. The worst sign is the lack of seriousness in the body of the people; its triviality, and its indifference to moral principle.

Norton was not consistent, you will say; and rightly. There is a question to ask of a man who finds a new source of responsibility in a creed destructive of the very principle of authority, yet laments the lack of responsibility in a world that acts in accordance with such a creed; there is a beautiful inconsistency in the heart of one who professes complete agnosticism, yet spends his life in the devoted study of Dante. It is the inconsistency of a conscience that has outlived faith and not found philosophy, the will of New England working out in its own peculiar manner the problem of the nineteenth century. To Adams the question of meaning in the world came with a somewhat different emphasis. Norton was the product of a long line of theologians, and doubt, when it crept in, took primarily the form of philosophical scepticism. But Adams was not born into the Brahmin caste. From the beginning, as seen in his great-grandfather and in his ancestral cousin, the revolt against traditional authority had been rather in the field of politics, and it was in his blood, so to speak, that his agnosticism should strike first upon the belief in a providential purpose in history. That indeed is the stimulus of what he calls his education. His inquiry was to branch out into a wider sphere, and in the end was to make its return to a medieval mysticism, as Norton's did to a medieval aestheticism; but in his earlier years he was sufficiently absorbed in seeking some theory to explain the sequence of historical events. What was the meaning of this opposition which his forbears and his father had maintained against the settled institutions of government? To whose profit did it accrue, or was there any profit to be found anywhere? In what way had the world grown wiser and truer from this struggle and from all the struggles of men since the beginning of time? Where should he put his finger on the thread of progress in the terrible tangle of human misadventure?

He began his inquiry—at least in old age, looking back over his experience, he seemed to himself to have begun it—when as a boy he watched the political manoeuvres of the Abolitionists. At home he "lived in the atmosphere of the Stamp Act, the Tea Tax, and the Boston Massacre"; only now "the Slave Power took the place of Stuart Kings and Roman Popes." He observed his father and Charles Sumner and their clique play the game of politics against the entrenched aristocracy of Boston; he saw from the inside the working of the coalition which sent Sumner to the Senate and made George Boutwell the Democratic governor of Massachusetts; he thought their ends noble, such as his great-grandfather would have approved, but he knew that their means were ignoble; and he wondered. "Thus before he was fifteen years old, he had managed to get himself into a state of moral confusion from which he never escaped."

Formal instruction gave him no clue to the labyrinth. "Four years of Harvard College, if successful, resulted in an autobiographical blank, a mind on which only a water-mark had been stamped." He got no wisdom from his teachers, none from his fellow students, though these included such promising names as Alexander Agassiz, Phillips Brooks, H. H. Richardson, and O. W. Holmes. "The chief wonder of education," he remarks, "is that it does not ruin everybody connected with it, teachers and taught." That is the world-old ingratitude of the scholar, commonly pronounced most vigorously by those who have profited most from instruction; it falls naturally from the lips of Henry Adams, and perhaps with him means something. At any rate he left college still "watching vaguely for a path and a direction." Travel might bestow what the class-room had withheld. He travelled. In Rome, more than once, he sat at sunset on the steps of the church of Santa Maria di Ara Coeli—there where Gibbon had mused on the fall of empire—sat, and reflected, and concluded nothing:

Rome was a bewildering complex of ideas, experiments, ambitions, energies; without her, the Western world was pointless and fragmentary; she gave heart and unity to it all; yet Gibbon might have gone on for the whole century, sitting among the ruins of the Capitol, and no one would have passed, capable of telling him what it meant. Perhaps it meant nothing.

We need not follow Adams through all the stages of his historical education. One great lesson in negative wisdom he was to learn in London, while helping his father to unravel the machinations of Palmerston and Lord John Russell and Gladstone against the government of the United States. He was to observe men sensitive to any imputation of untruth and otherwise highly moral, yet in public speaking one thing while in private acting another, men whose courage, as it seemed to him, lay in subterfuge and whose honour went no further than indignation. "If one could not believe them, Truth in politics might be ignored as a delusion"; and he had ample grounds for not believing any word of Gladstone at least, the most righteous of them all. What was to be made out of such a contradiction in terms by a student of life who "liked lofty moral principles and cared little for political tactics"? "Here, then, appeared in its fullest force, the practical difficulty in education which a mere student could never overcome; a difficulty not in theory, or knowledge, or even want of experience, but in the sheer chaos of human nature."

That difficulty was not diminished when he returned to Washington and saw a blunt plain soldier like Grant entangled in the most questionable business. For one moment, indeed, at the time of our Spanish War, he felt a sense of possible purpose working itself out in history. To him, if to no one else, "still living in the atmosphere of Palmerston and John Russell, the sudden appearance of Germany as the grizzly terror which, in twenty years, effected what Adamses had tried for two hundred in vain,—frightened England into America's arms,—seemed as melodramatic as any plot of Napoleon the Great." But his satisfaction was more temperamental than intellectual—than intelligent, one might say—and in the imbroglio of foreign intrigue that followed, and that wrecked the health of his dearest friend, John Hay, he was forced to see again only the conflict of blind wills and the shifting combinations of chance.

If Adams's observation of history in the making, supplemented by his study of history in the past, led to these sceptical conclusions, a sudden event of a more personal sort seemed, as it were, to rend the veil of cosmic charity and to show him that the foolishness of human affairs was but a little centre of chaos encompassed by a vast and malignant chaos of nature. Called from London to Italy by a telegram, he found his beloved sister, a woman of forty, for whom life had been gay and brilliant, dying in extreme torture from a miserable accident. As he sat by her bedside and watched the agony of her dissolution, while out of doors the world was glowing with the sensuous joys of an Italian summer, it seemed to him that now for the first time he beheld Nature face to face; and what he saw in that vision was to haunt him for the rest of his years:

Impressions like these are not reasoned or catalogued in the mind; they are felt as part of violent emotion; and the mind that feels them is a different one from that which reasons; it is thought of a different power and a different person. The first serious consciousness of Nature's gesture—her attitude towards life—took form then as a fantasm, a nightmare, an insanity of force. For the first time, the stage-scenery of the senses collapsed; the human mind felt itself stripped naked, vibrating in a void of shapeless energies, with resistless mass, colliding, crushing, wasting and destroying what these same energies had created and laboured from eternity to perfect. Society became fantastic, a vision of pantomime with a mechanical motion; and its so-called thought merged in the mere sense of life, and pleasure in the sense. The usual anodynes of social medicine became evident artifice. Stoicism was perhaps the best; religion was the most human; but the idea that any personal deity could find pleasure or profit in torturing a poor woman, by accident, with a fiendish cruelty known to man only in perverted and insane temperaments, could not be held for a moment. For pure blasphemy, it made pure atheism a comfort. God might be, as the Church said, a Substance, but he could not be a Person.

In those hours of biting agony, while the individual life so dear to him was wrestling unequally with the unsympathetic powers of death, Adams saw the destiny of mankind merged into the destiny of the sum of things. At an early period he had added to his reading of history a faithful study of science, and as he had sought for a thread of providential guidance in the one, so, under the influence of the newly based theory of evolution, he looked for signs of design and progress in the non-human order of creation. At first the two fields of inquiry had lain apart, but now, as I say, they appeared as phases only of the one problem which engaged his passionate attention. But the search baffled him, baffled him the more as it became more complex. As in history he thought he saw the evil persisting unchanged along with the good, so in the field of science he beheld the lower order of existence continuing on with the higher and throwing an element of stable confusion into progressive mutation. More than that. When he went beyond the material of biology into the dark background of inorganic forces he learned that the physicists themselves acknowledged only an inexpressible mystery. In Germany he heard Haeckel avowing that "the proper essence of substance appeared to him more and more marvellous and enigmatic as he penetrated further into the knowledge of its attributes, —matter and energy,—and as he learned to know their innumerable phenomena and their evolution." In France he heard the clearer and more authoritative voice of Poincaré making the same confession of ignorance: "[in science] we are led to act as though a simple law, when other things were equal, must be more probable than a complicated law. Half a century ago one frankly confessed it, and proclaimed that nature loves simplicity. She has since given us too often the lie. To-day this tendency is no longer avowed, and only so much of it is preserved as is indispensable so that science shall not become impossible." Then, turning to England, he read such words as these: "In the chaos behind sensation, in the 'beyond' of sense-impressions, we cannot infer necessity, order, or routine, for these are concepts formed by the mind of man on this side of sense-impressions. . . . Briefly, chaos is all that science can logically assert of the super-sensuous." Thus as the "unknowable" came nearer to man's inquiry it seemed to put on positive and menacing hues; the pronouncements of the most advanced physical thinkers echoed to Adams what he had learnt from his own study in history—chaos in the background here and there. And if he went to the pseudo-science of psychology he was faced with another "sub-conscious chaos below the mind"; man's "normal thought," he learned, "was dispersion, sleep, dream, inconsequence; the simultaneous action of different thought-centres without central control. His artificial balance was acquired habit. He was an acrobat, with a dwarf on his back, crossing a chasm on a slack-rope, and commonly breaking his neck." Here was a question that sprang from something very far from idle curiosity. Had Adams not witnessed the terror of the mystery, when this thing called chaos had suddenly lurched forward out of its background of mystery and enveloped his little oasis of well-loved order?

What was the proper attitude towards this enigma? Was it that no one can reach beyond himself? "All that Henry Adams ever saw in man was a reflection of his own ignorance"—such was his political discernment far back in his London days; should that be the final verdict of all his seeing? In a way he had acquired what ages ago had been proclaimed by Socrates as the beginning of wisdom: not to think we know what we do not know. Into this sea of negation he had sailed from the ancient moorings of his people; but not even the New Englander of the nineteenth century could rest in pure negation. Emerson, like Socrates, had found no difficulty in combining scepticism with an intuition of pure spirituality, though, unlike Socrates, to maintain his inner vision intact he shut his eyes resolutely on the darker facts of nature. That serene indifference to evil was the last thing possible to Adams. Another New Englander, nearer to Adams in date, John Fiske, had accepted the most rigid deductions of biological evolution, and then on Darwin's law of natural selection, which for humanly felt good and evil substituted a conception of blind unfeeling mechanism, had superimposed the conception of a cosmic deity unfolding the world to

> one far-off divine event,
> To which the whole creation moves.

Whatever may be said of such a philosophy, it was meaningless to Henry Adams; he could not marry the faith in a benignant pantheistic will with the sort of chaos that lurked for him behind every door of our ignorance. Still another New Englander, Charles Eliot Norton, as we have seen, was content to profess a complete agnosticism of theory along with an unswerving belief in human responsibility—to what? Alas, that "what" was the little irksome word that Adams could not get out of his mind.

The answer, or the direction towards an answer, came to him as he walked the halls of the Paris Exposition of 1900. There, at least, under the guidance of his scientific friend, Langley, if he saw nothing that pointed to a rational design at the end of things, he beheld in the great gallery of machines a symbol of what science had substituted for design. "The planet itself seemed less impressive, in its old-fashioned, deliberate, annual or daily revolution, than this huge wheel, revolving within arm's-length at some vertiginous speed, and barely murmuring, —scarcely humming an audible warning to stand a hair's-breadth further for respect of power,—while it would not wake the baby lying close against its frame. Before the end, one began to pray to it; inherited instinct taught the natural expression of man before silent and infinite force. Among the thousand symbols of ultimate energy, the dynamo was not so human as some, but it was the most expressive." Force, he would say, blind whirling force, strapped and bound in iron, is supreme over all:

> Dinos has driven out Zeus and rules as king.

We should need, in fact, a living Aristophanes to celebrate this step of a New Englander's education. Other men of the century had discovered this same god, but their worship had taken strangely different forms. "Power is power," says Tolstoy, reading for himself the lesson of history at the conclusion of his *War and Peace,* "that is Power is a word, the true meaning of which is to us incomprehensible"; and then, as a good humanitarian, he personifies this Unknowable in the instinctive soul of the People. Nietzsche, too, had found only *Macht* at the heart of the world, but he worshipped this Power not at all in the impulse of the People—quite the contrary; and some of his interpreters have deified a *Schrecklichkeit* very different from the pity of Tolstoy. Perhaps the true lesson of our age would be to learn why and how this modern Janus of Power has tricked us into believing that he has only one face. But Adams was too knowing to bow the knee with Tolstoy, and too timid to salute with Nietzsche. He took another way.

Norton, as we have seen, had found agnosticism compatible with devotion to Dante, being able at least to sympathize with the energetic moral sense and the aesthetic vision of that poet; and Adams, like him, turned at last for consolation to the age of Dante, if not to Dante himself, though with a difference. From the Exposition, "caring but little for the name, and fixed only on tracing Force, Adams had gone straight to the Virgin at Chartres, and asked her to show him God, face to face, as she did for St. Bernard." What the Virgin revealed to him is told clearly enough in the autobiography, but for its fullest elucidation one should read that extraordinary disquisition on the art and poetry and philosophy and religion of the twelfth and thirteenth centuries which he entitles *Mont-Saint-Michel and Chartres.* In the Virgin Mother of God, to whose honour the cathedrals pointed their arches towards heaven, before whose throne the windows were made to glow like the jewels of a queen, for whose delight romance wove its shimmering web of words, to whom great scholars sacrificed their learning, our far-travelled New Englander saw at last the one symbol of Force comprehensible to the human heart, if not to the human brain. "The Puritans," he says, "abandoned the New Testament and the Virgin in order to go back to the beginning, and renew the quarrel with Eve"; our latest Puritan rediscovers woman on her medieval throne, and chants to her in modern speech the ancient paean to Alma Venus Genetrix. It would be a pretty business to unravel the various motives that had impelled him on this devious way from the sturdy, if unloving, protestantism of his race. He himself makes much of the motive of love as the aspect of infinite power which man can understand. That may be; but I suspect that another attribute of the Virgin meant even more to his mind. Read, if you will, his charming pages on her interventions and miracles; you will observe that they were almost without exception performed to override the course of law and justice, and you will learn that behind her woman's pity there was another quality which Adams, at any rate, does not hesitate to glorify as equally feminine:

The fact, conspicuous above all other historical certainties about religion, that the Virgin was by essence illogical, unreasonable, and feminine, is the only fact of any ultimate value worth studying, and starts a number of questions that history has shown itself clearly afraid to touch. . . . She was imposed unanimously by all classes, because what man wanted most in the Middle Ages was not merely law or equity, but also and particularly favour. . . . The individual rebelled against restraint; society wanted to do what it pleased; all disliked the laws which Church and State were trying to fasten on them. . . . If the Trinity was in its essence Unity, the Mother alone could represent whatever was not Unity; whatever was irregular, exceptional, outlawed; and this was the whole human race.

Conscience was the last tie of New England to its past. Was it the perfect irresponsibility of the Virgin, human no doubt, feminine perhaps, certainly not Puritan, that gave to our tired sceptic the illusion of having reached a comfortable goal after his long voyage of education? There is a fateful analogy between the irresponsibility of unreasoning Force and unreasoning love; and the gods of Nietzsche and of Tolstoy are but the two faces of one god. To change the metaphor, if it may be done without disrespect, the image in the cathedral of Chartres looks perilously like the ancient idol of Dinos decked out in petticoats.

If we regard Adams's scholarship, his imagination, his verbal dexterity, his candour, his cynical vivacity, his range of reflection, we must give him a high place in the American literature of the past generation, a higher place probably than his present limited popularity would indicate. But one winces a little at acknowledging that the latest spokesman of the Adamses and of New England ends his career in sentimental nihilism. From Harvard College, which to Adams had been only one stage in the way of disillusion, the boy John Fiske had written: "When we come to a true philosophy, and make *that* our standpoint, all things become clear. We know what things to learn, and what, in the infinite mass of things, to leave unlearned; and then the Universe becomes clear and harmonious." The tragedy of Adams's education is that of a man who could not rest easy in negation, yet could find no positive faith to take its place. From one point of view he may appear to be the most honest and typical mind of New England in its last condition; yet withal some manlier voice, some word of deeper insight that yet faces the facts of life, we must still expect to hear from the people of Mather and Edwards and Channing and Emerson.

Comments and Questions

1. In his third paragraph Paul Elmer More suggests that the moral of *The Education of Henry Adams* is "the baffled sense of mystery behind the veil of apparent design." More then proceeds to analyze the contents of *The Education*. Study the ways in which the analysis of Adams's book reflects this "moral."

2. The paragraph beginning "But it is not as a gallery of character etchings . . ." reiterates More's interpretation of the "moral" of *The Education*, previously voiced in the third paragraph. Why does More feel the need to reiterate the moral at this point? Study the two paragraphs from the point of view of form and technique. What use does More make of the comparison between Adams and Henry James in the latter paragraph?

3. More opens his essay by suggesting that the tone of Adams's writing is one of "cynicism." Study the quotations from Adams's book, and decide how strong the note of cynicism sounds in them. Is "cynicism" an appropriate label for the tone?

4. A basic technique used by More is that of contrast. There is the contrast between Adams and James; between the spirit of seventeenth-century and nineteenth-century New England; between Adams and other New Englanders of his time (Emerson, Fiske, Norton); between the religiously oriented and the politically oriented. What contribution do these contrasts make toward a definition of Adams?

5. Particularly praiseworthy is More's ability to give a very complete synopsis of the contents of *The Education*, while yet making everything he tells about the book contribute to his interpretation of it. Make a study of how the writer effects this.

6. A good principle to keep in mind, both in reading and in writing, is that any piece of literature defines a reader (i.e., is written for a certain kind of reader). From a reading of More's essay, decide, as explicitly as you can, the nature of the reader whom More is addressing. Describe him. How old is he; or could he be any age? What has he read? What are his interests? How much formal schooling has he had? Then decide what relationship you bear to More's ideal reader. If you do not correspond entirely to the reader defined by More's essay, do you hope to become increasingly like him?

Suggestions for an Essay

Taking a work which you have read, analyze the various kinds of subject matter with which the author deals. That is, indicate what he tells his reader. Does he come to any conclusions about his subject matter? (For instance, if he writes about the country, does he suggest that the country is better than the city?) Does he write about the things you expected him to, or are you surprised by his choice of subject matter?

Write a paper that will give the reader unfamiliar with the work a good idea of what the author writes about. You will be obliged to decide whether to comment on the aesthetic quality of the work, or whether to confine yourself entirely to an analysis of its contents. Generally speaking, a more exciting essay results when a writer includes some evaluation of the work discussed. Not only does this make for a richer essay, but it also allows a reader familiar with the work discussed to compare his own interpretation of it with that of the critic he is reading.

Center your essay around which of the author's subjects interest you, which do not, and why. Which of his subjects would you like to know more about? Which do you hope you will run across in his other selections you propose to read?

If you propose to read further in the works of this author, your paper should represent an important step in defining your subsequent area of study; however, keep in mind that your task here, as in all writing, is to produce an interesting and enjoyable essay.

3

A COMPARISON OF TWO WORKS

Introduction

Literary critics frequently draw comparisons and contrasts between two works. Ordinarily, such comparisons and contrasts help the critic evaluate the aesthetic worth of the works in question, and serve, as well, to throw into relief the peculiar quality of each work.

Below is an excerpt from Chapter V of Henry James's critical biography of Nathaniel Hawthorne, in which James draws comparisons between Hawthorne's *The Scarlet Letter* and *The House of the Seven Gables*, as well as between *The Scarlet Letter* and John Gibson Lockhart's *Adam Blair*.

HENRY JAMES

from chapter v *of* HAWTHORNE

The Three American Novels

. . . [*The Scarlet Letter*] has the tone of the circumstances in which it was produced. If Hawthorne was in a sombre mood, and if his future were painfully vague, *The Scarlet Letter* contains little enough of gaiety or of hopefulness. It is densely dark, with a single spot of vivid colour in it; and it will probably long remain the most consistently gloomy of English novels of the first order. But I just now called it the author's masterpiece, and I imagine it will continue to be, for other

54

generations than ours, his most substantial title to fame. The subject had probably lain a long time in his mind, as his subjects were apt to do; so that he appears completely to possess it, to know it and feel it. It is simpler and more complete than his other novels; it achieves more perfectly what it attempts, and it has about it that charm, very hard to express, which we find in an artist's work the first time he has touched his highest mark—a sort of straightness and naturalness of execution, an unconsciousness of his public, and freshness of interest in his theme. It was a great success, and he immediately found himself famous. The writer of these lines, who was a child at the time, remembers dimly the sensation the book produced, and the little shudder with which people alluded to it, as if a peculiar horror were mixed with its attractions. He was too young to read it himself; but its title, upon which he fixed his eyes as the book lay upon the table, had a mysterious charm. He had a vague belief, indeed, that the "letter" in question was one of the documents that come by the post, and it was a source of perpetual wonderment to him that it should be of such an unaccustomed hue. Of course it was difficult to explain to a child the significance of poor Hester Prynne's blood-coloured A. But the mystery was at last partly dispelled by his being taken to see a collection of pictures (the annual exhibition of the National Academy), where he encountered a representation of a pale, handsome woman, in a quaint black dress and a white coif, holding between her knees an elfish-looking little girl, fantastically dressed, and crowned with flowers. Embroidered on the woman's breast was a great crimson A, over which the child's fingers, as she glanced strangely out of the picture, were maliciously playing. I was told that this was Hester Prynne and little Pearl, and that when I grew older I might read their interesting history. But the picture remained vividly imprinted on my mind; I had been vaguely frightened and made uneasy by it; and when, years afterwards, I first read the novel, I seemed to myself to have read it before, and to be familiar with its two strange heroines. I mention this incident simply as an indication of the degree to which the success of The Scarlet Letter had made the book what is called an actuality. Hawthorne himself was very modest about it; he wrote to his publisher, when there was a question of his undertaking another novel, that what had given the history of Hester Prynne its "vogue" was simply the introductory chapter. In fact, the publication of The Scarlet Letter was in the United States a literary event of the first importance. The book was the finest piece of imaginative writing yet put forth in the country. There was a consciousness of this in the welcome that was given it—a satisfaction in the idea of America having produced a novel that belonged to literature, and to the forefront of it. Something might at last be sent to Europe as exquisite in quality as anything that had been received, and the best of it was that the thing was absolutely American; it belonged to the soil, to the air; it came out of the very heart of New England.

It is beautiful, admirable, extraordinary; it has in the highest degree that merit which I have spoken of as the mark of Hawthorne's best things—an indefinable purity and lightness of conception, a quality which in a work of art affects one in the same way as the absence of grossness does in a human being. His fancy, as I just now said, had evidently brooded over the subject for a long time; the situation to be represented had disclosed itself to him in all its phases. When I say in all its phases, the sentence demands modification; for it is to be remembered that if Hawthorne laid his hand upon the well-worn theme, upon the familiar combination of the wife, the lover, and the husband, it was, after all, but to one period of the history of these three persons that he attached himself. The situation is the situation after the woman's fault has been committed, and the current of expiation and repentance has set in. In spite of the relation between Hester Prynne and Arthur Dimmesdale, no story of love was surely ever less of a "love-story." To Hawthorne's imagination the fact that these two persons had loved each other too well was of an interest comparatively vulgar; what appealed to him was the idea of their moral situation in the long years that were to follow. The story, indeed, is in a secondary degree that of Hester Prynne; she becomes, really, after the first scene, an accessory figure; it is not upon her the *dénoûment* depends. It is upon her guilty lover that the author projects most frequently the cold, thin rays of his fitfully-moving lantern, which makes here and there a little luminous circle, on the edge of which hovers the livid and sinister figure of the injured and retributive husband. The story goes on, for the most part, between the lover and the husband—the tormented young Puritan minister, who carries the secret of his own lapse from pastoral purity locked up beneath an exterior that commends itself to the reverence of his flock, while he sees the softer partner of his guilt standing in the full glare of exposure and humbling herself to the misery of atonement—between this more wretched and pitiable culprit, to whom dishonour would come as a comfort and the pillory as a relief, and the older, keener, wiser man, who, to obtain satisfaction for the wrong he has suffered, devises the infernally ingenious plan of conjoining himself with his wronger, living with him, living upon him; and while he pretends to minister to his hidden ailment and to sympathise with his pain, revels in his unsuspected knowledge of these things, and stimulates them by malignant arts. The attitude of Roger Chillingworth, and the means he takes to compensate himself—these are the highly original elements in the situation that Hawthorne so ingeniously treats. None of his works are so impregnated with that after-sense of the old Puritan consciousness of life to which allusion has so often been made. If, as M. Montégut says, the qualities of his ancestors *filtered* down through generations into his composition, *The Scarlet Letter* was, as it were, the vessel that gathered up the last of the precious drops. And I say this not because the story happens to be of so-called historical cast, to be told of the early days of Massachusetts, and of people in steeple-crowned hats and sad-coloured garments. The historical colouring is rather weak than otherwise; there is little elaboration of detail, of the modern realism of research; and the author has made no great point of causing his figures to speak the English of their period. Nevertheless, the book is full of the moral presence of the race that invented Hester's penance—diluted and complicated with other things, but still perfectly recognisable. Puritanism, in a word, is there, not only objectively, as Hawthorne tried to place it there, but subjectively as well. Not, I mean, in his judgment of his characters in any harshness of prejudice, or in the obtrusion of a moral lesson; but in the very quality of his own vision, in the tone of the picture, in a certain coldness and exclusiveness of treatment.

The faults of the book are, to my sense, a want of reality and an abuse of the fanciful element—of a certain superficial symbolism. The people strike me not as characters, but as representatives, very picturesquely arranged, of a single state of mind; and the interest of the story lies, not in them, but in the situation, which is insistently kept before us, with little progression, though with a great deal, as I have said, of a certain stable variation; and to which they, out of their reality, contribute little that helps it to live and move. I was made to feel this want of reality, this over-ingenuity, of *The Scarlet Letter*, by chancing not long since upon a novel which was read fifty years ago much more than to-day, but which is still worth reading—the story of *Adam Blair*, by John Gibson Lockhart. This interesting and powerful little tale has a great deal of analogy with Hawthorne's novel—quite enough, at least, to suggest a comparison between them; and the comparison is a very interesting one to make, for it speedily leads us to larger considerations than simple resemblances and divergences of plot.

Adam Blair, like Arthur Dimmesdale, is a Calvinistic minister who becomes the lover of a married woman, is overwhelmed with remorse at his misdeed, and makes a public confession of it; then expiates it by resigning his pastoral office and becoming a humble tiller of the soil, as his father had been. The two stories are of about the same length, and each is the masterpiece (putting aside, of course, as far as Lockhart is concerned, the *Life of Scott*) of the author. They deal alike with the manners of a rigidly theological society, and even in certain details they correspond. In each of them, between the guilty pair, there is a charming little girl; though I hasten to say that Sarah Blair (who is not the daughter of the heroine, but the legitimate offspring of the hero, a widower) is far from being as brilliant and graceful an apparition as the admirable little Pearl of *The Scarlet Letter*. The main difference between the two tales is the fact that in the American story the husband plays an all-important part, and in the Scottish plays almost none at all. *Adam Blair* is the history of the passion, and *The Scarlet Letter* the history of its sequel; but nevertheless, if one has read the two books at a short interval, it is impossible to avoid confronting them. I confess that a large portion of the interest of *Adam Blair*, to my mind, when once I had perceived that it would repeat in a great measure the situation of *The Scarlet Letter*, lay in noting its difference of tone. It threw into relief the passionless quality of Hawthorne's novel, its element of cold and ingenious fantasy, its elaborate imaginative delicacy. These things do not precisely constitute a weakness in *The Scarlet Letter*; indeed, in a certain way they constitute a great strength; but the absence of a certain something warm and straightforward, a trifle more grossly human and vulgarly natural, which one finds in *Adam Blair*, will always make Hawthorne's tale less touching to a large number of even very intelligent readers, than a love-story told with the robust, synthetic pathos which served Lockhart so well. His novel is not of the first rank (I should call it an excellent second-rate one), but it borrows a charm from the fact that his vigorous, but not strongly imaginative, mind was impregnated with the reality of his subject. He did not always succeed in rendering this reality; the expression is sometimes awkward and poor. But the reader feels that his vision was clear, and his feeling about the matter very strong and rich. Hawthorne's imagination, on the other hand, plays with his theme so incessantly, leads it such a dance through the moon-lighted air of his intellect, that the thing cools off, as it were, hardens and stiffens, and, producing effects much more exquisite, leaves the reader with a sense of having handled a splendid piece of silversmith's work. Lockhart, by means much more vulgar, produces at moments a greater illusion, and satisfies our inevitable desire for something, in the people in whom it is sought to interest us, that shall be of the same pitch and the same continuity with ourselves. Above all, it is interesting to see how the same subject appears to two men of a thoroughly different cast of mind and of a different race. Lockhart was struck with the warmth of the subject that offered itself to him, and Hawthorne with its coldness; the one with its glow, its sentimental interest—the other with its shadow, its moral interest. Lockhart's story is as decent, as severely draped, as *The Scarlet Letter;* but the author has a more vivid sense than appears to have imposed itself upon Hawthorne, of some of the incidents of the situation he describes; his tempted man and tempting woman are more actual and personal; his heroine in especial, though not in the least a delicate or a subtle conception, has a sort of credible, visible, palpable property, a vulgar roundness and relief, which are lacking to the dim and chastened image of Hester Prynne. But I am going too far; I am comparing simplicity with subtlety, the usual with the refined. Each man wrote as his turn of mind impelled him, but each expressed something more than himself. Lockhart was a dense, substantial Briton, with a taste for the concrete, and Hawthorne was a thin New Englander, with a miasmatic conscience.

In *The Scarlet Letter* there is a great deal of symbolism; there is, I think, too much. It is overdone at times, and becomes mechanical; it ceases to be impressive, and grazes triviality. The idea of the mystic *A* which the young minister finds imprinted upon his breast and eating into his flesh, in sympathy with the embroidered badge that Hester is condemned to wear, appears to me to be a case in point. This suggestion should, I think, have been just made and dropped; to insist upon it and return to it, is to exaggerate the weak side of the subject. Hawthorne returns to it constantly, plays with it, and seems charmed by it; until at last the reader feels tempted to declare that his enjoyment of it is puerile. In the admirable scene, so superbly conceived and beautifully executed, in which Mr. Dimmesdale, in the stillness of the night, in the middle of the sleeping town, feels impelled to go and stand upon the scaffold where his mistress had formerly enacted her dreadful penance, and then, seeing Hester pass along the street, from watching at a sick-bed, with little Pearl at her side, calls them both to come and stand there beside him—in this masterly episode the effect is almost spoiled by the introduction of one of these superficial conceits. What leads up to it is very fine—so fine that I cannot do better than quote it as a specimen of one of the striking pages of the book.

"But before Mr. Dimmesdale had done speaking, a light gleamed far and wide over all the muffled sky. It was doubtless caused by one of those meteors which the night-watcher may so often observe burning out to waste in the vacant regions of the atmosphere. So powerful was its radiance that it thoroughly illuminated the dense medium of cloud betwixt the sky and earth. The great vault brightened, like the dome of an immense lamp. It showed the familiar scene of the street with the distinctness of midday, but also with the awfulness that is always imparted to familiar objects by an unaccustomed light. The wooden houses, with their jutting stories and quaint gable-peaks; the doorsteps and thresholds, with the early grass springing up about them; the garden-plots, black with freshly-turned earth; the wheel-track, little worn, and, even in the market-place, margined with green on either side;—all were visible, but with a singularity of aspect that seemed to give another moral interpretation to the things of this world than they had ever borne before. And there stood the minister, with his hand over his heart; and Hester Prynne, with the embroidered letter glimmering on her bosom; and little Pearl, herself a symbol, and the connecting link between these two. They stood in the noon of that strange and solemn splendour, as if it were the light that is to reveal all secrets, and the daybreak that shall unite all that belong to one another."

That is imaginative, impressive, poetic; but when, almost immediately afterwards, the author goes on to say that "the minister looking upward to the zenith, beheld there the appearance of an immense letter—the letter *A*—marked out in lines of dull red light," we feel that he goes too far, and is in danger of crossing the line that separates the sublime from its intimate neighbour. We are tempted to say that this is not moral tragedy, but physical comedy. In the same way, too much is made of the intimation that Hester's badge had a scorching property, and that if one touched it one would immediately withdraw one's hand. Hawthorne is perpetually looking for images which shall place themselves in picturesque correspondence with the spiritual facts with which he is concerned, and of course the search is of the very essence of poetry. But in such a process discretion is everything, and when the image becomes importunate it is in danger of seeming to stand for nothing more serious than itself. When Hester meets the minister by appointment in the forest, and sits talking with him while little Pearl wanders away and plays by the edge of the brook, the child is represented as at last making her way over to the other side of the woodland stream, and disporting herself there in a manner which makes her mother feel herself, "in some indistinct and tantalising manner, estranged from Pearl; as if the child, in her lonely ramble through the forest, had strayed out of the sphere in which she and her mother dwelt together, and was now vainly seeking to return to it." And Hawthorne devotes a chapter to this idea of the child's having, by putting the brook between Hester and herself, established a kind of spiritual gulf, on the verge of which her little fantastic person innocently mocks at her mother's sense of bereavement. This conception belongs, one would say, quite to the lighter order of a story-teller's devices, and the reader hardly goes with Hawthorne in the large development he gives to it. He hardly goes with him either, I think, in his extreme predilection for a small number of vague ideas which are represented by such terms as "sphere" and "sympathies." Hawthorne makes too liberal a use of these two substantives; it is the solitary defect of his style; and it counts as a defect partly because the words in question are a sort of specialty with certain writers immeasurably inferior to himself.

I had not meant, however, to expatiate upon his defects, which are of the slenderest and most venial kind. *The Scarlet Letter* has the beauty and harmony of all original and complete conceptions, and its weaker spots, whatever they are, are not of its essence; they are mere light flaws and inequalities of surface. One can often return to it; it supports familiarity, and has the inexhaustible charm and mystery of great works of art. It is admirably written. . . .

The House of the Seven Gables was written at Lenox, among the mountains of Massachusetts, a village nestling, rather loosely, in one of the loveliest corners of New England, to which Hawthorne had betaken himself after the success of *The Scarlet Letter* became conspicuous, in the summer of 1850, and where he occupied for two years an uncomfortable little red house, which is now pointed out to the inquiring stranger. The inquiring stranger is now a frequent figure at Lenox, for the place has suffered the process of lionisation. It has become a prosperous watering-place, or at least (as there are no waters), as they say in America, a summer-resort. It is a brilliant and generous landscape, and thirty years ago a man of fancy, desiring to apply himself, might have found both inspiration and tranquility there. Hawthorne found so much of both that he wrote more during his two years of residence at Lenox than at any period of his career. He began with *The House of the Seven Gables,* which was finished in the early part of 1851. This is the longest of his three American novels; it is the most elaborate, and in the judgment of some persons it is the finest. It is a rich, delightful, imaginative work, larger and more various than its companions, and full of all sorts of deep intentions, of interwoven threads of suggestion. But it is not so rounded and complete as *The Scarlet Letter;* it has always seemed to me more like a prologue to a great novel than a great novel itself. I think this is partly owing to the fact that the subject, the *donnée,* as the French say, of the story, does not quite fill it out, and that we get at the same time an impression of certain complicated purposes on the author's part, which seem to reach beyond it. I call it larger and more various than its companions, and it has, indeed, a greater richness of tone and density of detail. The colour, so to speak, of *The House of the Seven Gables* is admirable. But the story has a sort of expansive quality which never wholly fructifies, and as I lately laid it down, after reading it for the third time, I had a sense of having interested myself in a magnificent fragment. Yet the book has a great fascination; and of all of those of its author's productions which I have read over while writing this sketch, it is perhaps the one that has gained most by reperusal. If it be true of the others that the pure, natural quality of the imaginative strain is their great merit, this is at least as true of *The House of the Seven Gables,* the charm of which is in a peculiar degree of the kind that we fail to reduce to its grounds—like that of the sweetness of a piece of music, or the softness of fine September weather. It is vague, indefinable, ineffable; but it is the sort of thing we must always point to in justification of the high claim that we make for Hawthorne. In this case, of course, its vagueness is a drawback, for it is difficult to point to ethereal beauties; and if the reader whom we have wished to inoculate with our admiration inform us, after looking awhile, that he perceives nothing in particular, we can only reply that, in effect, the object is a delicate one.

The House of the Seven Gables comes nearer being a picture of contemporary American life than either of its companions; but on this ground it would be a mistake to make a large claim for it. It cannot be too often repeated that Hawthorne was not a realist. He had a high sense of reality—his Note-Books superabundantly testify to it; and fond as he was of jotting down the items that make it up, he never attempted to render exactly or closely the actual facts of the society that surrounded him. I have said—I began by saying—that his pages were full of its spirit, and of a certain reflected light that springs from it; but I was careful to add that the reader must look for his local and national qualities between the lines of his writing and in the *indirect* testimony of his tone, his accent, his temper, of his very omissions and suppressions. *The House of the Seven Gables* has, however, more literal actuality than the others, and if it were not too fanciful an account of it, I should say that it renders, to an initiated reader, the impression of a summer afternoon in an elm-shadowed New England town. It leaves upon the mind a vague correspondence to some such reminiscence, and in stirring up the association it renders it delightful. The comparison is to the honour of the New England town, which gains in it more than it bestows. The shadows of the elms, in *The House of the Seven Gables,* are exceptionally dense and cool; the summer afternoon is peculiarly still and beautiful; the atmosphere has a delicious warmth, and the long daylight seems to pause and rest. But the mild provincial quality is there, the mixture of shabbiness and freshness, the paucity of ingredients. The end of an old race—this is the situation that Hawthorne has depicted, and he has been admirably inspired in the choice of the figures in whom he seeks to interest us. They are all figures rather than characters—they are all pictures rather than persons. But if their reality is light and vague, it is sufficient, and it is in harmony with the low relief and dimness of outline of the objects that surrounded them. They are all types, to the author's mind, of something general, of something that is bound up with the history, at large, of families and individuals, and each of them is the centre of a cluster of those ingenious and meditative musings, rather melancholy, as a general thing, than joyous, which melt into the current and texture of the story and give it a kind of moral richness. A grotesque old spinster, simple, childish, penniless, very humble at heart, but rigidly conscious of her pedigree; an amiable bachelor, of an epicurean temperament and an enfeebled intellect, who has passed twenty years of his life in penal confinement for a crime of which he was unjustly pronounced guilty; a sweet-natured and bright-faced young girl from the country, a poor relation of these two ancient decrepitudes, with whose moral mustiness her modern freshness and soundness are contrasted; a young man still more modern, holding the latest opinions, who has sought his fortune up and down the world, and, though he has not found it, takes a genial and enthusiastic view of the future: these, with two or three remarkable accessory figures, are the persons concerned in the little drama. The drama is a small one, but as Hawthorne does not put it before us for its own superficial sake, for the dry facts of the case, but for something in it which he holds to be symbolic and of large application, something that points a moral and that it behoves us to remember, the scenes in the rusty wooden house whose gables give its name to the story, have something of the dignity both of history and of tragedy. Miss Hephzibah Pyncheon, dragging out a disappointed life in her paternal dwelling, finds herself obliged in her old age to open a little shop for the sale of penny toys and gingerbread. This is the central incident of the tale, and, as Hawthorne relates it, it is an incident of the most impressive magnitude and most touching interest. Her dishonoured and vague-minded brother is released from prison at the same moment, and returns to the ancestral roof to deepen her perplexities. But, on the other hand, to alleviate them, and to introduce a breath of the air of the outer world into this long unventilated interior, the little country cousin also arrives, and proves the good angel of the feebly distracted household. All this episode is exquisite—admirably conceived and executed, with a kind of humorous tenderness, an equal sense of everything in it that is picturesque, touching, ridiculous, worthy of the highest praise. Hephzibah Pyncheon, with her near-sighted scowl, her rusty joints, her antique turban, her map of a great territory to the eastward which ought to have belonged to her family, her vain terrors, and scruples, and resentments, the inaptitude and repugnance of an ancient gentlewoman to the vulgar little commerce which a cruel fate has compelled her to engage in—Hephzibah Pyncheon is a masterly picture. I repeat that she is a picture, as her companions are pictures; she is a charming piece of descriptive writing, rather than a dramatic exhibition. But she is described, like her companions, too, so subtly and lovingly that we enter into her virginal old heart and stand with her behind her abominable little counter. Clifford Pyncheon is a still more remarkable conception, though he is, perhaps, not so vividly depicted. It was a figure needing a much more subtle touch, however, and it was of the essence of his character to be vague and unemphasised. Nothing can be more charming than the manner in which the soft, bright, active presence of Phoebe Pyncheon is indicated, or than the account of her relations with the poor, dimly sentient kinsman for whom her light-handed sisterly offices, in the evening of a melancholy life, are a revelation of lost possibilities of happiness. "In her aspect," Hawthorne says of the young girl, "there was a familiar gladness, and a holiness that you could play with, and yet reverence it as much as ever. She was like a prayer offered up in the homeliest beauty of one's mother-tongue. Fresh was Phoebe, moreover, and airy, and sweet in her apparel; as if nothing that she wore—neither her gown, nor her small straw bonnet, nor her little kerchief, any more than her snowy stockings—had ever been put on before; or, if worn, were all the fresher for it, and with a fragrance as if they had lain among the rose-buds." Of the influence of her maidenly salubrity upon poor Clifford, Hawthorne gives the prettiest description, and then, breaking off suddenly, renounces the attempt in language which, while pleading its inadequacy, conveys an exquisite satisfaction to the reader. I quote the passage for the sake of its extreme felicity, and of the charming image with which it concludes.

"But we strive in vain to put the idea into words. No adequate expression of the beauty and profound pathos with which it impresses us is attainable. This being, made only for happiness, and heretofore so miserably failing to be happy—his tendencies so hideously thwarted that, some unknown time ago, the delicate springs of his character, never morally or intellectually strong, had given way, and he was now imbecile—this poor forlorn voyager from the Islands of the Blest, in a frail bark, on

a tempestuous sea, had been flung by the last mountain-wave of his ship-
wreck into a quiet harbour. There, as he lay more than half lifeless on the
strand, the fragrance of an earthly rose-bud had come to his nostrils, and,
as odours will, had summoned up reminiscences or visions of all the
living and breathing beauty amid which he should have had his home.
With his native susceptibility of happy influences, he inhales the slight
ethereal rapture into his soul, and expires!"

I have not mentioned the personage in *The House of the Seven
Gables* upon whom Hawthorne evidently bestowed most pains, and
whose portrait is the most elaborate in the book; partly because he is,
in spite of the space he occupies, an accessory figure, and partly because,
even more than the others, he is what I have called a picture rather than
a character. Judge Pyncheon is an ironical portrait, very richly and
broadly executed, very sagaciously composed and rendered—the portrait
of a superb, full-blown hypocrite, a large-based, full-nurtured Pharisee,
bland, urbane, impressive, diffusing about him a "sultry" warmth of
benevolence, as the author calls it again and again, and basking in the
noontide of prosperity and the consideration of society; but in reality
hard, gross, and ignoble. Judge Pyncheon is an elaborate piece of description, made up of a hundred admirable touches, in which satire is
always winged with fancy, and fancy is linked with a deep sense of
reality. It is difficult to say whether Hawthorne followed a model in
describing Judge Pyncheon; but it is tolerably obvious that the picture
is an impression—a copious impression—of an individual. It has evidently a definite starting-point in fact, and the author is able to draw,
freely and confidently, after the image established in his mind. Holgrave,
the modern young man, who has been a Jack-of-all-trades, and is at the
period of the story a daguerreotypist, is an attempt to render a kind
of national type—that of the young citizen of the United States whose
fortune is simply in his lively intelligence, and who stands naked, as it
were, unbiased and unencumbered alike, in the centre of the far-
stretching level of American life. Holgrave is intended as a contrast;
his lack of traditions, his democratic stamp, his condensed experience,
are opposed to the desiccated prejudices and exhausted vitality of the
race of which poor feebly-scowling, rusty-jointed Hephzibah is the
most heroic representative. It is, perhaps, a pity that Hawthorne should
not have proposed to himself to give the old Pyncheon qualities some
embodiment which would help them to balance more fairly with the
elastic properties of the young daguerreotypist—should not have painted
a lusty conservative to match his strenuous radical. As it is, the mustiness
and mouldiness of the tenants of the House of the Seven Gables crumble
away rather too easily. Evidently, however, what Hawthorne designed
to represent was not the struggle between an old society and a new,
for in this case he would have given the old one a better chance; but
simply, as I have said, the shrinkage and extinction of a family. This
appealed to his imagination; and the idea of long perpetuation and sur-

vival always appears to have filled him with a kind of horror and disapproval. Conservative, in a certain degree, as he was himself, and fond
of retrospect and quietude and the mellowing influences of time, it is
singular how often one encounters in his writings some expression of
mistrust of old houses, old institutions, long lines of descent. He was
disposed, apparently, to allow a very moderate measure in these respects,
and he condemns the dwelling of the Pyncheons to disappear from the
face of the earth because it has been standing a couple of hundred years.
In this he was an American of Americans; or, rather, he was more
American than many of his countrymen, who, though they are accustomed to work for the short run rather than the long, have often a
lurking esteem for things that show the marks of having lasted. I will
add that Holgrave is one of the few figures, among those which Hawthorne created, with regard to which the absence of the realistic mode
of treatment is felt as a loss. Holgrave is not sharply enough character-
ised; he lacks features; he is not an individual, but a type. But my last
word about this admirable novel must not be a restrictive one. It is a
large and generous production, pervaded with that vague hum, that
indefinable echo, of the whole multitudinous life of man, which is the
real sign of a great work of fiction. . . .

Comments and Questions

1. In paragraph one, Henry James calls *The Scarlet Letter* Hawthorne's masterpiece; hence, he must feel that *The House of the Seven
Gables* is of lesser worth. Does his treatment of the two books adequately
demonstrate the reasons for his preference?

2. In paragraph two, James speaks of *The Scarlet Letter* as having
an "indefinable purity and lightness of conception. . . ." Is James skirt-
ing his responsibility as a critic here, or does his subsequent treatment of
The Scarlet Letter convince you that there *is* an indefinable quality about
it?

3. In paragraph two, James speaks of Hawthorne's having laid his
hand upon a "well-worn theme." In what ways does James suggest that
Hawthorne was able to create originality out of something well worn?

4. Notice, in paragraph two, the metaphorical use of the "fitfully-
moving lantern." How does James make this, and other metaphors, work
for him throughout the course of his criticism? Is there a possible connection between James's use of metaphorical expression and his suggestion concerning the "indefinable" quality of *The Scarlet Letter*?

5. One of the most striking qualities in James's comparison of
The Scarlet Letter and Lockhart's *Adam Blair* is James's ability to move

effortlessly back and forth between the two works, keeping both continually before the reader. Make a study of the methods James has used
to attain this difficult end. Contrast this method of comparing two works
with James's treatment of *The Scarlet Letter* and *The House of the
Seven Gables*, where the discussion of the two books is kept more
separate. What accounts for the difference in technique between the two
sets of comparisons?

6. James obviously feels that *The Scarlet Letter* (which he calls
a masterpiece) is a greater work than *Adam Blair* (which he calls a good
second-rate novel). Yet *Adam Blair*, which occupies a prominent place
in James's essay, is brought into the discussion to throw into relief what
seem to James to be weaknesses in Hawthorne's work. Is James wise
in using *Adam Blair* as he does? Or does his treatment of Lockhart's
novel work against what he is attempting to say about Hawthorne?

7. James's treatment of Hawthorne's two novels is rather long.
The tone is relaxed, somewhat informal. Would you prefer a shorter,
crisper, more concise, formal treatment, or do James's treatment and
tone aid him in saying what he wants to say about Hawthorne?

Suggestions for an Essay

Write an essay comparing some analogous aspect of two works
by your writer. As you compare the two works, try to *interpret* the
significance of what you say, so that a reader will know what to do
with the information you give him.

4

AN ANALYSIS OF THE FORM OF A WORK

Introduction

Much critical writing, particularly during the twentieth century, has concerned itself with analyzing the form (or structure) of literary works. *Form,* although much used as a technical, critical term, need not appear formidable. It is, of course, essentially a metaphor, since we ordinarily think of form in connection with tangible objects. (A chair, for instance, has form—legs, a back, rungs, a seat, upholstery, all arranged in certain relationships to one another.) Applied to a piece of literature, *form* signifies simply the way the work is put together, the relationship the parts bear to one another.

One way to throw the form of a piece of writing into bolder relief is to imagine the work constructed differently. Take Nathaniel Hawthorne's *The Scarlet Letter,* for example. Hawthorne could have begun his story before the adultery had been committed, and have shown the steps which led to Hester's and Dimmesdale's guilty passion. Or he could have shown Hester, as an old woman, looking back over her past, retelling her story. Or the story, instead of being told from the point of view of the author, could have been told from the point of view of Dimmesdale, or Chillingworth, or Pearl. Instead of relying largely on a dramatic method, presenting vignette after vignette, Hawthorne could have relied largely on exposition, simply telling in his own words the fortunes of his characters while occasionally interspersing a dramatic scene. Chillingworth's mental torture of Dimmesdale, which Hawthorne dwells on at length, could have been passed over lightly, in a single sentence even. And so on. But the fact is that Hawthorne did not write any of these imagined books, because the form of these books is different from the form Hawthorne gave his material.

Below are two essays in which the authors discuss the forms of two novels.

E. K. BROWN

an analysis of

THE PROFESSOR'S HOUSE

*I*n the summer of 1923, *A Lost Lady* completed, Willa Cather left for a long stay in France. She went almost at once to Ville-d'Avray, where Jan and Isabelle Hambourg had arranged a study for her in the house they had bought since her previous visit to France, when she was absorbing impressions for *One of Ours*. Miss Lewis writes: "The Hambourgs had hoped that she would make Ville-d'Avray her permanent home. But although the little study was charming, and all the surroundings were attractive, and the Hambourgs themselves devoted and solicitous, she found herself unable to work at Ville-d'Avray. She felt indeed that she would never be able to work there."

One outcome of this summer was the portrait by Leon Bakst, which hangs in the Public Library at Omaha. When funds had been subscribed, the first striking recognition Willa Cather had from people in her own state, she was asked to choose a painter. On the advice of friends she chose Bakst, though such a portrait was far from the usual round of his work. It was an unfortunate choice, though Willa Cather was immediately delighted with the man and enjoyed the talks she had with him and his friends during the twenty sittings. At one of these Nijinsky appeared. After he had been introduced and had kissed her hand, he withdrew to a corner and stood with his face to the wall. He believed himself to be a horse. It was plain to Willa Cather that Bakst, who was supporting a number of White Russians, was in great need of money, and she could not bring herself to cancel the commission. At each sitting she felt the portrait become more mistaken—stiff, dark, dead, lifeless—and she could tell from Bakst's desperation that he knew better than she how bad it was. She felt that she was behaving unworthily to the kind admirers in Omaha, but she could not say the word that would have extricated her from the false position. No expression of complaint, reproach, or even regret ever came from Omaha, and she was deeply touched by the magnanimous silence. After the sittings were over she escaped to Aix-les-Bains, where she stayed for several weeks of the early fall. It was here that the idea of *The Professor's House* began to take shape, and on her return to the apartment in Bank Street in November, she began at once to write that novel.

The Professor's House, at which she worked steadily through 1924, in Bank Street and, during the summer, at Grand Manan, is among the most revealing of her novels. Toward the end of the book Professor St. Peter reflects on what Tom Outland was spared in escaping by an early death "the trap of worldly success." "What change," the professor wonders, "would have come in his blue eye, in his fine long hand with the back-springing thumb, which had never handled things that were not the symbols of ideas? A hand like that, had he lived, must have been put to other uses. His fellow-scientists, his wife, the town and State, would have required many duties of it. It would have had to write thousands of useless letters, frame thousands of false excuses. It would have had to 'manage' a great deal of money." No writer of her time was more successful than Willa Cather in keeping freedom and anonymity. She never became an official personage, and the crucial decisions were taken in the years of her first popular success, from 1923 to 1927. She declined to join societies, no matter who asked her, no matter what their aim; she declined to recommend books, and wrote a review so rarely that she could decently avoid pressures to be nice and helpful. Instead of working for charities she gave as if from a bottomless purse to old friends fallen on hard times, or institutions in Webster County. If a letter appeared useless, she did not write it; and instead of a false excuse she preferred a frank explanation, which usually saved her from repetition of a request she could not grant or an invitation she could not accept. Her royalties mounted substantially with the popular success of *One of Ours* and she handled all money matters herself; anything, she felt, was better than living like the singer in "Coming, Aphrodite!" who used to drive down to Wall Street and review her holdings in the light of the latest oscillations of the market. Miss Lewis writes:

The struggle to preserve the integrity of her life as an artist, its necessary detachment and freedom, cost her something—cost a considerable expenditure of nervous energy, for it meant a steady exertion of her will against the will of the public. But it was not disdain for the tributes people wished to pay her, or a feeling of superiority or indifference, that caused her to withdraw more and more from the world. It was self-preservation.

Into Professor St. Peter Willa Cather poured her grief at the decline of so many of the values she cherished. The postwar students at the small Midwestern college where he has taught since before the end of the last century are now, he thinks, a common lot. The young professors are utilitarian, political, self-interested. The programs have suffered by the pressure of the will of the state legislature and the community, for whom the ideal in higher education is a trade school passing under the name of college. The war which had taken the life of Tom Outland had, "in one great catastrophe, swept away all youth and all palms, and almost Time itself." [1]

The novel is a revelation of an attitude in Willa Cather more desolate by far than any fear of the price that worldly success tries to impose, or a disapproval of new forces in American life. There is a startling com-

---

[1] This sentence was deleted from the collected edition.

ment on its meaning in Alexander Porterfield's essay on Willa Cather, perhaps the most considered English estimate of her fiction. Mr. Porterfield says: "Briefly, it is the story of a scholarly professor at a Middle Western University passing through that critical, uneasy period between middle and old age—at least, it should be taken as a study of such, otherwise its meaning is difficult to perceive exactly." *The Professor's House* is a study of the passing, prematurely, from middle to old age, and St. Peter, at fifty-two, is exactly at the age the author reached in the year of the novel's appearance. But it is disquieting to find a critic shutting the door on his perception that there is in a book more than he can comprehend, and deciding that his comprehension is the measure of its meaning.

It is by a scrutiny of the approach to houses that the deepest meaning in the novel will disclose itself, and by the same token clarify the beautiful relation among the three parts in which it is arranged. At the outset Willa Cather presents St. Peter living between two houses. There is the expensive conventional house that he has built because his wife wanted it and into which he has moved with reluctance, with indeed a positive distaste that greatly surprises him; and there is the old rented frame house, ugly, inconvenient, run down, in which he has lived for thirty years—for the whole of his adult life, the whole of his career, the whole of his marriage. He finds that he can write, and think, only in his attic study, encumbered with the forms on which a dressmaker has fitted clothes for his wife and daughters ever since he was a young husband. It is oil-lit and stove-heated; it has almost every disadvantage a room can have; but it has been the home of his mind and spirit. It is very easy to mark the two houses as symbols of no apparent depth, nor do they acquire in the first part of the novel any depth beyond the practice of a Sinclair Lewis or a James T. Farrell.

The obviously surprising element in the structure of *The Professor's House* is its second part, a long story inserted after the fashion of Cervantes or Smollett, and giving, as Willa Cather has said, an effect similar to those Dutch pictures of an interior where a square window offers a contrasting vista of a gray sea or the masts of ships. The length, vitality, and power of the intercalated tale are surprising, and not only at a first reading. The substance in this middle part of the novel is the crucial episode in the life of Tom Outland. Once and once only in the thirty years of his teaching St. Peter encountered a mind and personality of the first order, a student from whom he learned, and whose impress is strong upon the many-volumed history of Spanish exploration in America which brought St. Peter his fame, gave him his full mental and personal growth, and as a by-product provided the new house, built with literary prize money. When the novel opens, Tom is dead.

That crucial episode in Tom's life was the discovery of a Cliff-Dweller village in a New Mexican canyon. The discovery gave a new dimension to American life for Tom Outland. "I had read of filial piety in the Latin poets," he says, "and I knew that was what I felt for this place." Here was beauty, the beauty of pure and noble design, unspoiled by clutter or ornament, undistracted by cosiness, uncontradicted by the ugliness of machinery or industry. An expert to whom Tom showed some of the pottery was struck by its likeness to the decorative art of early Crete. The effect Willa Cather produces in her account of the Cliff-Dwellers, so much more vivid, so much more austere, than in the parallel passages in *The Song of the Lark,* is very near the evocation of the Greek town in the "Ode on a Grecian Urn." "It was as still as sculpture—and something like that. . . . The tower was the fine thing that held all the jumble of houses together and made them mean something. . . . That village sat looking down into the cañon with the calmness of eternity. The falling snowflakes, sprinkling the piñons, gave it a special kind of solemnity . . . preserved in the dry air and almost perpetual sunlight like a fly in amber, guarded by the cliffs and the river and the desert." The houses of the Cliff-Dwellers are never overtly contrasted with those in the Middle Western college town where the first and third parts of the novel are laid; and in the modern town the emphasis falls on individual buildings, in the ancient village, significantly, on the architectural as well as the social unity of the whole.

A light but telling touch will show how firmly the novel has been stitched together. Between his discovery of the village in the canyon and his death a few years later, Tom made physics his principal study. He devised and patented a bulkheaded vacuum, which after his death became the nucleus of a great improvement in aircraft. He had willed everything to his fiancée, one of the professor's daughters, but with not a particle of the professor in her make-up. With some of the immense fortune the invention brought, she and her entrepreneur husband, a born front-office man, built a country house and called it Outland. The professor's new house is a wrong house, but wrong only by its acceptance of prevailing convention. Outland is much more deeply a wrong house. Although it stood on a high site, it held no reminiscence of the village in the canyon—it was a Norwegian manor-house set down in the sultry Middle West, without a vestige of American feeling. We are spared a sight of its interior, but are told what is to furnish it—the loot of the antique shops of Europe imported by way of a Spanish-American port in a dodge to avoid customs duties. This is the worst of all the houses in the novel, but there are a number of wrong modern houses—for instance, that in which the head of the physics department lived, "in the most depressing and unnecessary ugliness"—and none has any affinity with the village of the Cliff-Dwellers. With the kind of past it stands for, the ugly insensitive present seems to have no conceivable bond.

But in the third and final part of the novel the bond is suddenly revealed. The first and second parts, which have seemed so boldly unrelated, are brought into profound unity. In the first part it was plain that the professor did not wish to live in his new house, and did not wish to enter into the sere phase of his life correlative with it. At the beginning of the third part it becomes plain that he cannot indefinitely continue to make the old attic study the theater of his life, that he cannot go on prolonging or attempting to prolong his prime, the phase of his life correlative with that. The personality of his prime—the personality that had expressed itself powerfully and in the main happily in his teaching, his scholarship, his love for his wife, his domesticity—is now quickly receding, and nothing new is flowing in. What begins to dominate St. Peter is something akin to the Cliff-Dwellers, something primitive that had ruled him long ago when he was a boy on a pioneer farm in the rough Solomon Valley in western Kansas. To this primitive being not many things are real. What counts above all is nature, seen as a web of life and finally of death.

The binding passage is in terms of houses:

[The Professor] . . . really didn't see what he was going to do about the matter of domicile. He couldn't make himself believe that he was ever going to live in the new house again. He didn't belong there. He remembered some lines of a translation from the Norse he used to read long ago in one of his mother's few books, a little two-volume Ticknor and Fields edition of Longfellow, in blue and gold, that used to lie on the parlour table:

> For thee a house was built
> Ere thou wast born;
> For thee a mould was made
> Ere thou of woman camest.[2]

Lying on his old couch, he could almost believe himself in that house already. The sagging springs were like the sham upholstery that is put in coffins. Just the equivocal American way of dealing with serious facts, he reflected. Why pretend that it is possible to soften that last hard bed?

He could remember a time when the loneliness of death had terrified him, when the idea of it was insupportable. He used to feel that if his wife could but lie in the same coffin with him, his body would not be so insensible that the nearness of hers would not give it comfort. But now he thought of eternal solitude with gratefulness; as a release from every obligation, from every form of effort. It was the Truth.

All that had seemed a hanging back from the future—the clinging to the old attic study, the absorption in Tom Outland's quality and the civilization of the Cliff-Dwellers, the ways of the missionary fathers, the revival of interest in the occupations of childhood and its pleasures—was

---

[2] Miss Cather was quoting from memory the opening of Longfellow's translation of the Anglo-Saxon "Grave":

> For thee was a house built
> Ere thou wast born,
> For thee was a mould meant
> Ere thou of mother camest.

something very unlike what it had seemed. It was profound, unconscious preparation for death, for the last house of the professor.

Willa Cather had begun on the surface with a record of mediocrities, of the airless prosaic world of a small college town—how airless, how prosaic, only those who have lived in one know; and with the disenchantment a distinguished spirit felt in the narrowing utilitarianism of the postwar years. The mediocrities and the utilitarians do not have everything their own way. For all his shortcomings on the surface, the head of the physics department is as sound in essence as one of Willa Cather's pioneers. Even through the first part of the novel the aura about Tom Outland's name is an assurance of other values, not as yet defined. St. Peter himself cannot be hemmed in by what is here and now: the descendant of a Napoleonic soldier, he has the look and many of the tastes of a Latin, and on him is the mark of his preoccupation with the Mediterranean culture and the Spanish explorers. Yet he and those who belong with him do not dominate this first part of the novel; they belong to a minority not only weak numerically but edging to extinction. In the second part the balance is reversed: the mediocrities and utilitarians— in the main civil servants, remembered with contempt and pity from Willa Cather's stays in Washington a quarter century earlier—are few and feeble; and against them is set something that is quite overwhelming —the life the Cliff-Dwellers lived, and the understanding of that life by the sensitive and civilized Belgian priest Father Duchene, to whom Tom turned for interpretation; and, in the foreground throughout, Tom's own ever growing understanding of the Cliff-Dwellers and everything else.

The profound surprise for the reader is in the strange, short third part. Between the life of the Middle Western college town and the life of the Cliff-Dwellers' village the common quality is simply that both end in death. Guided by the feeling that they both end in death, we know how to measure them. What aspect of beauty, of dignity, even of interest would the ruins of the college town hold for Macaulay's New Zealander if he were to pause on this continent on his way to sketch the ruins of St. Paul's?

Not by any answers it proposes, but by the problems it elaborates, and by the atmosphere in which they are enveloped, *The Professor's House* is a religious novel. The parallels in Willa Cather's earlier fiction for the depth of self-scrutiny and the anxiety about alternatives in St. Peter all have to do with the rendering of artists, with the development of Thea Kronborg's talent or that of the sculptor from Kansas in *The Troll Garden*. In the one specimen of St. Peter's lecture we are permitted to overhear, the link between art and religion is forged in our presence:

As long as every man and woman who crowded into the cathedrals on Easter Sunday was a principal in a gorgeous drama with God, glittering angels on one side and the shadows of evil coming and going on the other, life was a rich thing. The king and the beggar had the same chance at miracles and great temptations and revelations. And that's what makes men happy, believing in the mystery and importance of their own little individual lives. It makes us happy to surround our creature needs and bodily instincts with as much pomp and circumstance as possible. Art and religion (they are the same thing, in the end, of course) have given man the only happiness he has ever had.

The shift is not a weakening in Willa Cather's belief in the primacy of art, but a bracketing of religion with art. The same bracketing occurs when Father Duchene sums up the distinction between the Cliff-Dwellers and other tribes of the region. On their mesa he feels, with reverence, humanity "lifted itself out of mere brutality," and the agencies by which it did so were art (as expressed in the ancient people's "distinct feeling for design," whether in the shaping of a water-pot or the grouping of the village) and religion (as expressed in their "manifold ceremonies and observances"). Less explicitly, Tom Outland makes the same response: for him the mesa, which was at first a stimulus to "adventure," assumed a beauty like that of sculpture, and finally aroused "a religious emotion." So it is with the novel as a whole; one passes from a record of happenings to the achievement of startling and satisfying form, and then to the suggestion of essential feeling about final issues.

. Comments and Questions

1. E. K. Brown, before undertaking his discussion of *The Professor's House*, offers a somewhat extended biographical discussion of various occurrences in Willa Cather's life prior to her writing of the novel. Is this discussion extraneous, or does Brown integrate this historical criticism with what he says about the book?

2. Consider the use to which Brown puts Alexander Porterfield's essay on Willa Cather. What function does the allusion to Porterfield perform? Does the allusion prejudice you in favor of Brown's imminent interpretation of *The Professor's House*, or against it?

3. Throughout his analysis of the novel, Brown writes rather extended passages in which he re-creates portions of the novel. Do you feel that he is doing this simply for the benefit of readers who may not have read *The Professor's House* (i.e., that he is merely offering a synopsis of the action) and that a reader who had read the novel would find these passages boring? Or do these passages of re-creative criticism actively aid the critic in his interpretation of the novel?

4. Examine the closing statement carefully: "So it is with the novel as a whole; one passes from a record of happenings to the achievement of startling and satisfying form, and then to the suggestion of

essential feeling about final issues." This sentence may be taken as a summation of the essay as a whole. Looking back over the essay, decide exactly *how* Brown has defined "form," and in what ways he finds it "startling" and "satisfying." The grammar of Brown's sentence ("and then to . . .") implies that the "suggestion of essential feeling about final issues" grows out of Willa Cather's "achievement of startling and satisfying form." Has the critic so defined cause and effect throughout the essay? If so, how?

5. The essay on *The Professor's House* concerns itself explicitly with one novelistic technique: *form.* Yet Brown, in discussing this technique, makes it plain that he finds the novel artistically satisfying. Does he rely too much on his praise of the novel's form to carry conviction concerning the novel's merit, or does he succeed in making out a convincing case for the stature he accords the work?

6. The author obviously feels that *The Professor's House* is a significant novel by virtue of the symbolic depths it achieves. Yet halfway through the essay he says that the first two houses about which the book concerns itself are "symbols of no apparent depth." How do these, and the other houses in the book, ultimately achieve their apparent depth?

7. Note the literary allusions to Sinclair Lewis, James T. Farrell, Cervantes, Smollett, and Keats. Decide how Brown makes these references work for him, and the degree of success he achieves in their use.

8. Brown nowhere gives his reader a list of the critical standards by which he judges the worth of a novel. Yet certain criteria are implicit throughout what he says. Try to pick them out, and arrive at an understanding of them. Compare them, if you like, with the standards of judgment implicit in the article by Lauriat Lane, Jr. on *Huckleberry Finn* (see Chapter 2), and the selection from Henry James's *Hawthorne* in which James discusses *The Scarlet Letter* and *The House of the Seven Gables* (see Chapter 3).

I. B. CAUTHEN, JR.

Fielding's Digressions in JOSEPH ANDREWS

*I*n his *Henry Fielding* F. Homes Dudden has criticized the novel *Joseph Andrews* for four "evident" weaknesses. For him, the novel is "too rambling and haphazard," and its denouement is unsatisfactory;

moreover, he censures Fielding for too frequently indulging "in farcical absurdities" in the episodes of the book. Finally, he condemns the "digressions":

the main narrative is interrupted by the interpolation of two independent stories—'The History of Leonora, or the Unfortunate Jilt,' and 'The History of Two Friends'—and by the extensive life-history of Mr. Wilson. The introduction of such digressions, though in accord with the common usage of the Spanish and French fiction-writers—to say nothing of earlier examples in classical epics, medieval romances, and Eastern tales—can hardly be justified on artistic grounds. Moreover, in the first of his intercalated stories (which is also the more interesting and humorous) Fielding absurdly causes the narrator to repeat no fewer than five whole letters from memory. Wilson's history, indeed, comprises some matter relevant to the plot . . . ; but it would have been definitely an advantage had the greater part of it been omitted. (I, 351–352)

Mr. Dudden's fellow-commentators agree with such a criticism of the digressions, although they advance various excuses for them. Ethel Thornbury, like Mr. Dudden, sees them as only a manifestation of the contemporary practice which had the sanction of epic usage; but she concedes that Fielding works them into his central story by making them "have an ethical bearing upon the problem of the hero's life." Cross, however, sees the stories introduced only to fill up an uneventful hour, although "at times perhaps Fielding lets his narrative stand perfectly still as a burlesque of the suspense characteristic of Richardson." Saintsbury's excuse for them (in his Everyman introduction) is likewise traditional: "divagations of this kind existed in all Fielding's Spanish and French models, . . . [and] the public of the day expected them." But if these digressions can be defended on other grounds, we may be able to give them a virtue other than Saintsbury's "grand and prominent [one] of being at once and easily skippable."

The three stories are placed at almost regular intervals throughout the novel: Leonora's story appears in Book II, chapters 4 and 6, Mr. Wilson's life-history occurs in III, 3, and the story of Paul and Leonard in IV, 10. The third and last story is not finished, perhaps for a reason other than that Beau Didapper "offered a rudeness to [Fanny] with his hands," for which he received from Joseph "a sound box on the ear." The two completed stories and the interrupted third one, I believe, are closely related to Fielding's aesthetic theory of his novel—the exposure of ridiculous human frailty and folly. By holding "the glass to thousands in their closets, . . . they may contemplate their deformity, and endeavor to reduce it, and thus by suffering private mortification may avoid public shame." The novel, therefore, is designed both to entertain and, more importantly, to instruct by laying bare the "only true source of the ridiculous"—affectation. This affectation, according to Fielding, proceeds either from vanity or from hypocrisy: vanity makes men affect "false characters, in order to purchase applause," while hypocrisy is the concealing of "our vices under an appearance of their opposite virtues" in an endeavor to avoid censure. Vanity is thus a disproportional exaggeration of a trait which, in itself, may be virtuous enough; hypocrisy is the living lie.

From the discovery of this affectation [Fielding declares] arises the Ridiculous, which always strikes the reader with surprise and pleasure; and that in a higher and stronger degree when the affectation arises from hypocrisy, than when from vanity; for to discover any one to be the exact reverse of what he affects, is more surprising, and consequently more ridiculous, than to find him a little deficient in the quality he desires the reputation of.

If the "digressions" can be related to this theory which underlies the novel, they furnish their own justification.

The first story, told to while away a journey, concerns the lovely Leonora, "an extreme lover of gaiety" who never missed a public assembly "where she had frequent opportunities of satisfying a greedy appetite of vanity." She is attracted by Horatio, a young barrister, to whom she always listens attentively "and often smiled even when [his compliments were] too delicate for her comprehension." When Horatio proposes to her, Leonora is "covered with blushes" and refuses him with "as angry a look as she could possibly put on"—although, of course, she "had very much suspected what was coming." But eventually she accepts Horatio. At this inopportune moment, a stranger who owns a coach and six arrives in town and Leonora is attracted to him because of his pretty equipage. He is the French fop Bellarmine who immediately becomes interested in Leonora: she "saw herself admired by the fine stranger, and envied by every woman. . . . Her little heart began to flutter within her, and her head was agitated with a convulsive motion. . . . She could not disengage her thoughts one moment from the contemplation of [her present triumph]. She had never tasted anything like this happiness." Thus Bellarmine's gaiety and gallantry possessed the heart of the vain Leonora in a day, demolishing poor Horatio's work of a year. Upon the advice of her aunt, Leonora jilts Horatio, who in turn wounds Bellarmine in a duel, which, of course, makes Leonora love her foppish heart-flutterer more than ever.

However, when Bellarmine goes to Leonora's father to draw up the marriage papers, he learns that he is to get Leonora without a shilling of dowry; he breaks off his engagement, and Leonora, broken-hearted over losing both him and Horatio, "left the place where she was the subject of conversation and ridicule" and retired to a small place in the country.

In this digression, Leonora is held up as an object of ridicule for her vanity in her beauty, her pleasure in being admired by other women for Bellarmine's attentions, her pride in his coach and six, his French clothes, his superficial culture, and for her refusal of the honest and unaffected Horatio. Bellarmine is the hypocrite—his love is not for Leonora, but for Leonora's father's money. He gives the appearance of a sincere lover, but he is in reality only a fortune hunter. The unmasking of the hypocrite and the exposure of Leonora's vanity carry out Fielding's general purpose for the novel in this digression.

In the same way, Mr. Wilson's story contributes to the general purpose. Like Leonora, Mr. Wilson is a vain young person who is excessively ambitious of obtaining a fine character. By frequenting public places in London, he learned to master "fashionable phrases, . . . to cry up the fashionable diversions, and [to know] the names and faces of the most fashionable men and women." His reputation for intrigue he made secure by writing letters to himself; his life was one of sauntering about the streets, going to coffee-houses, attending Drury Lane and Lincoln's Inn Fields, and indulging in small talk in drawing rooms. In such a life, he confesses, he admired himself. Nor was he unique: at the Temple, where he lived, he found the beaus "the affection of affection." Here he met "with smart fellows who drank with lords they did not know, and intrigued with women they never saw." Where they talked and did nothing, Wilson seems to have done everything and talked little: he kept a series of mistresses, intrigued with the "wife to a man of fashion and gallantry," received "some advances . . . by the wife of a citizen," and fell in with "a set of jolly companions, who slept all day and drank all night." Later, he "became a great frequenter of playhouses" and continued to accomplish his own ruin until he could be saved only by the *deus ex machina* of a lottery ticket. He then reformed, married the woman who generously gave him the lottery ticket, and managed her father's estate until he saw he was no business man. He then retired to the country where he now leads an idyllic life with his family.

Midway in this story of a typical fop, Fielding gives us the moral of it and its purpose. By his observations of London life, Wilson concludes that

the general observation, that wits are most inclined to vanity, is not true. Men are equally vain of riches, strength, beauty, honours, etc. But these appear of themselves in the eyes of beholders, whereas the poor wit is obliged to produce his performance to show you his perfection. . . . Vanity is the worst of passions, and more apt to contaminate the mind than any other: for, as selfishness is much more general than we please to allow it, so it is natural to hate and envy those who stand between us and the good we desire. Now, in lust and ambition these are few; and even in avarice we find many who are no obstacles to our pursuits; but the vain man seeks preeminence; and everything which is excellent or praise-worthy in another renders him the mark of his antipathy.

Wilson's story thus is the biography of a vain wit, a ridiculous, affected, and at times hypocritical fop. He suffers for his vanity, and the reader is both amused and instructed by the edifying account of his own unmasking and his reform. He no more deserves Harriet Hearty than Dorimant in Etherege's *Man of Mode* deserves his Harriet. But he has sense enough to reform himself, even as Fielding's readers were encouraged to amend their ways by "private mortification."

The third story, the interrupted tale of Leonard and Paul, has reached its climax when Joseph Andrews throws the listeners into consternation by his defense of Fanny. Read to visitors by Parson Adams' small son, the story concerns a couple who bicker incessantly over every detail of their lives; a friend advises them on this marital problem, first telling the husband to surrender to his wife when he is most convinced that he is in the right. Unfortunately, he gives the same advice a little later to the wife, and consequently he finds himself "the private referee of every difference." When the couple, however, compare his decisions, they find he has decided in favor of each upon every occasion, and he becomes, of course, the only thing the couple has in common—a mutual enemy.

Here again, as in the stories of Leonora and of Mr. Wilson, is an exposure of vanity, this time about the vanity of being preëminently correct. Both Leonard and his wife are so insistent upon their correctness that they become equally vain: as Mr. Wilson had said, men are vain of "riches, strength, beauty, honours, &c." He could have easily added "and of truth as they want to see it." Certainly the vanity of Leonard and his wife contaminates their minds as they each seek preëminence over the other in each argument. Nor is the hypocritical attitude that their friend Paul proposes a solution to their vanity. Indeed, no solution is given, nor is there one to give except the self-reform or the consequent suffering that concludes the other two digressions that precede this one. No wonder Fielding, manipulating his characters, lets Didapper offer that rudeness to Fanny only to be rewarded with a box on the ear. The conclusion of the story is for the reader to write: the way the reader lets the story end is an exercise in how well he has learned from what he has already read in the novel.

These three digressions, therefore, need not be so utterly condemned nor half-heartedly defended as they have been. Although they may not be as artistically successful today as they were in the eighteenth century, they are closely related to Fielding's aesthetic of the novel, the exposure of affectation that arises from vanity or hypocrisy. By the very nature of this relationship, they assume an artistic purpose that should be considered historically as well as in the light of Fielding's own avowed intention in writing the novel. And while the "digressions" probably cannot be made acceptable to modern aestheticians of the unified novel, they are far from the traditional digression—they are, instead, much more akin to the exemplum, a story told with moral intent. Although such a device had often been used in literature before the time of Fielding, there is no model as far as I know in the novel for such stories. In this genre-making novel Fielding uses three structurally discrete stories as a means of playing a variation upon a basic theme, hostility to pretension. He had no model in the young art of novel-making for this kind of thematic repetition, the exemplum whose characters, setting, and events are completely unconnected with the main story.

Admittedly these digressions—or exempla—stand outside the episodic structure of the book, but they are discussions that go even beyond the announced theme of affectation. They are concerned with three important phases of life which the novel proper cannot include. For here we have a discussion of courtship, of married life, and of the vain young man beginning his career. In these three discussions Fielding continues his exposure of affectation that underlies the whole novel; in the novel itself this exposure takes place in character and incident: Mr. Wilson may inveigh against vanity and Parson Adams, agreeing with him, may be vain enough to want to read a sermon on vanity; Peter Pounce may be the uncharitable hypocrite who would turn the poor out to pasture, an unmasking that drives Parson Adams from the carriage; Mrs. Slip-slop may affect learning as Lady Booby affects chastity—they all are victims of Fielding's stripping of a character to its essentials. In the same way, these stories unmask the vices of hypocrisy and vanity in courtship, in marriage, and in the life of the rake. By their inclusion Fielding has doubled his emphasis on his theme—the laying bare of the only true source of the ridiculous. As Parson Adams commented upon Steele's *Conscious Lovers,* this novel—with its exempla—has things in it "solemn enough for a sermon."

Comments and Questions

1. In developing the idea that Fielding's three digressions reinforce the "theory which underlies the novel," I. B. Cauthen, Jr. recounts and analyzes the three digressions in considerable detail, yet is virtually silent concerning the plot of the novel itself. Does the author need to demonstrate in more detail his feeling that the purpose of the novel is "the exposure of ridiculous human frailty and folly"? Or does he do well to avoid a detailed analysis of the novel itself?

2. In recounting the three digressions, Cauthen makes considerable use of phrases taken directly from the novel. A notable feature of the article is the manner in which these short quotations are smoothly woven into the texture of the article. Make a study of the writer's technique at this point. In addition, consider whether or not these direct quotations are necessary; whether they add to the force of what is said. Why did Cauthen not simply paraphrase the digressions in his own words?

3. In his final paragraph, after having underscored the point that the digressions reinforce the moral of the novel, Cauthen says that they "go even beyond the announced theme of affectation." Exactly how does Cauthen define the way they "go . . . beyond"? Does this "going beyond" make the digressions artistically more justifiable? Or does the author say?

4. The digressions in *Joseph Andrews,* according to Cauthen, "probably cannot be made acceptable to modern aestheticians of the unified novel." Does Cauthen imply an attitude toward these "modern aestheticians"? What do you understand Cauthen to mean by "unified novel"?

5. Cauthen calls *Joseph Andrews* a "genre-making" novel. How is "genre-making" defined? What is the new genre ushered in by *Joseph Andrews?* Should Cauthen have mentioned later novels written in this genre, to substantiate his interpretation?

6. The article seems very little concerned with the artistic worth of *Joseph Andrews.* In fact, it is difficult to tell from reading the article whether we are to regard the novel as a masterpiece, or as a rather ordinary performance. (Compare, in this connection, E. K. Brown's high praise of Willa Cather's *The Professor's House.*) Do you consider this lack of evaluation a weakness in Cauthen's article, or would evaluation have taken him outside the limits he set for himself?

7. Cauthen's essay bears some interesting similarities to E. K. Brown's essay on *The Professor's House,* since both critics suggest that the novels they are discussing possess a unity which a superficial reading might overlook. Compare the two essays in this and other respects, from the point of view of deciding which of the two—if either—is the more successful. Consider, among other aspects of the works, the question of length. Why is E. K. Brown's essay somewhat longer?

Suggestions for an Essay

Write an essay analyzing the form of a work you have read. Try to make the essay *interpretive.* That is, tell what effect the form has on your response to the work. Note in this connection how E. K. Brown interprets the significance of form in Willa Cather's *The Professor's House:* the novel, says Brown, is an artistically unified work despite its apparently loose structure because what on the surface appear to be unrelated sections of the novel are really held together by the central image of houses, which Willa Cather works with in such a way that they ultimately come to symbolize one's attitude toward death.

This essay should afford a good opportunity to practice using direct quotations (see Chapter 10), since any analysis of the form of a work naturally leads to a close examination of the text of that work. Study "The Use of Quotations" in Chapter 10; then consider using some direct quotations in your essay on form.

THE EVOLUTION OF A WRITER'S THOUGHT

Introduction

Scholars who have made a study of the entire body of a writer's work frequently comment on the evolution of his art. An essay on this subject provides an admirable exercise in synthesis, at the same time that it presents some challenging problems in exposition. Since a number of works will have to be considered, there obviously will not be time to go into the text of any single work in much detail. How to discuss the writings in a general way while still suggesting the essence of the writer's contribution becomes, then, one of the major problems in this kind of essay. Another, and allied, problem is how to keep the body of a writer's work before a reader, so that he may see it in focus, while still giving adequate attention to the specific titles which constitute that body. Another task is that of maintaining a proper balance between information, interpretation, and evaluation.

Below are two essays which discuss, chronologically, a considerable number of works by the authors treated.

VIRGINIA WOOLF

The Novels of Thomas Hardy

*W*hen we say that the death of Thomas Hardy leaves English fiction without a leader, we mean that there is no other writer whose supremacy would be generally accepted, none to whom it seems so fitting

and natural to pay homage. Nobody of course claimed it less. The un-
worldly and simple old man would have been painfully embarrassed by the
rhetoric that flourishes on such occasions as this. Yet it is no less than the
truth to say that while he lived there was one novelist at all events who
made the art of fiction seem an honourable calling; while Hardy lived
there was no excuse for thinking meanly of the art he practised. Nor was
this solely the result of his peculiar genius. Something of it sprang from
his character in its modesty and integrity, from his life, lived simply down
in Dorsetshire without self-seeking or self-advertisement. For both
reasons, because of his genius and because of the dignity with which
his gift was used, it was impossible not to honour him as an artist and
to feel respect and affection for the man. But it is of the work that
we must speak, of the novels that were written so long ago that they
seem as detached from the fiction of the moment as Hardy himself was
remote from the stir of the present and its littleness.

We have to go back more than a generation if we are to trace the
career of Hardy as a novelist. In the year 1871 he was a man of thirty-
one; he had written a novel, *Desperate Remedies,* but he was by no
means an assured craftsman. He "was feeling his way to a method",
he said himself; as if he were conscious that he possessed all sorts of
gifts, yet did not know their nature, or how to use them to advantage.
To read that first novel is to share in the perplexity of its author. The
imagination of the writer is powerful and sardonic; he is book-learned
in a home-made way; he can create characters but he cannot control
them; he is obviously hampered by the difficulties of his technique and,
what is more singular, he is driven by some sense that human beings
are the sport of forces outside themselves, to make use of an extreme
and even melodramatic use of coincidence. He is already possessed
of the conviction that a novel is not a toy, nor an argument; it is a
means of giving truthful if harsh and violent impressions of the lives
of men and women. But perhaps the most remarkable quality in the
book is the sound that echoes and booms through its pages of a water-
fall. It is the first manifestation of the power that was to assume such
vast proportions in the later books. He already proves himself a minute
and skilled observer of nature; the rain, he knows, falls differently as
it falls upon roots or arable; he knows that the wind sounds differently
as it passes through the branches of different trees. But he is aware in
a larger sense of Nature as a force; he feels in it a spirit that can
sympathise or mock or remain the indifferent spectator of human fortunes. Already that sense was his; and the crude story of Miss Aldclyffe
and Cytherea is memorable because it is watched by the eyes of the gods,
and worked out in the presence of Nature.

That he was a poet should have been obvious; that he was a novelist
might still have been held uncertain. But the year after, when *Under
the Greenwood Tree* appeared, it was clear that much of the effort of
"feeling for a method" had been overcome. Something of the stubborn

originality of the earlier book was lost. The second is accomplished, charming, idyllic compared with the first. The writer, it seems, may well develop into one of our English landscape painters, whose pictures are all of cottage gardens and old peasant women, who lingers to collect and preserve from oblivion the old-fashioned ways and words which are rapidly falling into disuse. And yet what kindly lover of antiquity, what naturalist with a microscope in his pocket, what scholar solicitous for the changing shapes of language, ever heard the cry of a small bird killed in the next wood by an owl with such intensity? The cry "passed into the silence without mingling with it". Again we hear, very far away, like the sound of a gun out at sea on a calm summer's morning, a strange and ominous echo. But as we read these early books there is a sense of waste. There is a feeling that Hardy's genius was obstinate and perverse; first one gift would have its way with him and then another. They would not consent to run together easily in harness. Such indeed was likely to be the fate of a writer who was at once poet and realist, a faithful son of field and down, yet tormented by the doubts and despondencies bred of book-learning; a lover of old ways and plain countrymen, yet doomed to see the faith and flesh of his forefathers turn to thin and spectral transparencies before his eyes.

To this contradiction Nature had added another element likely to disorder a symmetrical development. Some writers are born conscious of everything; others are unconscious of many things. Some, like Henry James and Flaubert, are able not merely to make the best use of the spoil their gifts bring in, but control their genius in the act of creation; they are aware of all the possibilities of every situation, and are never taken by surprise. The unconscious writers, on the other hand, like Dickens and Scott, seem suddenly and without their own consent to be lifted up and swept onwards. The wave sinks and they cannot say what has happened or why. Among them—it is the source of his strength and of his weakness—we must place Hardy. His own word, "moments of vision", exactly describes those passages of astonishing beauty and force which are to be found in every book that he wrote. With a sudden quickening of power which we cannot foretell, nor he, it seems, control, a single scene breaks off from the rest. We see, as if it existed alone and for all time, the wagon with Fanny's dead body inside travelling along the road under the dripping trees; we see the bloated sheep struggling among the clover; we see Troy flashing his sword round Bathsheba where she stands motionless, cutting the lock off her head and spitting the cater-pillar on her breast. Vivid to the eye, but not to the eye alone, for every sense participates, such scenes dawn upon us and their splendour remains. But the power goes as it comes. The moment of vision is succeeded by long stretches of plain daylight, nor can we believe that any craft or skill could have caught the wild power and turned it to a better use. The novels therefore are full of inequalities; they are lumpish and dull and inexpressive; but they are never arid; there is always about them a little blur of unconsciousness, that halo of freshness and margin of the unexpressed which often produce the most profound sense of satisfaction. It is as if Hardy himself were not quite aware of what he did, as if his consciousness held more than he could produce, and he left it for his readers to make out his full meaning and to supplement it from their own experience.

For these reasons Hardy's genius was uncertain in development, uneven in accomplishment, but, when the moment came, magnificent in achievement. The moment came, completely and fully, in *Far from the Madding Crowd*. The subject was right; the method was right; the poet and the countryman, the sensual man, the sombre reflective man, the man of learning, all enlisted to produce a book which, however fashions may chop and change, must hold its place among the great English novels. There is, in the first place, that sense of the physical world which Hardy more than any novelist can bring before us; the sense that the little prospect of man's existence is ringed by a landscape which, while it exists apart, yet confers a deep and solemn beauty upon his drama. The dark downland, marked by the barrows of the dead and the huts of shepherds, rises against the sky, smooth as a wave of the sea, but solid and eternal; rolling away to the infinite distance, but sheltering in its folds quiet villages whose smoke rises in frail columns by day, whose lamps burn in the immense darkness by night. Gabriel Oak tending his sheep up there on the back of the world is the eternal shepherd; the stars are ancient beacons; and for ages he has watched beside his sheep.

But down in the valley the earth is full of warmth and life; the farms are busy, the barns stored, the fields loud with the lowing of cattle and the bleating of sheep. Nature is prolific, splendid, and lustful; not yet malignant and still the Great Mother of labouring men. And now for the first time Hardy gives full play to his humour, where it is freest and most rich, upon the lips of country men. Jan Coggan and Henry Fray and Joseph Poorgrass gather in the malthouse when the day's work is over and give vent to that half-shrewd, half-poetic humour which has been brewing in their brains and finding expression over their beer since the pilgrims tramped the Pilgrims' Way; which Shakespeare and Scott and George Eliot all loved to overhear, but none loved better or heard with greater understanding than Hardy. But it is not the part of the peasants in the Wessex novels to stand out as individuals. They compose a pool of common wisdom, of common humour, a fund of perpetual life. They comment upon the actions of the hero and heroine, but while Troy or Oak or Fanny or Bathsheba come in and out and pass away, Jan Coggan and Henry Fray and Joseph Poorgrass remain. They drink by night and they plough the fields by day. They are eternal. We meet them over and over again in the novels, and they always have something typical about them, more of the character that marks a race than of the features which belong to an individual. The peasants are the great sanctuary of sanity, the country the last stronghold of happiness. When they disappear, there is no hope for the race.

With Oak and Troy and Bathsheba and Fanny Robin we come to the men and women of the novels at their full stature. In every book three or four figures predominate, and stand up like lightning conductors to attract the force of the elements. Oak and Troy and Bathsheba; Eustacia, Wildeve, and Venn; Henchard, Lucetta, and Farfrae; Jude, Sue Bridehead, and Phillotson. There is even a certain likeness between the different groups. They live as individuals and they differ as individuals; but they also live as types and have a likeness as types. Bathsheba is Bathsheba, but she is woman and sister to Eustacia and Lucetta and Sue; Gabriel Oak is Gabriel Oak, but he is man and brother to Henchard, Venn, and Jude. However lovable and charming Bathsheba may be, still she is weak; however stubborn and ill-guided Henchard may be, still he is strong. This is a fundamental part of Hardy's vision; the staple of many of his books. The woman is the weaker and the fleshlier, and she clings to the stronger and obscures his vision. How freely, nevertheless, in his greater books life is poured over the unalterable frame-work! When Bathsheba sits in the wagon among her plants, smiling at her own loveliness in the little looking-glass, we may know, and it is proof of Hardy's power that we do know, how severely she will suffer and cause others to suffer before the end. But the moment has all the bloom and beauty of life. And so it is, time and time again. His characters, both men and women, were creatures to him of an infinite attraction. For the women he shows a more tender solicitude than for the men, and in them, perhaps, he takes a keener interest. Vain might their beauty be and terrible their fate, but while the glow of life is in them their step is free, their laughter sweet, and theirs is the power to sink into the breast of Nature and become part of her silence and solemnity, or to rise and put on them the movement of the clouds and the wildness of the flowering woodlands. The men who suffer, not like the women through dependence upon other human beings, but through conflict with fate, enlist our sterner sympathies. For such a man as Gabriel Oak we need have no passing fears. Honour him we must, though it is not granted us to love him quite so freely. He is firmly set upon his feet and can give as shrewd a blow, to men at least, as any he is likely to receive. He has a prevision of what is to be expected that springs from character rather than from education. He is stable in his temperament, steadfast in his affections, and capable of open-eyed endurance without flinching. But he, too, is no puppet. He is a homely, hum-drum fellow on ordinary occasions. He can walk the street without making people turn to stare at him. In short, nobody can deny Hardy's power—the true novelist's power—to make us believe that his characters are fellow-beings driven by their own passions and idiosyncrasies, while they have—and this is the poet's gift—something symbolical about them which is common to us all.

And it is when we are considering Hardy's power of creating men and women that we become most conscious of the profound differences that distinguish him from his peers. We look back at a number of these characters and ask ourselves what it is that we remember them for. We recall their passions. We remember how deeply they have loved each other and often with what tragic results. We remember the faithful love of Oak for Bathsheba; the tumultuous but fleeting passions of men like Wildeve, Troy, and Fitzpiers; we remember the filial love of Clym for his mother, the jealous paternal passion of Henchard for Elizabeth Jane. But we do not remember how they have loved. We do not remember how they talked and changed and got to know each other, finely, gradually, from step to step and from stage to stage. Their relationship is not composed of those intellectual apprehensions and subtleties of perception which seem so slight yet are so profound. In all the books love is one of the great facts that mould human life. But it is a catastrophe; it happens suddenly and overwhelmingly, and there is little to be said about it. The talk between the lovers when it is not passionate is practical or philosophic, as though the discharge of their daily duties left them with more desire to question life and its purpose than to investigate each other's sensibilities. Even if it were in their power to analyse their emotions, life is too stirring to give them time. They need all their strength to deal with the downright blows, the freakish ingenuity, the gradually increasing malignity of fate. They have none to spend upon the subtleties and delicacies of the human comedy.

Thus there comes a time when we can say with certainty that we shall not find in Hardy some of the qualities that have given us most delight in the works of other novelists. He has not the perfection of Jane Austen, or the wit of Meredith, or the range of Thackeray, or Tolstoy's amazing intellectual power. There is in the work of the great classical writers a finality of effect which places certain of their scenes, apart from the story, beyond the reach of change. We do not ask what bearing they have upon the narrative, nor do we make use of them to interpret problems which lie on the outskirts of the scene. A laugh, a blush, half a dozen words of dialogue, and it is enough; the source of our delight is perennial. But Hardy has none of this concentration and completeness. His light does not fall directly upon the human heart. It passes over it and out on to the darkness of the heath and upon the trees swaying in the storm. When we look back into the room the group by the fireside is dispersed. Each man or woman is battling with the storm, alone, revealing himself most when he is least under the observation of other human beings. We do not know them as we know Pierre or Natasha or Becky Sharp. We do not know them in and out and all round as they are revealed to the casual caller, to the Government official, to the great lady, to the general on the battlefield. We do not know the complication and involvement and turmoil of their thoughts. Geographically, too, they remain fixed to the same stretch of the English country-side. It is seldom, and always with unhappy results, that Hardy leaves the yeoman or farmer to describe the class above theirs in the social scale. In the drawing-room and clubroom and ballroom, where people of leisure and education come together, where comedy is bred and shades of character revealed, he is awkward and ill at ease. But the opposite is equally true. If we do not know his men and women in their relations to each other, we know them in their relations to time, death, and fate. If we do not see them in quick agitation against the lights and crowds of cities, we see them against the earth, the storm, and the seasons. We know their attitude towards some of the most tremendous problems that can confront mankind. They take on a more than mortal size in memory. We see them, not in detail but enlarged and dignified. We see Tess reading the baptismal service in her nightgown "with an impress of dignity that was almost regal". We see Marty South, "like a being who had rejected with indifference the attribute of sex for the loftier quality of abstract humanism", laying the flowers on Winterbourne's grave. Their speech has a Biblical dignity and poetry. They have a force in them which cannot be defined, a force of love or of hate, a force which in the men is the cause of rebellion against life, and in the women implies an illimitable capacity for suffering, and it is this which dominates the character and makes it unnecessary that we should see the finer features that lie hid. This is the tragic power; and, if we are to place Hardy among his fellows, we must call him the greatest tragic writer among English novelists.

But let us, as we approach the danger-zone of Hardy's philosophy, be on our guard. Nothing is more necessary, in reading an imaginative writer, than to keep at the right distance above his page. Nothing is easier, especially with a writer of marked idiosyncrasy, than to fasten on opinions, convict him of a creed, tether him to a consistent point of view. Nor was Hardy any exception to the rule that the mind which is most capable of receiving impressions is very often the least capable of drawing conclusions. It is for the reader, steeped in the impression, to supply the comment. It is his part to know when to put aside the writer's conscious intention in favour of some deeper intention of which perhaps he may be unconscious. Hardy himself was aware of this. A novel "is an impression, not an argument", he has warned us, and, again

Unadjusted impressions have their value, and the road to a true philosophy of life seems to lie in humbly recording diverse readings of its phenomena as they are forced upon us by chance and change.

Certainly it is true to say that, at his greatest, he gives us impressions;

at his weakest, arguments. In *The Woodlanders, The Return of the Native, Far from the Madding Crowd,* and, above all, in *The Mayor of Casterbridge,* we have Hardy's impression of life as it came to him without conscious ordering. Let him once begin to tamper with his direct intuitions and his power is gone. "Did you say the stars were worlds, Tess?" asks little Abraham as they drive to market with their beehives. Tess replies that they are like "the apples on our stubbard-tree, most of them splendid and sound—a few blighted". "Which do we live on—a splendid or a blighted one?" "A blighted one", she replies, or rather the mournful thinker who has assumed her mask speaks for her. The words protrude, cold and raw, like the springs of a machine where we had seen only flesh and blood. We are crudely jolted out of that mood of sympathy which is renewed a moment later when the little cart is run down and we have a concrete instance of the ironical methods which rule our planet.

That is the reason why *Jude the Obscure* is the most painful of all Hardy's books, and the only one against which we can fairly bring the charge of pessimism. In *Jude the Obscure* argument is allowed to dominate impression, with the result that though the misery of the book is overwhelming it is not tragic. As calamity succeeds calamity we feel that the case against society is not being argued fairly or with profound understanding of the facts. Here is nothing of that width and force and knowledge of mankind which, when Tolstoy criticises society, makes his indictment formidable. Here we have revealed to us the petty cruelty of men, not the large injustice of the gods. It is only necessary to compare *Jude the Obscure* with *The Mayor of Casterbridge* to see where Hardy's true power lay. Jude carries on his miserable contest against the deans of colleges and the conventions of sophisticated society. Henchard is pitted, not against another man, but against something outside himself which is opposed to men of his ambition and power. No human being wishes him ill. Even Farfrae and Newson and Elizabeth Jane whom he has wronged all come to pity him, and even to admire his strength of character. He is standing up to fate, and in backing the old Mayor whose ruin has been largely his own fault, Hardy makes us feel that we are backing human nature in an unequal contest. There is no pessimism here. Throughout the book we are aware of the sublimity of the issue, and yet it is presented to us in the most concrete form. From the opening scene in which Henchard sells his wife to the sailor at the fair to his death on Egdon Heath the vigour of the story is superb, its humour rich and racy, its movement large-limbed and free. The skimmity ride, the fight between Farfrae and Henchard in the loft, Mrs. Cuxsom's speech upon the death of Mrs. Henchard, the talk of the ruffians at Peter's Finger with Nature present in the background or mysteriously dominating the foreground, are among the glories of English fiction. Brief and scanty, it may be, is the measure of happiness allowed to each, but so long as the struggle is, as Henchard's was, with the decrees of fate and not with the laws of man, so long as it is in the open air and calls for activity of the body rather than of the brain, there is greatness in the contest, there is pride and pleasure in it, and the death of the broken corn merchant in his cottage on Egdon Heath is comparable to the death of Ajax lord of Salamis. The true tragic emotion is ours.

Before such power as this we are made to feel that the ordinary tests which we apply to fiction are futile enough. Do we insist that a great novelist shall be a master of melodious prose? Hardy was no such thing. He feels his way by dint of sagacity and uncompromising sincerity to the phrase he wants, and it is often of unforgettable pungency. Failing it, he will make do with any homely or clumsy or old-fashioned turn of speech, now of the utmost angularity, now of a bookish elaboration. No style in literature, save Scott's, is so difficult to analyse; it is on the face of it so bad, yet it achieves its aim so unmistakably. As well might one attempt to rationalise the charm of a muddy country road, or of a plain field of roots in winter. And then, like Dorsetshire itself, out of these very elements of stiffness and angularity his prose will put on greatness; will roll with a Latin sonority; will shape itself in a massive and monumental symmetry like that of his own bare downs. Then again, do we require that a novelist shall observe the probabilities, and keep close to reality? To find anything approaching the violence and convolution of Hardy's plots one must go back to the Elizabethan drama. Yet we accept his story completely as we read it; more than that, it becomes obvious that his violence and his melodrama, when they are not due to a curious peasant-like love of the monstrous for its own sake, are part of that wild spirit of poetry which saw with intense irony and grimness that no reading of life can possibly outdo the strangeness of life itself, no symbol of caprice and unreason be too extreme to represent the astonishing circumstances of our existence.

But as we consider the great structure of the Wessex novels it seems irrelevant to fasten on little points—this character, that scene, this phrase of deep and poetic beauty. It is something larger that Hardy has bequeathed to us. The Wessex novels are not one book, but many. They cover an immense stretch; inevitably they are full of imperfections— some are failures, and others exhibit only the wrong side of their maker's genius. But undoubtedly, when we have submitted ourselves fully to them, when we come to take stock of our impression of the whole, the effect is commanding and satisfactory. We have been freed from the cramp and pettiness imposed by life. Our imaginations have been stretched and heightened; our humour has been made to laugh out; we have drunk deep of the beauty of the earth. Also we have been made to enter the shade of a sorrowful and brooding spirit which, even in its saddest mood, bore itself with a grave uprightness and never, even when most moved to anger, lost its deep compassion for the sufferings of men and women. Thus it is no mere transcript of life at a certain time and place that Hardy has given us. It is a vision of the world and of man's lot as they revealed themselves to a powerful imagination, a profound and poetic genius, a gentle and humane soul.

Comments and Questions

1. In tracing the evolution of her writer's thought, Virginia Woolf begins by discussing his early novel, *Desperate Remedies*. What she says about this novel, necessarily, constitutes a forecast of what is to follow. Study the various weaknesses as well as the strong points which the critic sees in *Desperate Remedies*. To what extent does the writer follow up these strong points in discussing the later novels?

2. The critic says that in Hardy's early novels "first one gift would have its way with him and then another," and that the moment for the flowering of his genius came in *Far from the Madding Crowd*. What virtues does Virginia Woolf see in the novels preceding *Far from the Madding Crowd*, and to what extent does she demonstrate Hardy's fusion of these in the latter novel?

3. The essay denominates Hardy an "unconscious" writer, and says that this unconsciousness "is the source of his strength and of his weakness." How central is this paradox to the essay as a whole? How does the critic develop this idea?

4. Particularly notable is the manner in which this essay fuses information and evaluation. The essay obviously is highly appreciative. In nearly every sentence the writer reflects, directly or indirectly, her deep admiration for Hardy's novels. Yet nearly every sentence, as well, advances our understanding of the evolution of Hardy's art. Study carefully the writer's technique at this point.

5. Comparisons and contrasts permeate the essay. Not only are Hardy's various novels compared, but Hardy's work as a whole is set over against the works of Jane Austen, Meredith, Thackeray, and Tolstoy. What is Virginia Woolf able to say about Hardy by using these other writers?

6. Although her essay is deeply appreciative, Virginia Woolf points out several weaknesses inherent in Hardy's fiction. Decide on the advisability of this approach.

7. Review the Introduction to this chapter, where a number of difficulties are mentioned which face the critic who traces the evolution of a writer's thought. Take these up in turn, and decide to what extent, and in what way, the critic has succeeded in overcoming them.

HOWARD W. WEBB, JR.

The Meaning of Ring Lardner's Fiction: A Re-evaluation

*O*ur judgments of Ring Lardner and of his work have become stereotyped and thus distorted. Because of the seeming finality of Clifton Fadiman's argument that "Except Swift, no writer has gone farther on hatred alone," [1] we have come to think of Lardner as a man who despised his fellowman. Because of the clarity with which he caught the social, professional, and linguistic traits of his characters—his "athletes, salesmen, suburbanites, song writers, barbers, actresses, stenographers, and the like" [2]—we have come to believe that his achievement went no further. So long as we rest with these conclusions, we will miss the more fundamental, and far subtler, point of his writing. The dominant theme in Ring Lardner's writing was not the pettiness and meanness of modern life; it was the problem of communication. In his work he analyzed, more in amusement and pity than in anger, the flaws and failures that impede its smooth and even flow.

This theme is manifest in both the matter and the manner of Lardner's work. Such factors as debasing of standard English, banality of vocabulary and ideas, confusion and absence of meaning, all of which tend to jeopardize or destroy the process of successful linguistic communion, provide the substance of many of his comic sketches, his nonsense compositions and parodies, and even of his radio reviews. [3] The same factors define the essence of his style, that imaginative synthesis of vulgate Americanese. Matter and manner were most significantly combined in Lardner's short stories. There the substance is mirrored by the very nature of the style. [4] Usually embodied in an oral narrative, a series of letters or a diary, or in conversations, the style creates a host of personalities who cannot communicate successfully. Each of them is hopelessly confined within a prison of self which no word or touch or gesture ever quite penetrates. These are the figures who dramatize Ring Lardner's theme: the comedy, the pain, the terror of being incommunicado.

---

[1] Clifton Fadiman, "Ring Lardner and the Triangle of Hate," *Nation,* CXXXVI, 315 (March 22, 1933). See also Maxwell Geismar, "Ring Lardner: Like Something Was Going to Happen," *Writers in Crisis* (New York, 1942), pp. 3–36.

[2] George F. Whicher, "Analysts of Decay," *The Literature of the American People,* ed. A. H. Quinn (New York, 1951), p. 880. Similar lists can be found in almost all anthologies, articles, and reviews.

[3] See Ring Lardner, *First and Last* (New York, 1934), for a representative selection of such pieces.

[4] I have dealt with Lardner's style in "The Development of a Style: The Lardner Idiom," which will appear in *American Quarterly.*

Lardner's typical character has an image of himself which bears little resemblance to the one he actually presents to others. So long as he can interpret, in terms of his private self-image, the realities that surround him, he is safe and happy; but more often than not, because image and reality collide, he feels threatened and insecure. Thus, within his prison he is, paradoxically, tormented by the possibility of invasion and assault. Depending upon his response to his predicament, he may be viewed as comic or vicious or pathetic.

No one story comprehends all these possibilities. Rather, all of them together describe various aspects of a single situation, a situation best instanced by an experience Lardner recalled from his junior year in high school:

They was a ½ witted boy in town that thought the school yard was his amusement park. For many yrs. he had spent all his days roaming the grounds and picking up stones which he throwed at no special targets, but finely one day the janitor told him to get off the grounds and stay off by orders of the school board. Well my father was on the school board and after that whenever I hove in sight of the boy, who incidentally ignored the janitor's advice, he would say to me your father is on the school board and follow up the remark with a shower bouquet of specially selected stones. My sudden death would not of changed the make-up of the school board, but I never had time to stop and tell him that.[5]

Because his understanding of the normal world was vague at best, the half-wit felt generally threatened; because he lived in his own private world, he was able to respond to the threat—to communicate his unhappiness—only by finding a target for his stones. Lardner understood very clearly the threat he faced—those were real stones; but because of the half-wit's predicament, and his response to it, Lardner too was unable to communicate. Both parties felt assaulted and both were incommunicado.

In his fiction Lardner examined this situation from four perspectives, emphasizing one at the start of his career, another in the early twenties, a third at the end of that decade, and a fourth in the last few years of his life. In the beginning, most of his stories regarded only the half-wit, who thus appears to be a harmless fellow throwing stones "at no special targets." Encased within his distorted personal universe, he goes his way heedless, even unaware, of others; and his eccentric behavior is merely ridiculous. The best-known embodiment of this figure is Jack Keefe, the rookie pitcher of *You Know Me Al*.[6]

---

[5] Ring Lardner, "What I Ought to of Learnt in High School," *American Magazine*, XCVI, 80, 82 (Nov., 1923).

[6] *You Know Me Al* (New York, 1916; reissued New York, 1925). All references are to the reissue of 1925. Two other collections of "busher" stories are *Treat 'Em Rough* (Indianapolis, 1918) and *The Real Dope* (Indianapolis, 1919); two uncollected groups of stories appeared serially in the *Saturday Evening Post* in 1915 and 1919.

Jack perceives reality through the thick shield of his enormous ego. When he wins a game, his pitching must triumph over the errors of other players and misjudgments of the umpires: "I had everything and the Dubs done well to score a run. . . . The umps give them their run. . . . Then Schulte the lucky stiff happened to get a hold of one and pulled it past first base. I guess Chase must of been asleep" (p. 80). When he loses, the fates and his teammates have played him false: "I had a sore arm which I was warming up. . . . Weaver and Lord and all of them kept kicking them round the infield and Collins and Bodie couldn't catch nothing. . . . Crawford got the luckiest three-base hit I ever see. He popped one way up in the air and the wind blowed it against the fence" (pp. 38, 41). When the manager taunts: "Don't work no harder than you have to or you might get hurt and the league would blow up," Jack concludes: "I guess he thinks pretty well of me" (p. 27).

Jack's only security, in a seemingly treacherous world, is his conception of himself. When this is challenged, as it frequently is, by the battering of reality, Jack's reaction is compounded of fear and hostility. A friendly bit of advice from an Ed Walsh or a Christy Mathewson he regards as a sign of jealousy. When his wife Florrie wants to hire a nurse to watch the baby, Jack refuses because "I would not trust no nurse to take care of the baby because how do I know the nurse is not nothing but a grafter or a dope fiend maybe and should ought not to be left with the baby" (p. 186). When the force of reality overwhelms his bastion, Jack retreats into illusion. For example, he rejoins the White Sox after World War I determined not to sign for less than five thousand dollars, although he quickly reduces the amount he will accept to three thousand. His contract, however, calls for only twenty-four hundred dollars, and Jack is incensed. "I was getting $2500.00 per annum before I went to the war," he writes; but after all efforts to raise the amount have failed, he decides to sign for "$2400.00 which is the same money I was getting when I quit and that's going some Al. . . ." [7]

From the time he leaves Terre Haute to join the White Sox, in the first "busher" story, until, in the last, he is sold to the Athletics, Jack Keefe remains unchanged. Never is he able to move beyond the confines of his private self-image, to establish any meaningful relationship with the world which seems to threaten him. But his frustration, his outrage, and his antics are comic, for they bring harm only to him. He is the smart wisecracker—who answers the bantering of others with the threat of a punch in the jaw; the unbeatable pitcher—who cannot win regularly; the irresistible lover—whose affairs end with someone else's getting the girl; the model husband—who cannot get along with his wife. He is Jack Keefe, able and all-knowing, for whom life is forever going

---

[7] "The Busher Re-enlists," *Saturday Evening Post,* CXCI, 151, 155 (April 19, 1919).

wrong. "You know me Al," he boasts, and the words, which run like a refrain through the stories, form an ironic assertion of what he is not.

This first portrait in Lardner's gallery was followed by similar ones: Alibi Ike, Gullible of *Gullible's Travels* (Indianapolis, 1917), Fred Gross of *Own Your Own Home* (Indianapolis, 1919), and the wife and the sister-in-law of *The Big Town* (Indianapolis, 1921). In another group of stories, however, a new perspective emerges; here the scope has been enlarged to include both the half-wit and his victim. The half-wit is still heedless of others, but he is not unaware of them. He regards them as invaders and thus as appropriate targets for his "specially selected stones." Seen in this broader view, his behavior is no longer merely eccentric; it is dangerous.

The first of these vicious half-wits to appear in Lardner's writing was Midge Kelly of "Champion." [8] Midge, like Jack Keefe, has an enormous ego; but he is never afraid, nor does he ever retreat. Reality must conform to his view of it—or else. When his private self-image is threatened, he becomes aggressive, striking out violently at anyone who seems to intrude upon his demesne. Indeed, he is capable of only two responses: arrogance or anger. His associates ultimately learn this, but not always before they have been hurt. Midge seduces the sister of his best friend and, after being forced to "do right by her," delivers "a crushing blow" (p. 114) to her cheek and abandons her. Midge's manager, Tommy Haley, has no contract; he relies instead upon the champion's gratitude. "He knows it was me that drug him out o' the gutter," Tommy remarks, "and he ain't goin' to turn me down now. . . . Where'd he of been at if I hadn't listened to him when he first come to me?" (p. 116). But the time arrives when Tommy is of no further use; and Midge tells him: "Get out o' here before they have to carry you out. You been spongin' off o' me long enough" (p. 122). Tommy has failed to understand that for Midge Kelly other people are either extensions of or threats to himself, and that when they cease to be the former they automatically become the latter, and appropriate targets for his punches.

The obvious loathing Lardner felt for Midge Kelly, and for the other vicious half-wits he created, may account for the impression that he hated the human race. Actually, however, completely vicious characters occupy central positions in very few of his stories. Besides Midge Kelly, there are only Conrad Green and Jim Kendall, the practical joker of "Haircut." Similar characters, like the miserable mates of "The Love Nest" and the garrulous bridge player of "Who Dealt?" are careless or thoughtless rather than vicious. They represent a modification of the

[8] The story first appeared in the *Metropolitan Magazine*, XLIV, 14–16, 62–64 (Oct., 1916). It was subsequently included in *How to Write Short Stories* (New York, 1924) and in *Round Up* (New York, 1929), pp. 109–127. Unless otherwise noted, all references to individual stories are to the last named collection.

original image, even though their stones land with the same force and cause as much harm. Perhaps even more important, many of these characters bring pain to themselves as well as to their victims. Conrad Green ends his day defeated on every front; Jim Kendall brings on his own death; the "love nest" turns out to be a chamber of horrors; and with her chatter the bridge player ruins her own marriage as well as that of her friends. Whether by viciousness or carelessness, these people despoil or destroy the territory they wish to protect.

Perhaps a further explanation for the undue emphasis given Lardner's hatred may be found in a third group of stories which present still another view of the total situation. Here, dangerous or thoughtless stone-throwers are an integral part of the action, but the central figures are their victims. Several uncollected early tales present this view;[9] it is most fully set forth, however, in a number of stories which appeared between 1927 and 1929.

The significance of these stories derives from the behavior of the victims themselves. Some of them, like the provincial poet of "The Maysville Minstrel" and the neglected wife of "Now and Then," suffer passively, resigning themselves to persecution. Others strike back; and their action casts the half-wit in the role of the invader: a coarse boor who, brandishing his weapons of crude manners and vulgar language, charges into the world of decency and common sense. This situation may be illustrated by the behavior of Mr. Shelton, the central character in "Contract." [10] After enduring baby talk, faulty grammar, bad cocktails, and constant criticism of his bridge playing for an entire evening, he decides that he has had enough. A week later, when the bridge club meets once more, he takes delight in pointing out flaws in his companions' table manners, pronunciation, and usage; to his delight, he is not invited again. His triumph, however, is brief, for at the next bridge party he attends, his partner ends the first game by inquiring: "Oh, Mr. Shevlin . . . why *didn't* you lead me a club? You *must* watch the discards!" (p. 139).

Like so many of the others in this third group,[11] "Contract" is an essentially trivial story, little more, in fact, than the pettish expression of a personal irritation. But this should not blind us to the importance of the perspective here presented, for, as Donald Elder points out, "In many cases the very flaws in the stories are clues to [Lardner's] anger, his exasperations, his disappointments. . . ." [12] The images of invasion

---

[9] See, for example, "Back to Baltimore," *Redbook,* XXIV, 29–41 (Nov., 1914), and "The Crook," *Saturday Evening Post,* CLXXXVIII, 18–20, 52–53 (June 24, 1916).

[10] The story first appeared in *Harper's Bazaar,* LXIII, 100–101, 142, 144, 149 (March, 1929), and was reprinted in *Round Up,* pp. 129–139.

[11] See, for example, "Nora," "Liberty Hall," "Dinner," and "Ex Parte," all reprinted in *Round Up.*

[12] Donald Elder, *Ring Lardner* (New York, 1956), p. 307.

and assault and the situations in which communication is distorted or breaks down were more for Lardner than literary devices. They were central to his view of life; they spoke his own fears. The stone-throwing episode that he recalled was not an isolated instance; his writing about himself is filled with anecdotes in which he, as an unoffending man of decency and common sense unable to communicate with those who threaten him, is the victim of the brutish people and forces of the world. In "Jersey City Gendarmerie Je T'aime" he relates his unhappy encounters with Jersey City policemen; in "All Quiet on the Eastern Front" his troubles with the insistently noisy boats outside the New York hospital where he is staying; and in "A Slow Train Through Arizona" his trials on a trip from Tucson to Phoenix.[13]

And Lardner's fear of assault was compounded by his apparent inability to forestall or halt it. Just as Mr. Shelton never fully triumphed over his bridge partners, so Lardner was not able to make the Jersey City police comprehend his plights and needs, or to silence the noisy boats. Just so, he could not pause to argue with the half-wit. His personal world, like his fictional world, was one in which people did not listen or would not understand. The predicament is forcefully illustrated in the macabre sketch "Large Coffee," [14] which describes the frustrating, twelve-week effort of a writer to make clear to room service that he wants for breakfast "enough coffee to fill one cup four times" (p. 73). Although he finally gets an order clerk who understands his request, she lasts less than two weeks; and soon after her departure, his body is found in his room, "his head crushed in by a blow from some blunt instrument" (p. 72), presumably, and appropriately, the telephone.

In the light of these sketches, the stone-throwing situation—clear enough when seen in terms of a Jack Keefe, a Midge Kelly, or even a Mr. Shelton—becomes wholly ambiguous. In a world where one is victimized by policemen, plagued by boat whistles, and unable to make clear a simple order—in such a world, where do reality and normality lie; where is meaning to be found? In such a world, how does one distinguish between the half-wits and the men of decency and common sense? How, in fact, does a man judge what he himself is? These are precisely the problems posed in the fourth group of Lardner's stories. In this group there are no stone-throwers; there are only victims. And whether they are wildly unbalanced, comically stupid, or quietly reasonable, they all face the same predicament. Although they seek desperately for adequate definitions of self, theirs is a world where meaning is not possible. Thus, unarmed against the stones of fate and circumstance which rain down upon them, they surrender to despair or madness and submit themselves to chaos.

---

[13] *New Yorker,* V, 24–25 (Nov. 2, 1928); *ibid.,* VII, 14–17 (June 27, 1931); *Cosmopolitan,* XCI, 86–87 (Sept., 1931). See also the series of autobiographical articles that appeared in the *Saturday Evening Post* in 1931–1932.

[14] *First and Last,* pp. 71–77.

The first instance of this perspective is again to be found in an early story, "My Roomy."[15] Mr. Elliott, the central character, is a major-league rookie, and he is in search of an identity. He wants very much to be a successful ball player so that he can make enough money to marry his girl. His teammates regard him as "just a plain nut and li'ble to break out any time" (p. 341); and his irrational behavior seems to justify their assumption. Although he is a power with a bat, Elliott refuses to learn to field. Off the diamond, his actions are even stranger: he runs water in the bathtub all night, shaves in the middle of the night, and sings as loudly as possible regardless of the lateness of the hour; only his roommate, the sympathetic but detached narrator of the story, will put up with him. Elliott's bizarre behavior is never explained, but clearly it is a twisted cry for recognition.

Unlike Jack Keefe and Midge Kelly, Mr. Elliott is not trying to maintain an image of self but to establish one. If he is a success and gets to marry his girl, he tells the narrator, he will "settle down. I'd be so happy that I wouldn't have to look for no excitement" (p. 342). And he seems to have a chance to find himself; for in spite of his eccentricities, he is kept on the team as a pinch hitter, because, as his roommate says, "He sure can bust 'em" (p. 330). Indeed, the self-image that Elliott is trying to establish is that of a "buster." In part he triumphs; he can "bust" the ball and "bust up" ball games. He cannot understand, however, that his demands for recognition, his inability to communicate with normality, "bust up" the routine activities of his teammates. When his roommate scolds him for breaking up a poker game, Elliott replies: "That's my business—bustin' things" (p. 338), and hurls a pitcher of ice water through a closed window.

His tragedy is that in striving to be a "buster" he succeeds only in being a "bust." When his antics on the diamond become intolerable and he is sold to Atlanta, he decides to quit baseball. Before he leaves, however,

he goes up to the lookin'-glass and stares at himself for five minutes. Then, all of a sudden, he hauls off and takes a wallop at his reflection in the glass. Naturally he smashed the glass all to pieces and he cut his hand somethin' awful.

Without lookin' at it he come over to me and says: "Well, good-by, sport!"—and holds out his other hand to shake. When I starts to shake with him he smears his bloody hand all over my map. Then he laughed like a wild man and run out o' the room and out o' the hotel. (p. 344)

The symbolic overtones of the scene are obvious: in smashing his reflected image, Elliott is acknowledging his failure and "busting" what he has sought to become; in smearing his blood on his roommate, he is

[15] The story first appeared in the *Saturday Evening Post*, CLXXXVI, 17–19, 61–62, 65 (May 9, 1914). It was reprinted in *How to Write Short Stories* and in *Round Up*, pp. 327–346.

cursing the world of normality which he has sought so unsuccessfully
to enter. Nor is the irony of his failure yet at an end. Returning to
his home town to discover that his girl has already married, he assaults
the happy couple with a baseball bat; and again he fails. From the
asylum where he is sent, Elliott writes his roommate: "I was at bat twice
and made two hits; but I guess I did not meet 'em square. They tell
me they are both alive yet, which I did not mean 'em to be." He signs
himself "B. Elliott," significantly, the first indication of a given name,
and adds in a post script that the "B stands for Buster" (p. 346). Thus,
with complete defeat and total insanity comes fulfilment.

"My Roomy" is Lardner's most revealing story. Taken together with
the Jack Keefe stories and "Champion," it defines Lardner's total view
of life; for while Elliott has much in common with both the "busher"
and Midge Kelly, he is not comic or vicious; he is pathetic. Also, seen
in terms of the high-school anecdote, he joins the problems of the half-
wit with those of Ring Lardner. Like the former, he wants to assert
his right to a plot of ground, a place in the world; like the latter, he
wants to shout his name and halt the rain of stones; and like both, he
cannot find any successful means to communicate. Mr. Elliott's is, to
be sure, a special case; the normal, reasonable world does exist in
"My Roomy," and Elliott is cut off from it by his own eccentricities as
well as by the circumstances that assail him. This does not, however,
vitiate the story's fundamental point: the horror and terror of being
perpetually and irrevocably incommunicado.

Lardner did not employ this perspective again until the last three
or four years of his life. Then, overwhelmed by physical disease and
intellectual despair,[16] he resigned himself to what he apparently regarded as an indifferent, if not malevolent, and chaotic world. A persistent motif in his final stories is the impossibility of establishing any
rational and enduring image of self. Three stories in particular—
"Mamma," [17] Lose With a Smile (New York, 1933), and "Poodle" [18]
—make clear the extent of his resignation. In "Mamma" the central
character, a Mrs. Carns, shaken by the deaths of her husband and two
children, wanders aimlessly about New York, telling anyone who tries
to help her that her name is Mamma and that her husband will take
her home to their beautiful children after he leaves his office. Ultimately,
at the hospital where she is taken, Mamma remembers her last name,
and a nurse learns the facts of the case. Later, when Mamma asks
whether her husband has been called, the nurse replies: "There's no
such name. . . . I looked in the book and couldn't find it" (p. 252).
This is the only humane answer possible, for Mamma has not been
denied, she has been deprived of her self-image. The world no longer

---

[16] See Elder, pp. 293–378.
[17] "Mamma," Good Housekeeping, XC, 52–54, 252 (June, 1930).
[18] "Poodle," Delineator, CXXIV, 8–9, 30, 32–33 (Jan., 1934).

holds any meaning for her; only in the haven of insanity can she continue to assert the identity she has lost.

Nor is there any joy in *Lose With a Smile*. This series of letters between a rookie and his girl, as Gilbert Seldes has aptly observed, "is not amusing. It is melancholy." [19] Danny Warner, the rookie, aspires to a regular position on the Brooklyn club and honestly tries to follow the instructions of the manager and the coach; and he hopes, too, to make a name for himself in the music world. But, in contrast with Jack Keefe, he has limited talents and less self-confidence. On the diamond, he is unsuccessful even as a pinch-hitter, and the qualities of his voice and songs spell obvious disaster for his musical ambitions. Even his chances for a happy marriage seem dim, for at the end, having been released to Jersey City, Danny writes his girl that he is through with baseball and may see her "in 10 days and may be never" (p. 172). On the same day, she writes that she is coming to New York on "Saturday morning and please meet me as I will be scared to death if you dont" (p. 174). They may get together; but since their letters will inevitably cross, it is just as likely that while the girl waits forlornly in the station Danny will be wandering about New York, as lost in his way as Mamma is in hers.

For the foolish, as for the mad, Lardner offered little solace. For the man of decency and common sense he offered none at all. Such a figure is the nameless narrator of "Poodle," a victim of the depression whose only weapon against his helpless state is self-derision. After losing his job, he begins the dreary, hopeless round of the unemployed: answering want ads, sleeping in hotel lobbies, and watching cheap movies. One day, treating himself to a more expensive show at the Paramount, he encounters an eccentric millionaire who calls him Poodle and insists that they are old friends. The millionaire needs a companion "to prevent him buying the corner of Forty-second and Fifth Avenue and starting a rival Radio City" (p. 32), and the narrator is hired for the job. "I'm a seventy-two hundred-dollar day nurse named Poodle," he concludes. "I spend eight hours a day with a crazy person . . ." (p. 33). In a world gone mad, a world from which certainty and solid definitions have departed, the reasonable man has no choice but to assume whatever identity insanity will grant him.

From this conclusion we may gauge the depth of Lardner's own despair. He had insisted upon the necessity for self-knowledge and successful communication; and in the beginning, the "busher" had been able to be Jack Keefe and Midge Kelly to be "champion," however comic or vicious they might thus appear. In the end, however, Lardner conceded that neither self-knowledge nor successful communication was possible; what had seemed the special plight of "Buster" Elliott had become the common predicament of all men. Mrs. Carns could be only

[19] "Editor's Introduction," *The Portable Ring Lardner* (New York, 1946), p. 5.

"Mamma"; Danny and his girl could have, at best, only the anonymity of life in the city; the nameless victim of the depression could be only "Poodle." In these final stories even Lardner's style has lost its zest; its flatness and lack of emphasis reveal more of the author than of his characters. Had he lived longer, Lardner might have found another perspective from which to regard that stone-throwing situation; or he might have explored in greater depth and with more linguistic effectiveness his final, Olympian view which merged the half-wit and the victim into a single lost and helpless figure. We may regret the loss, but we should not, in reviewing what he accomplished, obscure his achievement.

Lardner's writings present a unified view of life. We need not accept that view, but we should at least recognize it as that of a man who has raised serious questions about the nature of experience. Nor should we allow the settings of his stories to blind us to the significance of his dominant theme. The problems with which he dealt were no more acute among the semi-literate and inarticulate who ran the base paths, trod the boards, or lounged in the broad expanse of middle-class suburbia than they were among the rest of America's citizens. Finally, we should dismiss the charges of misanthropy which have long been lodged against Lardner. His creations, even those he loathed, were the product of his sympathetic understanding of the catastrophe that befalls anyone who is cut off from communication with his fellowmen. We should, at last, allow Ring Lardner to communicate with us.

Comments and Questions

1. In his opening paragraph Howard W. Webb, Jr. seeks to justify his article: a re-evaluation of Ring Lardner's fiction is needed because our judgments of Lardner have become distorted. How convincing is the justification? Should the writer have speculated concerning why critics as knowledgeable as Clifton Fadiman and George F. Whicher have focused attention on matters which he deems secondary?

2. Webb makes considerable use of short quotations from various of Ring Lardner's stories. Decide how these quotations contribute to Webb's thesis that Lardner's characters fail in their attempts to communicate.

3. Notice that phrases from, and references to, the early quotation about the half-wit throwing stones turn up periodically. This quotation, then, becomes a unifying device. What relation, exactly, does this stone-throwing incident bear to the four stages through which Webb sees Ring Lardner's fiction passing?

4. At the beginning of his second paragraph, Webb suggests that

Ring Lardner's basic theme of the problem of communication "is manifest in both the matter and the manner of Lardner's work." Throughout the remainder of the article, does the emphasis fall equally on "matter" and "manner," or is the emphasis predominantly in one direction?

5. The author bases his analysis of Lardner's fiction on a fourfold evolutionary pattern through which he sees Lardner's fiction moving. What *interpretation* does he put on this fourfold analysis? That is to say, what does he suggest we are to *do* with this information?

6. Almost the only specific aesthetic judgment contained in the article is found in Webb's comment in his next to last paragraph, where he indicates that the style of Ring Lardner's last stories has "lost its zest," and is characterized by "flatness and lack of emphasis." Is an aesthetic judgment of Lardner implicit in Webb's article? If so, what is it, and how is it implied? If no implicit evaluation is present, is its absence a weakness in the article?

7. Compare the opening and closing paragraphs to see what lines of inquiry suggested in the opening paragraph receive summation at the close of the article. Decide how effective the closing paragraph is, when viewed in the light of the whole article.

Suggestions for an Essay

Write an essay tracing the evolution in the art of a writer whose works you have studied. Even though you may not have read all of his works, pretend, for the purposes of this paper, that the titles with which you are familiar constitute his entire contribution. Make your essay interpretive; that is, present some sort of comparative evaluation of the worth of the selections you are considering.

6

AN ANALYSIS OF POINT OF VIEW

Introduction

Of considerable importance in the evaluation of fiction is a study of how an author handles *point of view*. This critical term, essentially a metaphor, means much the same thing when applied to literature as it does in ordinary conversation. Someone might say, "Well, from *my* point of view, a two-story house is nice in some ways, but it certainly is hard to take care of." What the person means, obviously, is that this is the way *he* looks at two-story houses. Similarly, every piece of fiction is "looked at" from someone's point of view; i.e., every story is *someone's* story.

Broadly considered, point of view in most pieces of fiction is handled in one of three ways:

1. *Omniscient author.* Historically, this is the oldest technique to enjoy wide usage. When we say that an author has employed the omniscient author technique we mean that the author, as storyteller, tells us the story, that it is *his* voice to which we are listening, that he is a person with whom we have to reckon, just as we have to reckon with the characters in the story. Many eighteenth- and nineteenth-century novels (Henry Fielding's *Tom Jones,* George Eliot's *Middlemarch,* Thomas Hardy's *The Return of the Native*) employ this technique. The term "omniscient author" derives from the fact that, since the author is telling the story, and since it is he who has created the characters about whom he is talking, he is in a position to know everything about his characters, and can, at will, take us into the minds of any of them, to show us what they are thinking.

2. *First person narrator.* In this technique, a character in the work of fiction tells the story, using the first person "I" throughout. Sometimes the "I" is a central character around whom the action revolves (Huck Finn in Mark Twain's *Huckleberry Finn*); at other times the "I" is what is sometimes called an observer (rather than

a participant), and remains relatively ill-defined in comparison to the other characters (David Copperfield in Charles Dickens' *David Copperfield*). Sometimes a writer, wishing to use his book as a vehicle for philosophical speculation, but fearing that a reader may object to the author qua author obtruding with interpolated observations, will let the story be told by a supernumerary character. No one, for example, has ever seriously doubted that when we listen to Ishmael narrate *Moby-Dick,* and offer philosophical speculations concerning man, God, and the universe, we are actually listening to Herman Melville.

3. *Third person restricted.* In this technique the writer tells the story, but tells it as though he were observing the action of the story by following one certain character around, looking over his shoulder. The author takes the reader into the mind of this character, but into the minds of none of the other characters. This central character—or "register," as Henry James called him—is therefore present throughout the entire work. Henry James (1843–1916) was the first significant novelist to practice this technique widely and successfully, and it has enjoyed widespread popularity among various important novelists since James.

Historically, various strengths and weaknesses have been urged for and against the various point of view techniques. It is frequently said that the reader has a right to object to the omniscient author interrupting the action to visit with his reader (a practice indulged in at great lengths by eighteenth-century novelists, while some more recent novelists, even though "omniscient," have kept themselves pretty much out of sight). The omniscient author, since he theoretically knows everything about all of his characters, is likewise open to the charge of withholding information from a reader, since he obviously cannot tell everything about every character.

Concerning the first person narrator, it is sometimes charged that the character who narrates the action can scarcely be developed into an interesting, third-dimensional character, since he cannot tell enough about himself to make us greatly interested in him without alienating himself from us. (It might be instructive to speculate how writers such as Mark Twain, in *Huckleberry Finn,* and Eudora Welty, in *The Ponder Heart,* avoid this difficulty.)

Concerning the third person restricted point of view, it is sometimes urged that—just as in the case of the first person narrator—the writer is obliged to refrain from dramatizing any of the action of the story in which his central character could not logically have figured.

Such criticisms of these point of view techniques, however, do not get very far considered in the abstract, apart from specific works. For point of view is simply *one* technique—albeit an important one—and the success or failure of a point of view technique has to be judged in the light of how it affects our reading of a given work. There have been good works of fiction, and bad ones, written using all the points of view mentioned, along with variations of them.

Following are two essays which discuss point of view. The way in which both writers, in their individual ways, link their authors' handling of point of view with the total meaning they derive from the works helps drive home a truism which is nevertheless worth repeating: that if a story were told from another point of view, it would be a different story and hence reflect a somewhat different reading of life.

MURRAY KRIEGER

Conrad's YOUTH: A Naive Opening to Art and Life

Youth is, for the uninitiated, a most helpful entry into the study of Joseph Conrad. It is, of course, not one of his most searching fictions, but it reveals in modest and undeveloped form many of his characteristic devices and themes. If these devices and themes are undeveloped here, they are also simple; as such they are useful to the student seeking to find a way to cope with Conrad's grander and graver works. For enough difficulty and complexity abound in his work generally so that the student can use whatever assistance he can get.

The most obvious, and thus the most frequently cited, of Conrad's devices is the narrator point of view, especially the use of his *alter ego*: the wise, the mature, the warmly sympathetic and understanding man of the world—and of the sea—Marlow. He will tell us a number of Conrad's stories, but in *Youth* he makes his first appearance. Conrad contributed in a major way to the reformulation of the problem in fiction that we term 'point of view'; that is, the manner in which the events of the tale are relayed to the reader—whether indirectly, through the intervening presence of an omniscient, unidentified author who leads us by the hand, or through the intervening presence of a first person, the "I" of the tale; or directly, by allowing the reader to witness the events and conversation without an intervening consciousness making its commentaries. Conrad wanted the last—the purely dramatic point of view—confined to the drama, since it did not exploit the special resources for narration that fiction made available to its author. And he was anxious somehow to avoid the limitations both of an "I" and of omniscience. The latter was for him too diffuse, lacking in focus, covering its story like a blanket. And if one were dealing, as he was, with delicate examinations of delicate moral beings—in which refined subjective responses were all-important—omniscience would be especially clumsy. Now it is true that with the first person the story comes to the reader subjectively refracted through a single consciousness. Unfortunately, however, there is no way of getting outside the "I," of permitting either a more objective view or other competing subjective views filtered through other sensibilities. Limited by the single set of perceptions available to an "I," Conrad would of course not be able to multiply dimensions and perspectives. For him, whose fictional world perhaps anticipated, if it did not reflect, the subjectivity of what was to be the ever-contingent universe of the relativity concept, more complex methods had to be found. Conrad felt he combined the advantages of the two opposed points of view, the omniscient and the first person, in his invention of Marlow, and with him the narrator point of view.

But, judging only from *Youth,* the reader may think that, in effect, Marlow is nothing more than the usual first person telling his story. Aside from a couple of paragraphs at the start and a short one at the end to frame his narration, it is all Marlow, speaking in his own person. But is this narrative frame needed? Why not simply start and finish with Marlow, have him simply transcribing his own youthful reminiscence? For one thing, we would lose the dramatic situation in which Marlow unfolds his tale: several successful, sedate, middle-aged men— all of them once long ago young and adventurous and at sea and thus now feeling this tight bond of kinship—are having an evening together over a bottle of wine. Marlow shares much with them: his career from romance to solid propriety, his attitudes both past and present, of youth and middle-age, his sense of what is lost and how necessary—if painful— it was to lose it. The rhetorical tone of the tale, and of the general philosophical commentaries that accompany it, arises in large part from Marlow's easy confidence of group understanding, from an exclusive, fraternal sense of belonging. This tone, permitted only by the dramatic situation that frames the monologue, helps Conrad establish the contrast between the then and the now, the freshness and idiocy of romance and the wrinkled weariness of solid, circumspect reality. So does the sense that this narration is being spoken aloud help him attain this effect. In addition, there are those significant returns to the present dramatic situation in Marlow's repeated requests for his hearers to "pass the bottle." At times these occur when the narration threatens to become too sentimental or dramatic, too lost, in its recollections. Marlow breaks the mood, indeed destroys it utterly—as Conrad means him to—with his most unsentimental and undramatic requests. He is jarring the reader— as he is jarring Marlow's listeners and even Marlow himself—out of the beckoning, tempting grasp of romance. What is being told us, we are forcibly reminded, is past, irrevocably behind us, faded and done with, despite the teasing and deceptive vividness of narration. For always the vividness is accompanied by Marlow's conversational rhetoric that establishes the perspective of time and of a sad, aging wisdom.

Besides allowing the dramatic framework, this point of view allows us to be at once outside and inside our narrator, his story and his view of it. Unlike an omniscient author, the narrator gives us a particular perspective upon the series of events. Further, unlike an "I," he has a specific identity, an objective reality, for us. Everything he says is in quotation marks: we see him from the outside as a character, before and after—if not during—his narration. This makes all the difference when there is a need for us to have several contrasting views upon a situation. After all, if we are limited to a first-person narrator and cannot get outside him, we cannot get an outside view of our lens so as to judge his judgment of the events he relates to us, to understand the refraction, the limitations produced by his single angle of vision. We see through the window but are not made sufficiently aware of the existence of the glass and its distorting properties.

There are in *Youth* ironies and incongruities which the distanced narrator's role can emphasize. Although there is a wide gap of time and of temperament between narrator and protagonist so that with gentle irony Marlow can condescend to his former, youthful self, at the same time the older Marlow sees in the younger one a certain value and validity that in his honesty he dare not evade. The fact that Marlow is spinning the tale and that it concerns his own earlier self—not that of someone else—enables him to be inside the young man's sensitive psyche even as Marlow's present age, with the skepticism it has brought, allows him to view the youthful dedication rather critically. And even as, through Marlow, we are allowed to look through the young man's eyes as well as to observe him looking through them, so we are allowed to look through the older Marlow's eyes and—since he is an objective character in the story—to observe him observing his own past, to judge the distortions produced by our lens, to understand his reactions in terms of his own limitations of age, sedateness, his mild and moderate disillusionment. And finally we cannot be certain which Marlow is our protagonist—the youthful or the middle-aged—which it is whose psyche is most worth observing. For indeed it is both, in their inter-relations. This multiplication of perspectives gives the story its values; and it is the narrator point of view that allows them so to multiply and to vie with each other for supremacy, and for our sympathy.

Yet, as I have suggested, Conrad's use of his narrative device in *Youth* is but a weak shadow of what this method becomes as he comes to live more familiarly with his talkative creature, Marlow. There is in this initial use of his narrator some stylistic difficulty in reconciling the flowery rhetoric the early Conrad so enjoyed using with the sense of colloquialism demanded by the oral narrative situation. How to be both lofty, even romantic, in diction and yet casually conversational in tone? There are inflated phrases like "rectitude of soul," "terrestrial globe," or "a pestiferous cloud defiling the splendour of sea and sky." How is language as pompous as this—and there is much of it—to be reconciled with the breezy carelessness of those passages in which Conrad is trying to emphasize the spontaneity of Marlow's extemporaneous narration? Perhaps the most objectionable of the latter is the refrain, "Pass the bottle." Its function, as I have observed, is evident enough—and of course crucial to Conrad's theme. But Conrad puts too heavy a strain on what is after all a rather crude mechanical contrivance all too obviously meant to shatter the reader's illusions even as time has shattered Marlow's. For the most part Conrad is in other writings more subtle in gaining his effects. While of course some of the contrast in the narrative itself between the pompous and the colloquial is consistent with Conrad's ironic intention, unfortunately the incongruities of style also occur, sometimes closely juxtaposed, in passages when Marlow's attitude seems constant. As he grew, Conrad was usually able more successfully to weld the tone of Marlow the descriptive polysyllabic *raconteur,* Marlow the pompous philosopher, and Marlow the breezy drinking companion.

Further, while I have tried at some length to justify Conrad's use of his peculiar narrator technique in *Youth,* I must admit that he gets far more out of it elsewhere, especially in *Lord Jim.* There he introduces characters and incidents that we see at times through Marlow, at times directly; he also uses other lenses besides Marlow; and, in using Marlow to tell his story, he accentuates certain aspects and suppresses others by turning about the time-sequence and proceeding in a way that is anything but chronological. Thus he manipulates time in order to emphasize subjective reality over objective and classifiable fact. But here it is *Youth* that concerns us. I have only wanted to indicate briefly some possibilities of this technical innovation that Conrad realizes in his more profound work. The number of perspectives upon a single action or single problem comes to be endlessly multiplied so that one's view of it is endlessly complex, as it should be, here in Conrad's world where relativity rules supreme and objects have reality not in themselves so much as in their effect upon the consciousness of the character concerned with them. Only in *Youth* does one find the narrator-Marlow's role so circumscribed as to be related only to a single other character, himself, and his technique of story-telling so inhibited as to restrict him to a simple chronological recital of a sequence of events. Yet even here, less exploited as he is, Marlow manages, as I have shown, to function for his master most effectively.

The theme of *Youth* is similarly related to themes in Conrad's other work. And Conrad had a most serious interest in his themes—themes of a special nature—as one might expect, of an especially complex nature.

All that Conrad had to say in his own voice on the subject of art and truth reveals that he is primarily concerned with how much his work can mean but that the meaning which concerns him is anything but simple, is indeed ineffable. There is no "clear logic of a triumphant conclusion": hence his circuitous method. He means us to feel that the density, the indefiniteness, the merest intimation of a frightfully complex moral reality escape the neat formulations of any simple code. This explains why he feels he has to tell us his tales: precisely to illustrate the many-sidedness that makes his stories more indispensable to our understanding and our living than the inadequate over-simplifications of moral philosophy. Thus in Conrad there is to be found no single-dimension of meaning. Always there is the qualification, the sense of balance, of irresolution, so that every gain has its loss and every loss its gain. All is dilemma; there is no best way; indeed, at times we may even doubt that there is an indisputably better way. For Conrad art is not designed to give answers, or at least his art is not.

In *Youth* too there is an ambivalence: in the balance between the romantic striving that may from a more sober view seem essentially aimless, and the sensible compromise with reality that speaks of an inglorious weariness even as it boasts of wisdom. We cannot choose any more than Marlow himself can. He would not return to the folly that alone permitted the blind courage he still admires. Nor can he give up his calm knowledge even though it has stripped from him the possibility of a heroism he knows he misses even if he has made his peace without it.

But again *Youth* is but a frail shadow of Conrad's other work. The symbolism by which he expresses his theme here is surprisingly transparent, indeed explicit. It neither demands nor deserves more than a superficial notice in passing. For it does not enrich the story which is only an illustration of it any more than it is enriched by the story which in no essential way adds to or deepens its meaning. It begins this way:

You fellows know there are those voyages that seem ordered for the illustration of life, that might stand for a symbol of existence. You fight, work, sweat, nearly kill yourself, sometimes do kill yourself, trying to accomplish something—and you can't. Not from any fault of yours. You simply can do nothing, neither great nor little—not a thing in the world—not even marry an old maid, or get a wretched 600-ton cargo of coal to its port of destination.

All this, at the outset of the story, is terribly grandiose. It puts a tremendous burden on any story that is to live up to this advance notice. And it supplies us with too calculated a commitment. Marlow reinforces this statement, and about as explicitly, a bit later: "To me she was not an old rattle-trap carting about the world a lot of coal for a freight—to me she was the endeavor, the test, the trial of life." And speaking of the old ship, whose worn body cannot support the glorious dream of youthful enthusiasm, he clearly demonstrates her symbolic place in the theme:

"Her youth was where mine is—where yours is—you fellows who listen to this yarn. . . ." There is also, of course, the obvious significance of the ship's motto, "Do or Die," and the finally conclusive characterization of "the sea that gives nothing except hard knocks—and sometimes a chance to feel your strength. . . ." There is one passage in which the theme achieves a more brilliant and metaphorical expression, but after a moment's study it should not be much less obvious than the others:

Oh, the glamour of youth! Oh, the fire of it, more dazzling than the flames of the burning ship, throwing a magic light on the wide earth, leaping audaciously to the sky, presently to be quenched by time, more cruel, more pitiless, more bitter than the sea—and like the flames of the burning ship surrounded by an impenetrable night.

This is effective, but one can make the evident equations readily enough to pass quickly on. Not that obviousness or clarity in literature is necessarily bad. Far from it. But the special virtue of Conrad's work generally is its complex treatment of our moral life; thus work as thin and as thematically limited as *Youth* seems to be in comparison with his other fictions has its special value in its capacity to initiate the reader into that absorbing world Conrad everywhere creates. For it is a world unique and revelatory enough to demand such initiation.

Most of the thematic elements that are, for Conrad, all too neatly contained in *Youth* appear more monumentally elsewhere, again nowhere more crucially than in *Lord Jim*. There too we have the story of an education, the fitting out for life of a dedicated young man. There too we have a trial, and it is also a self-imposed trial. That is, our hero's romantic mind, having projected itself outward upon common-sense reality so as to convert this reality into illusion, now sees this imagined outside world as imposing exaggerated romantic demands upon him. But unfortunately the cruelly indifferent, unromantic world refuses to cooperate with the sensitive dreamer, thus frustrating his unswerving and uncompromising quest for honor and for the highest and noblest fulfillment of moral duty.

Once again the problems are severely simplified in *Youth* and, unusual as it is in Conrad, simplified in a comic direction. The romanticism of the young Marlow is undercut by more than the ironic skepticism of the older Marlow who reconstructs him. It is undercut most immediately by the objective facts of the situation, by what is undeniably the triviality—indeed the farcicality, the sense of the ridiculous—that characterizes the ship, its captain, its cargo, the difficulties in getting under way: in short, the entire adventure. The whole affair is hardly respectable. There is no objective ground sufficient to sustain young Marlow's fervor, so that there is difficulty in our taking him seriously throughout the tale any more than we can take seriously his "first command," his captaincy of the lifeboat at the end. To be sure, this may be as the older Marlow meant it to be and why he is patronizing and ironic toward the memory of his younger self. Still, in his tribute to the glories of youth implied throughout the story and stated explicitly at the end, our narrator *is* being serious, perhaps more serious than the earlier situation has allowed for. For the challenge young Marlow sees thrust upon him is seen—by the older Marlow and by us—to be too illusory for us to admire his answer sufficiently. Granted that for awhile there is a real element of danger for the ship and its crew. But there is enough that is comic in the way this is presented to keep us from sympathizing fully with their devotion in the face of it.

But let Conrad stack the cards differently: Let him have much the same sort of young hero, but since this hero may not succeed let him be someone other than Marlow himself. After all, if we need to see inside the hero, Conrad can complicate his point of view so as to allow him also to function as a lens. Now let Conrad create as his situation one that inherently deserves, indeed demands, courage and devotion. And it thus becomes more than a matter of *pure* illusion. Our romantic youth, who makes such unrealistic demands upon his resources for heroism, is now confronted by a situation that has its own heartless demands. Must not some human failures reveal themselves—here in the real world with knighthood no longer in flower? And must not these failures be fearfully exaggerated by our hero's sensitive, uncompromising mind? All this is, in effect, what happens when we move from the relatively shallow world of *Youth* to the profound world of *Lord Jim,* from illusions deriving from a farcical reality to illusions deriving from a terrifying reality. Reality, we are told in *Lord Jim,* is "the destructive element." And the romantic hero, having failed his dream like most of us but, unlike most of us, unwilling to give it up, can learn to live with himself and in the world only by "immersing" himself in "the destructive element," reality, while cherishing still his youthful illusions of honor and courage. Of course at the hands of this reality, which lives up to Conrad's phrase, this hero can expect only his destruction, but a destruction through which his faithfulness shines and his truest self is realized. But here, in *Lord Jim,* in this profound modulation of the themes we find so modestly displayed in *Youth,* we are brought to the very edge of the tragic, that fearsome and lonely realm through which Joseph Conrad became one of our most moving and most instructive guides.

Comments and Questions

1. How important to the success of *Youth,* according to Murray Krieger, is Conrad's handling of point of view?

2. In what ways does Krieger link Conrad's handling of point of view with the theme and reading of life given in *Youth*?

3. Note the various point of view techniques which Krieger mentions, and the various reasons why he feels they would not have served Conrad's purpose in *Youth*.

4. Krieger writes that Conrad "contributed in a major way to the reformulation of the problem in fiction that we term 'point of view.'" What, according to Krieger, is the problem, and what, specifically, is the nature of Conrad's "reformulation"?

5. Although Krieger's article concerns itself basically with Conrad's handling of point of view in *Youth*, the critic also spends some little time comparing and contrasting *Youth* and *Lord Jim*. Krieger's article, therefore, may profitably be studied in connection with your study of Chapter 3 in this manual. In what way does Krieger integrate his analysis of Marlow as narrator with his feeling that *Lord Jim* is a more significant work than *Youth*?

QUENTIN ANDERSON

from

George Eliot in MIDDLEMARCH

*I*n *The Prelude* Wordsworth notes that while he was taken up with Godwinian rationalism he had discovered that rationalism had a special danger: it denied the existence of the passions which actually informed it. The briefest possible answer to the question, What is the greatness of George Eliot? is to say that she knew and could show that every idea is attended by a passion; that thought is a passional act. Of course it is on the showing, the accomplishment of the artist, that the emphasis must finally rest, but it seems politic to begin this account by suggesting to a somewhat unreceptive age how much she has to tell her readers. Widely read and highly respected during the last four decades of her century, George Eliot (1819–80) became schoolroom fare in ours; but the assumption that she is once more coming into the light is current, it may be the misleading consequence of the appearance of Professor Gordon Haight's monumental edition of her *Letters* and F. R. Leavis's fine chapters on her in *The Great Tradition*. There is a seeming paradox in the fact that, although admired, she is not much read, because no novelist in English has come closer to answering a question which is very important to us: How can a social world be felt and understood? It appears probable that there is some resistance in us against the terms in which George Eliot answers this question; we may well want a chance for vicarious or imagined mastery over the social order—a chance to judge and discriminate with sureness—but most of us find something remote, something truly 'Victorian', in a world so fully humanized as the world of *Middlemarch;* perhaps this is because it requires more love than we can give, more assurance than we can muster. . . .

This novel is subtitled 'A Study of Provincial Life', and the climax in the national life which it partly chronicles, the period in which the Reform Bill of 1832 was moving towards adoption, was selected with the apparent intention of giving the novel the representative quality which we associate with Flaubert's *Sentimental Education* and Tolstoy's *War and Peace.* But one of the first things we must note about the novel is that this particular intention masks a more general one. Flaubert's choice of the revolution of 1848 or Tolstoy's of Napoleon's invasion of Russia as events which bring together various strands of the national experience was motivated in part by a desire to put that experience before us. George Eliot's notebook for the novel shows that she looked up such matters as the stages in the passage of the Reform Bill, the medical horizons of the 1830s, the industrial uses of manganese, and various other details. But the uses to which she puts these things are not terminal; she is not concerned as Flaubert is to lodge firmly in the reader's sensibility a mass of impressions deliberately selected to inform us of the political, industrial, and social life of the time. She is, in fact, incapable of suggesting the tone of a given period or historical moment. In the Middlemarch world, as in George Eliot generally, change is something intrusive, an irruption from without. The more general intention of which I have spoken is the attempt to render in a novel her sense of the 'primitive tissue' of a community.

This term is employed by Tertius Lydgate, a surgeon with excellent training, who buys a Middlemarch practice and hopes to combine medical work with research in physiology. His studies in Paris have persuaded him that a promising line of inquiry lies in the attempt to find the primal tissue which is the basis of all those adapted to special bodily functions. The master image of the book precisely parallels Lydgate's physiological inquiry: this is the image of human relationships as a web. Each of us stands at what seems to us a centre, our own consciousness, though it is in fact but one of numerous nodes or junction points. This is further illustrated in George Eliot's figure of the metal mirror bearing many scratches, which when illuminated at any given point produces the illusion of concentric circles ranged about that point. This figure enriches the suggestion of the recurrent web image and those associated with it by enforcing the fact that in dealing with a particular person we must consider: his appearance in the eyes of each of the other persons whom he encounters; the way he appears among various social groups to which he is known or which know of him; and his own complex of feelings which leads him to offer the world a version (or various versions) of himself. This does not at first seem an epoch-making kind of viewpoint for a novelist, since all novelists must somehow convey the quality of each character's self-regard and the opinions that others have of him. But George Eliot's special success in *Middlemarch* is the consequence of making the reciprocal workings of self-regard and opinion primary—in effect an extraordinary economy of means, and not simply of means, for it appears when we look closely that the matter of the book is people's opinions about one another, and that its particular method consists in contriving scenes in which the disparity between the intentions of agents and the opinions of observers is dramatically exhibited. This consistency of method accounts for our sense of the unity of a book which embraces a whole social order and four, or by another reckoning, five principal stories.

Of course these stories are intertwined by the plot as well as by our developing sense of Middlemarch as a community. The first of these stories is that of Dorothea Brooke, which was begun as an independent tale and later worked into the plan of the larger novel. Dorothea is somewhat externally characterized in a brief 'Prelude'. She belongs to a group of great spirits who remain unknown and unsung: 'with dim lights and tangled circumstance they tried to shape their thought and deed in noble agreement; but, after all, to common eyes their struggles seemed mere inconsistency and formlessness; for these later-born Theresas were helped by no coherent social faith and order which could perform the function of knowledge for the ardently willing soul.' The account concludes: 'Here and there is born a Saint Theresa, foundress of nothing, whose loving heart-beats and sobs after an unattained goodness tremble off and are dispersed among hindrances, instead of centring in some long-recognizable deed.' F. R. Leavis discerns a tendency on the part of George Eliot to make rather too personal investments in her heroines, and the tone of this 'Prelude' bears him out. The reader ought to be assured that the Dorothea he meets in the opening scenes of the novel is not this portentous figure, but a young lady whose foible in marrying an elderly pedant has the consequences—comic, pathetic, and even, in a minor and domestic key, tragic—that we might expect it to have in life. As the novel goes forward, however, Dorothea's demand that the world afford chances for heroic achievement does begin to seem much too categorical. We must return to the question of her role in the imaginative economy of the novel at a later point.

Lydgate, the principal figure of the second intrigue, is closer to the working centre of the book than Dorothea, since his fate turns not simply on his marriage to Rosamond Vincy, but upon the sum of his actions and reactions in response to Middlemarch. His story is linked with the third in the group of four, the story of Bulstrode, the banker guilty of moral defalcations, whose self-arraignment is one of the finest episodes in the book (although the whole Bulstrode strand in the novel is less impressive than the others because his past is somewhat stagily rendered and the agents out of that past who hunt him down seem melodramatic conveniences). The fourth strand, closer in tone to the earlier Midland novels, functions in part to provide a standard by which the others may be placed and judged. It involves the Garth family, Mary, her father, Caleb, her successful suitor Fred Vincy, and the Reverend Farebrother, who also aspires to Mary. Here also belong the provincial humours of the book, which centre about old Peter Featherstone's disposition of his property.

Middlemarch is carefully (contemporary readers tend to say exhaustively) plotted. One or more of the characters in each of the four stories plays an important part in each of the other three. The Victorian reader was offered a multiplicity of occasions for sympathetic concern. One of the things about George Eliot and her readers which it is hardest for us to recapture is the artless and unashamed emotionalism of the latter over the fate of her characters, and the benign acceptance of this situation on the part of the writer. The century which wrenched Hamlet out of *Hamlet* had not the least scruple about lobbying for its favourite character while the novel was in the course of publication in parts—while it was in fact still being written. One may imagine that if the modern objection to such innocence about the fashion in which a work is made an artistic whole had been stated it would have been met with the response that the whole was really constituted by the assurance of moral conformity—George Eliot could be trusted. Blackwood, George Eliot's publisher, wrote her in this vein while *Middlemarch* was appearing; he sets down his hopes and fears for the characters, and tells her in effect that her interposition in their lives has been both touching and morally impeccable. The novelist and her fellows were of course affected by this atmosphere: they wrote with a consciousness of the awakened and palpitant sensibilities of the readers who were speculating about what would happen in the next part; they watched the sale of each part with anxiety, and made anxious inquiry about a falling-off. Some of the occasions for sympathetic concern in this novel may be listed: How will Dorothea awake to a consciousness of the meaning of her marriage to the pedant, Casaubon? Will Fred Vincy inherit old Featherstone's money? Failing that, will he reclaim himself and marry Mary Garth, or will Farebrother cut him out? Will Rosamond's 'torpedo contact' paralyse her vigorous husband, Lydgate? Can he succeed in medical practice in the face of the bigotry of Middlemarch? Can he extricate himself from his debts? How will Bulstrode be found out, and what will thereupon happen to him and his devoted wife? There is a cognate familiarity about many of the motifs of the story: the idealism of Dorothea, the earnest and rather wry Christianity of Farebrother, the weakling reclaimed in Fred Vincy, the dryness, harsh fun, and moral beauty of the plain Mary Garth. Neither plot nor traits of character taken alone are sufficiently distinctive to set this novel apart from others. I have found that youthful readers nowadays are restive when confronted by such careful plotting and such familiar traits of character; they shy away and quite miss the light which illumines all these things in their mutual relations, the voice of the wise woman. That voice is often heard speaking directly with an authority which makes use of the Victorian reader's involvement with the characters to make him look up and look about, to see how human relations are established within the world of the story—to see the whole of what the wise woman surveys.

What she surveys may be called a landscape of opinion, for it is not the natural landscape that is dominant here. In fact, there are only two fully realized natural landscapes, Lowick Manor and Stone Court, and in these cases the landscape is realized by an individual whose situation and interests make him aware of an external world at that particular moment. For the most part we may characterize the book's use of the physical world by referring to George Eliot's own sense of Warwickshire as a physical locale which has been wholly humanized, and to the Reverend Cadwallader's half-serious remark that it is a very good quality in a man to have a trout stream. This transposition of the natural into the moral and psychological is further illustrated by the novelist's use of snatches of poetry—Dorothea Brooke's hope for social betterment 'haunted her like a passion'—and we may say that the affectionate sense of nature and the objects that man makes and handles which suffuses *Adam Bede* has been deliberately subdued here. Nothing comparable to the description of Hetty Sorrel in Mrs Poyser's dairy can enter into *Middlemarch*, not because it is a more 'intellectual' book, but because its immediacies are not things seen but things felt and believed. It is striking that we know almost nothing of the appearance of Middlemarch itself, although our sense of the life of the town as a community is very full indeed, ranging as it does from a pot-house to the Green Dragon, the town's best inn, from horse-dealers, auctioneers, and grocers to the lawyers, physicians, merchants, clergymen, and landowners who stand at the head of the scale. Although we see little of the activities of all these people we hear their voices, each pitched to the tone of its own desire, each capable of dropping suggestively or rising assertively on grounds which George Eliot shows to be wholly inadequate when related to the facts of the particular case. Chapter 45 is a good instance of the masterly way in which she can demonstrate the drifts and swirls of opinion through the town. In this account of various responses to Lydgate's principled refusal to dispense drugs himself, each of the voices establishes a character so fully and with such economy that it is hard to believe that Mawmsey, the grocer, and Mrs Dollop of the Tankard have not always been known to us. Yet this single chapter does much more. In it we learn that the clouds of misapprehension and selfishness gathering about Lydgate cannot possibly be dispelled, that he is more than likely to get into debt, and that his wife's awful insularity will resist his earnest and even his desperate attempts to penetrate it. George Eliot had much earlier (Chapter 15) used her author's privilege to warn the reader of all these possibilities. 'For surely all must admit that a man may be puffed and belauded, envied, ridiculed, counted upon as a tool and fallen in love with, or at least selected as a future husband, and yet remain virtually unknown—known merely as a cluster of signs for his neighbours' false suppositions.' The novelist, writing of *Middlemarch*, says: 'I wanted to give a panoramic view of provincial life . . .'; but what she does give is something far more active, far more in accord with the image of the web—or perhaps a vast switchboard in which every signal is interpreted differently by each receiver, and each receiver is in its turn capable of propagating in response a signal of its own with equally dissonant consequences. Yet in the end, roughly but surely, the dissonances die out and a consensus of sorts emerges, for as George Eliot remarks at one point, not everyone is an originator, and there is a limit to the varieties of error people can fall into.

The characters move in a landscape of opinion, but those who concern us have an inner life; they can look within as well as without, and measure their sense of themselves against the world's demands and expectations. The economy of means and materials I have referred to consists in the use of the landscape of opinion as the scene of action. It does not exclude, it rather informs and gives depth to the conventional motifs and the conventional attributes of character mentioned above. A long quotation extracted from the description of Casaubon illustrates the method:

If to Dorothea Mr Casaubon had been the mere occasion which had set alight the fine inflammable material of her youthful illusions, does it follow that he was fairly represented in the minds of those less impassioned personages who have hitherto delivered their judgements concerning him? I protest against any absolute conclusion, any prejudice derived from Mrs Cadwallader's contempt for a neighbouring clergyman's alleged greatness of soul, or Sir James Chettam's poor opinion of his rival's legs, from Mr Brooke's failure to elicit a companion's ideas, or from Celia's criticism of a middle-aged scholar's personal appearance. I am not sure that the greatest man of his age, if ever that solitary superlative existed, could escape these unfavourable reflections of himself in various small mirrors; and even Milton, looking for his portrait in a spoon, must submit to have the facial angle of a bumpkin. Moreover, if Mr Casaubon, speaking for himself, has a rather chilling rhetoric, it is not therefore certain that there is no good work or fine feeling in him.

Did not an immortal physicist and interpreter of hieroglyphics write detestable verse? Has the theory of the solar system been advanced by graceful manners and conversational tact? Suppose we turn from outside estimates of a man, to wonder, with keener interest, what is the report of his own consciousness about his doings or capacity; with what hindrances he is carrying on his daily labours; what fading of hopes, or what deeper fixity of self-delusion the years are marking off within him; and with what spirit he wrestles against universal pressure, which will one day be too heavy for him, and bring his heart to its final pause. Doubtless his lot is important in his own eyes; and the chief reason that we think he asks too large a place in our consideration must be our want of room for him, since we refer him to the Divine regard with perfect confidence; nay it is even held sublime for our neighbour to expect the utmost there, however little he may have got from us. Mr Casaubon, too, was the centre of his own world; if he was liable to think others were providentially made for him, and especially to consider them in the light of their fitness for the author of a 'Key to all Mythologies', this trait is not quite alien to us, and, like the other mendicant hopes of mortals, claims some of our pity.

Certain aspects of this passage invite attention. George Eliot is here gathering up a series of notations about Casaubon which have been established in dialogue. In doing so she becomes a sharply marked present voice. We have come a long way from Fielding's interposed addresses to the reader in *Tom Jones*, a long way from Dickens and Thackeray as well—Thackeray cannot step on his stage without shaking it or dwarfing it; the effect is always of diminution, a voice which condescends to or coos about the pettiness or charm of the creatures displayed, while Dickens's effects in this kind involve facing about, leaving the characters to fend for themselves while he carries on his special pleading. George Eliot, however, speaks to the issues of her own work, and addresses the reader in terms which set her above it but never to one side. In her 'I protest against any absolute conclusion . . .' we find a gentle schoolmistress's irony which places her between the book and our apprehension of it. In this instance she is saying that we are guilty, not because we are all egocentrics by definition, but because these notations about Casaubon have indeed composed our picture of him. She goes on to indicate what she is about to do with the figure: we shall end by finding him pathetic; we are to be converted—to be forced to abandon the stereotyped social gesture which leads us to 'refer him [Casaubon] to the Divine regard' and refer him instead to our own failures to get the world to concede our majesty. Her own rhetoric, the somewhat heavy verbal play of 'solitary superlative', the clinical remoteness and buried scientific analogy of 'what deeper fixity of self-delusion the years are marking off within him', the carefully indicated central image of the mutually mirroring selves, the fact that she is playing prologue to her own action—for each of her generalities is a forecast of a part of Casaubon's fate—are all elements of that voice which frames the whole book. . . .

Professor Haight, in his introduction to a recent edition of *Middlemarch*, repudiates the figure of the Wise Woman, which he finds rampant in John Walter Cross's biography. It seems to him too heavy, too statuesque, to refer to George Eliot. However, George Eliot herself is partly responsible for the dissemination of this image (she aided the compiler of a book of wise and tender sayings from her work), and the Wise Woman, or whatever we wish to call her, is an indispensable figure in discussing her work. In fact, the only thing which can possibly balance, can possibly support *Middlemarch*, is this image of the writer which the novel creates in the reader. Were she not there we should not be attending.

George Eliot is present as the only fully realized individual in her book. This sounds like a harsh saying, but it may not be quite so harsh as it sounds. When one is reading *Middlemarch* there are many moments when one looks up and says, 'How intelligent, how penetrating this woman is!' And, of course, one is speaking of George Eliot. In reading the fine chapter of analysis which has to do with Lydgate's character and the situation in which he finds himself in Middlemarch, we come upon this passage:

He was at a starting-point which makes many a man's career a fine subject for betting, if there were any gentlemen given to that amusement who could appreciate the complicated probabilities of an arduous purpose, with all the possible thwartings and furtherings of circumstance, all the niceties of inward balance, by which a man swims and makes his point or else is carried headlong. The risk would remain, even with close knowledge of Lydgate's character; for character too is a process and an unfolding.

Those who like *Middlemarch* take pleasure in the writer's judiciousness. They are far more tempted to invest themselves with her sensibility than they are to identify themselves with that of any of her characters. It is notable that analytic passages like the one just quoted predominate among those chosen for quotation from Leslie Stephen's day to our own. The description of Caleb Garth, of Rosamond Vincy's terrible self-absorption, of Dorothea's aspirations and her blindness to her sister Celia's world, of Bulstrode's casuistical inner life, of Casaubon's tortured consciousness of inadequacy—all these are analytic though all are matched by passages of dialogue in which their substance is exemplified. Certain dramatic scenes—that between Dorothea and Rosamond in particular—are also favourites, but again the most familiar passage about Rosamond seems to be that which describes her reaction to the awful, the inconceivable fact that there is another self in the world, one which Ladislaw cherishes far more than hers. These fine and satisfying analytic passages are not additions or decorations, nor do they represent a division within George Eliot, rather they exhibit her sense of process at work within the frame of actuality; it is her life *in* the novel which lies at its heart; this is what we rejoice in. Admittedly this means that no character is freed to exist as Don Quixote or Julien Sorel are enfranchised; the very firmness and clarity of George Eliot's vision, extending to the edges of her canvas, quite preclude her granting to any one of her creatures the authority of existence. Like a goddess, she suffers them to exist in so far as they may be known through sympathy and comprehension. No more life than this can emerge—any further measure would make her characters novelists. Those who are her surrogates, her delegated voices, are in a sense independent of her, but they are wholly caught up within a system of morally and aesthetically statable responses—as is Mary Garth—and correspond rather to Mary Anne Evans, who had once lived within a provincial society, than to George Eliot, the novelist.

Those who live completely within the shelter of a community never apprehend it as an entity. In a sense, the very notion of 'society' came to imaginative fulfilment for the first time in nineteenth-century romanticism; the assumption of one of the roles of the romantic involved a reciprocal identification: here am I, a discriminable self, there is the world, the other to which I stand opposed. Of course such opposition was never total; the romantic was forced to call on some aspect of existence for support and sanction—on nature, on the philosophic status of the imagination, on libertarian politics, on the wider experience of the remote and exotic—whatever might give poetic actuality to the insights of the self. To George Eliot, a member of a succeeding generation, all these options were familiar, but none of them was acceptable. The experience which gave society objectivity for her was the loss of her religious faith. And the striking thing is that she did not thereupon become a rationalist, a scientific blue-stocking, or a lecturer on the rights of women. Only a few months after she had informed her father that she could not in conscience accompany him to church she realized that her fresh point of view towards the meaning of religion made such gestures unnecessary and foolish. She had made a massive discovery.

This discovery was very simple, but its effects were profound. Miss Evans repossessed the world imaginatively when she came to the conclusion that the creeds, formulae, practices, and institutions in which people shrouded themselves were no less significant if one saw that they were not absolute. With a feminine directness she now accepted everything she had momentarily rejected. But human behaviour was now seen as a set of symbolic gestures expressive of individual needs and desires. The positivism of Auguste Comte undoubtedly played a role in this, but it did not teach her to interpret human actions; it is clear that this was a spontaneous gift which was hers before she began to write fiction. She was able to see the emotional concomitants of churchgoing; able to make out what Diderot calls the 'professional idioms' of behaviour. Each of us is like the marine animal which borrows a shell; we borrow our shells for social purposes, but our feelers wave no less expressively for that. George Eliot found that she could translate the psychic gestures involved in our religion, our politics, our superstitions, our local traditions, and discover, as she had in herself, a common root of action and reaction. She wrote to the American novelist, Harriet Beecher Stowe, that her novel, *Oldtown Folks,* showed a comprehension of the 'mixed moral influence shed on society by dogmatic systems', which was 'rare even among writers'. She saw, in other words, that the interplay between creeds, ideas, and desires was the novelist's business. But we must still ask what binds the novelist's world together? What sanction remains after the absoluteness of creeds and institutions has been denied?

A curious inversion in a sentence from the 'Prelude' to *Middlemarch* which has been quoted above supplies an answer. In speaking of those whose career resembles Dorothea's, George Eliot remarks that the 'later-born Theresas were helped by no coherent social faith and order which could perform the function of knowledge for the ardently willing soul.' There is a suggestion here that if you find fulfilment through knowledge you do not need the pressure of an unquestioned social order and religious faith to sustain you. This brave assumption was written into George Eliot's work and acted out in her life. Her role as novelist involved finding and telling the truth. It was not a matter of occasional didactic interjections, but of a continuously present intelligence speaking in the declarative.

There is a famous sentence descriptive of Lydgate's character which will serve as a leading instance:

Lydgate's spots of commonness lay in the complexion of his prejudices, which in spite of noble intention and sympathy, were half of them such as are found in ordinary men of the world: that distinction of mind which belonged to his intellectual ardour, did not penetrate his feeling and judgement about furniture, or women, or the desirability of its being known (without his telling) that he was better born than other country surgeons.

The scenes in which Lydgate's character is rendered in dialogue do not have the power of this passage of commentary. The dialogue cannot render as much as George Eliot can see. I do not mean that we are not persuaded by her statement or that we feel that dialogue and statement are not in accord; it is simply the fact that she scores most heavily as commentator that we must recognize. The very best things in George Eliot are no doubt her account of Lydgate, Rosamond, and their marriage, in *Middlemarch,* the encounters between Mrs Transome and her former lover, Matthew Jermyn in *Felix Holt,* and the story of Gwendolen Harleth's struggle with Grandcourt in *Daniel Deronda.* In each case it is the voice of George Eliot the writer which is finally persuasive. It is absurd to say, as a good many people have, that her insight is intrusive or an aesthetic impropriety; it is her genius made manifest.

Middlemarch, the scene of this novel, is wholly dominated by the finely tempered mind which envisions it. But how is this scene framed and judged from without? What are the effectual boundaries of the landscape of opinion? The town—though it is a middling place from the point of view of one considering a group of provincial towns—lies on the marches, it is on the periphery of the great world, not simply the world of London or even Rome, but the world of science, the arts, and of history; realized human greatness does not enter it. We must inquire how the writer who herself moved in the great world acknowledged that world in *Middlemarch*.

There is a finely scaled scene in *Daniel Deronda* in which Gwendolen Harleth asks the musician, Klesmer, to help her to launch a musical career on nothing more than a feeble talent and her social pretensions. Klesmer confronts Gwendolen with the audacity and the ignorance of her claim. The scene has a wonderfully tonic effect—it is as if George Eliot had managed a dramatic confrontation of the austerities of art with the blind abundant energies of youth and beauty. Klesmer's treatment of Gwendolen is exquisitely modulated; it is at once a denunciation and a tribute to her as a woman. But she must be told that social lies and politeness have nothing to do with being an artist. In the world of art you must tell the truth; self-regard and the world's opinion must give way before realized mastery. There is an analogous scene in *Middlemarch*, though the standard invoked is not impersonal. Rosemary's flirtation with Ladislaw is abruptly ended when she discovers that Dorothea is all-important to him. She had found in Ladislaw a representative of the world outside Middlemarch to which she had ignorantly aspired, and Ladislaw thinks her of no account. She is momentarily awed into a generosity which brings Ladislaw and Dorothea together. Throughout the book Ladislaw speaks authoritatively about the world outside the town's awareness. It is he who tells Dorothea that Casaubon's work is useless because he has not read the German scholars; it is he who demands fidelity to a standard of artistic accomplishment; he alone has some sense of national politics.

Yet Ladislaw does not have the authority of Klesmer; he is the weakest of the major characters, not merely because he is made to behave like a dilettante, but because George Eliot's judiciousness does not extend to him; he is not understood. In fact, he is rather like a character in an ordinary novel. F. R. Leavis sees this as a consequence of the weakness of the figure of Dorothea. Since she is in part a self-indulgent fantasy of George Eliot's and not wholly disciplined by the demands of the novel, we may think of Ladislaw as an accessory required by the fantasy. Certainly the scenes they share are full of high-flown nonsense. But there is a good deal of evidence that Dorothea and Ladislaw represent something more than the unresolved longings of Mary Anne Evans. The leading characters in *Romola, Felix Holt, Middlemarch,* and *Daniel Deronda* all escape the circle of the author's judgement. It is claimed for each of them that they aspire to or escape into the great world. Dorothea is the partial exception. When confronted by her uncle, Casaubon, her sister Celia, or the Chettams, she is fully controlled, fully understood. But Romola, Felix Holt, and Deronda are all extravagantly moral or extravagantly spiritual or both. And Dorothea and Ladislaw in their scenes together have the same defect.

Instead of thinking of *Middlemarch* as showing two strains, an artistically responsible element and a neurotically compelled one, we must, I believe, adopt a fresh version of the traditional assertion that George Eliot's conception of her fiction is internally divided. Leavis has pointed to the meaninglessness of the form this assertion of a split took in the criticism of Henry James and Leslie Stephen. The disjunction between an 'intellectual' George Eliot and a George Eliot who has the novelist's sympathetic comprehension of human beings is, as we have seen, a clear-cut contradiction. It is the voice heard within the frame of her best fiction which has high intellectual distinction.

But there is an internal division in her conception of *Middlemarch* which corresponds to the far more serious split in *Daniel Deronda,* in which Deronda's mystical religiosity is given precedence over the fictionally superior story of Gwendolen Harleth. (The argument may also be applied to *Romola* and *Felix Holt.*) This split in the writer's conception of fiction appears to have a biographical root. The novels of George Eliot's maturity re-enact her own emancipation; the values which the Garths and Farebrother assert within the little world of Middlemarch are reasserted from the viewpoint of liberated intelligence by the voice of the narrator; her loss of faith, her translation to the metropolis, her defiance of propriety in living with Lewes, are all justified by the activity of the novelist who surveys Middlemarch. The right opinion of the Garths and Farebrother gives way before the knowledge of the novelist. But for George Eliot the re-enactment brought with it an irresistible impulse to include a character who could function as knower, an *embodied* voice.

She was unable, even in the years of her maturest art, to conceive of fiction as a truly independent form. It would seem to have been enough to bring that fine intelligence to bear on the enclosed world of Middlemarch, but she is never content with this. She must bring forward some instance of principled nonconformity, as if to feed an appetite for self-justification. We must conclude, I think, that the fairy-tale triumph of Romola over the physical and moral ills of a fever-stricken village, and the fantastic errand which takes Deronda to Jerusalem—he is, in effect, to build a culture!—are not merely tributes to a Victorian taste for moral exaltation. They are attempts on the part of the writer to give herself a recognizable moral status.

The English novel is so much the richer for George Eliot's contribution that one may be tempted into scolding her for not doing what no English novelist of the century did: for not taking possession of the great world. Her sense of community, her finely modulated articulation of passion and idea, the clarity and firmness of her characterization—these things alone justify Virginia Woolf's remark that *Middlemarch* was one of the few English novels written for grown-up people. Since the grown-up perspective includes Flaubert and Tolstoy, we are of course conscious that George Eliot did not share their power to incarnate the great world in the lesser one, to make the novel an instrument which can register the fate of a society in the perspective of history and heroic achievement. To exercise this power she would have had to take her own splendid powers for granted, and this she could not do.

Comments and Questions

1. Although Quentin Anderson does not happen to use the term itself, George Eliot in writing *Middlemarch* employs the so-called "omniscient author" technique, as that technique is defined in the Introduction to this chapter. Study this discussion of the omniscient author technique in preparation for your work on the questions which follow.

2. Anderson writes: ". . . for it appears when we look closely that the matter of the book is people's opinions about one another, and that its particular method consists in contriving scenes in which the disparity between the intentions of agents and the opinions of observers is dramatically exhibited." Does Anderson imply any connection between George Eliot's intention, as he interprets it, and her choice of the omniscient author point of view? What reasons does Anderson suggest for George Eliot's having chosen to use the omniscient author technique in *Middlemarch?* Are there other reasons, equally valid?

3. After giving the long quotation from *Middlemarch* beginning "If to Dorothea Mr Casaubon had been the mere occasion . . ." Anderson praises George Eliot for letting us listen to her own voice, while at the same time deprecating this same technique as used by Fielding, Dickens, and Thackeray. What, precisely, differentiates George Eliot's voice from those of the other novelists mentioned?

4. Anderson writes: "In her 'I protest against any absolute conclusion . . .' we find a gentle schoolmistress's irony which places her between the book and our apprehension of it." A coming between the reader and the book is precisely what many readers and critics have

objected to on the part of the omniscient author. How does Anderson suggest that George Eliot turns this theoretical weakness into a particular strength?

5. In praising what he calls George Eliot's "analytic passages," Anderson is careful to indicate that these passages "all are matched by passages of dialogue in which their substance is exemplified." Why does he feel it is important to establish this?

6. Anderson suggests that George Eliot's choice of the omniscient author technique carries with it certain unavoidable restrictions. What are they? Do you agree with Anderson at this point?

7. In the paragraph beginning "Those who live completely within the shelter of a community . . ." and in the two succeeding paragraphs, Anderson comments on the intellectual climate and social milieu in which George Eliot lived. How does he tie these aspects of the novelist's life up with her point of view technique?

8. The author remarks that "It is absurd to say, as a good many people have, that her [George Eliot's] insight is intrusive or an aesthetic impropriety; it is her genius made manifest." What methods has Anderson used to convince his readers of the truth of his statement? What part has been played by his quotations from *Middlemarch,* and his subsequent explications?

9. Does Anderson, in praising *Middlemarch* highly, imply that the omniscient author technique is inherently superior to other point of view techniques, or does he simply suggest that George Eliot's technique helps achieve the purpose of this particular novel?

10. From what you are able to gather about *Middlemarch* from reading Anderson's essay, or from what you may know of it already, speculate concerning what differences would inevitably have resulted had George Eliot employed some point of view technique other than the one she used.

Suggestions for an Essay

If you have made a study of a writer of fiction, write an essay analyzing the point of view technique he employs in one of his works. Interpret what you say by telling what effect the point of view has on the total impact of the work. If you feel the point of view technique was wisely chosen, you may wish to show why by illustrating how other techniques would have been inadequate (as Murray Krieger does in connection with Joseph Conrad's *Youth*). If, on the other hand, you object to your author's handling of point of view, you will presumably wish to show wherein his ineptness lies, or to indicate where he went astray.

THE WRITING OF A BOOK REVIEW

Introduction

An activity frequently engaged in by scholars and critics is that of writing book reviews. Although exceptions exist, most good book reviews contain three types of information:

1. A review should indicate accurately and completely what a book contains. Readers want to know what subjects are treated in the book, its organization, proportions, emphases, and limits.

2. A review ordinarily places a book in some sort of setting. If the author has written previous books, the reviewer may indicate the relation between the book under consideration and the author's other productions. If the book reflects influences, if the writer belongs to a certain school of thought (as in the case of books of philosophy, history, or criticism), these facts may be noted and their significance interpreted.

3. A review should evaluate the book and indicate whether or not it is worth reading. Many more books, even in one specialized area, are published each year than can be read by any one person. Readers of reviews expect to learn whether they should spend their time on this book, or that. Since time is valuable, the reviewer's responsibility is no small one.

Different books, obviously, demand different approaches: a novel one type, a technical treatise on nuclear fission another. But the primary aim of all reviews should be evaluation. The reader of a review will ordinarily not be interested in the subject matter of a book, or with its historical setting, apart from its value. Reviewers sometimes move, as their review progresses, from factual information to evaluation. But skilled reviewers frequently fuse the different types of information which have been mentioned into smoothly organic wholes.

The reviewer's response to a book will, necessarily, be entirely favorable, entirely unfavorable, or mixed. Each response presents its own difficulties. If the reviewer's response is entirely favorable, he must avoid giving the impression that he is undiscriminating, too easily impressed. If the review is entirely unfavorable, the reviewer must avoid giving the impression that he is disgruntled, that personal or private pique has motivated his unfavorable response. If the response is mixed, successful and unsuccessful elements must be clearly defined, and some suggestion given as to whether the strength or weakness of the book predominates. In a word, the reviewer must seek to give a reader confidence in what he says. Reviewers for established periodicals are frequently recognized authorities in their fields, whose names, affixed to reviews, themselves carry authority; but an inexperienced or unknown reviewer can establish confidence in his readers by writing well.

A responsibility which a review writer shares with any essayist is that of being interesting. A book review, to be sure, is utilitarian and can have no independent life apart from the book which has called it into being. But it does not follow that the review need be dull and pedestrian. The review, as a form of composition, lends itself well to imaginative treatment, since the reviewer, as is the case with any essayist, has the opportunity to reveal the personality behind the writing. The best reviews are those which not only tell a reader what he goes to a review to learn, but which, in the reading, afford satisfaction.

Following are four book reviews concerned with the type of book researchers frequently use in their work.

RANDALL STEWART

a review of Richard Harter Fogle's

HAWTHORNE'S FICTION: THE LIGHT AND THE DARK

*T*his is the first book of its kind on Hawthorne, and one of a comparatively few, perhaps, which deal in precisely this way with any writer. The uniqueness is owing, however, not so much to Mr. Fogle's novelty as to his beforehandedness, for with the rapid spread of the new criticism, with its emphasis on analysis, we may confidently expect an increasing number of works of similar scope and design. Mr. Fogle's book, that is to say, epitomizes pretty well the main trend in literary study at the present time.

The book consists of twelve chapters: an introductory and a concluding chapter, six chapters dealing with six of Hawthorne's tales, and four dealing with the four major novels. Mr. Fogle goes after Hawthorne a piece at a time; each chapter analyzes an individual work, and the book becomes, therefore, a collection of analyses. Each analysis is almost entirely confined to the work under consideration, though the author does not make quite the fetish of *nulla salus extra opus* which some of the new critics have made. He does on occasion venture beyond the work itself. In one or two instances he compares a character with similar characters in other stories by Hawthorne. He places one story briefly in the main stream of English romanticism. Occasionally he appeals to characteristic Hawthorne usages and attitudes. Once or twice a possible literary influence is mentioned. Once or twice a partial identification is suggested between a fictional character and the author himself, and in a single instance (and this is the farthest reach of Mr. Fogle's apostasy) biography, in the form of a quotation from a Hawthorne letter, is summoned to the aid of interpretation. But these aberrations from orthodox new-critical procedure are few and unobtrusive. Few books dealing with literature, I imagine, have been confined so strictly within the bounds of the works themselves, or have been so completely divorced from history and biography. Mr. Fogle does not mar his pages with a single date. His aim—and it is a noble one—is to see his material *sub specie aeternitatis*.

The test of a critical method is the degree of illumination which the critic manages to throw upon his subject, and by this test Mr. Fogle's book is deserving of high praise, for few, if any, books have illuminated Hawthorne's actual works as clearly and brightly as this one. The book is rich in insights. There are many passages which one marks in the reading, and to which one will recur again and again: passages on the ambiguities of "The Minister's Black Veil," the patterns of imagery and symbol in *The Marble Faun,* the ironies in *The Scarlet Letter,* the use of symbol and allegory in "Rappaccini's Daughter," the symbolic procession of the seasons in *The Blithedale Romance,* and many others. Everywhere the critic is subjecting the work to the closest and most sensitive scrutiny; everywhere he finds the symmetry and functional unity of carefully contrived literary art; everywhere he discovers the balance of thesis and antithesis.

For Hawthorne's meaning (Mr. Fogle makes this clearer than any previous writer on the subject has done) cannot be reduced to a few simple propositions. His fictions are embodiments of a rich complexity. Ambiguity is at the center of his vision of life. Is Beatrice Rappaccini demon or angel? Is Aylmer villain or hero? Is Hester Prynne more sinned against than sinning? Is Donatello's transformation for the better or worse? Is, indeed, Hawthorne's treatment of his subject "puritan" or "romantic"? These, and scores of other questions raised by his fictions, require double answers. Of such ambiguities is the substance of his art composed.

So far from being regarded as a mark of weakness and confusion (as they were by W. C. Brownell, and other able critics in the past), the ambiguities are now seen to be a source of great strength. Hawthorne has gained on other grounds, too. Allegory and symbolism are no longer in disfavor as they were when the "realism" of the late nineteenth century held sway. If ambiguity adds truth and dramatic tension, allegory and symbolism give to Hawthorne's work something of the timelessness of abstract art. These and other virtues, recently discovered, carry such weight with young critics today that Mr. Fogle can declare, roundly and without a shadow of qualification, "Hawthorne is a great writer."

RANDALL STEWART

a review of *William Bysshe Stein's*

HAWTHORNE'S FAUST: A STUDY OF THE DEVIL ARCHE-
TYPE

*H*awthorne continues to be critically re-examined with gusto and acuteness. The young critics of today are discovering in his writings things unseen, or imperfectly seen, before. In no area is the shift from the old scholarship to the new criticism more plainly perceptible than in Hawthorne studies. If one compares the articles on Hawthorne published in the last five years with those listed in Professor Lewis Leary's bibliography, one can note the change.

Mr. Stein objects to the procedure, currently popular in some quarters, of treating each of Hawthorne's stories as a separate entity. His aim is more comprehensive: he wishes to establish the interrelations of Hawthorne's thought in the various works. He is concerned, therefore, more with thematic development than with the minutae of method or technique. One result of such an approach is that Hawthorne's literary career is seen to have the unity of a continuous exploration.

The author of this incisive study has hit upon a unifying formula which proves to be immensely rewarding: "A simple mythic formula based on the devil archetype," says Mr. Stein, "provides Hawthorne with the medium of inquiry into the riddle of good and evil." It is basically the legend of Faust, who sold his soul to the devil in return for a certain *quid pro quo*. Repeatedly in Hawthorne's fiction the author finds the "devil image" and the "diabolic pact," the Faustian desire to know more than heavenly power permits, the ordeal of sin and the necessity of the evil principle.

Especially illuminating is the treatment of the "Five Fausts" (Aylmer, Rappaccini, Warland, Drowne, and Brand), the Faustian elements in *The Scarlet Letter* (Chillingworth is seen as the "Puritan Faust," Hester as "Fausta," the feminine counterpart, Dimmesdale as "the Lascivious Monk"), and the epic of the soul's growth in *The Marble Faun* and *Septimius Felton* (where the author detects the influence of Goethe's *Faust*). Mr. Stein praises *Septimius Felton,* and indeed the other unfinished works of the last phase, which "haunt the mind," he says, "like the scattered remains of a noble Gothic cathedral." It is interesting to note that the philosophical critic thus sees a kind of climactic conclusion in Hawthorne's last efforts, where the analytic or aesthetic critic is likely to find only anticlimax and failure.

Mr. Stein's study throws useful though not always conclusive light on Hawthorne's sources and influences. The treatment of the Mathers, the "Faust Chapbook" (much read in New England), and Marlowe seems a bit sketchy. More satisfactory, because more fully documented, is the exposition of the place in the Faust legend (and the influence on Hawthorne) of the writings of the Gothic romancers—Beckford, Lewis, Godwin, and Maturin. The importance of Goethe's *Faust* as a shaping influence on Hawthorne's creative mind is insisted upon throughout, but, I think, never quite demonstrated. The author believes, for example, that "Goethe and his *Faust* must often have been a topic of conversation" between Hawthorne and Longfellow. But there is apparently no record to that effect, and indeed there are almost no references to Goethe by Hawthorne anywhere. One wonders—especially in view of Hawthorne's comparative ignorance of German literature—if the tribute to Goethe in "The Hall of Fantasy" is not perfunctory, after all. But it should be said that an intimate knowledge of Goethe's *Faust* by Hawthorne is not necessary to Mr. Stein's thesis: the Faust myth, even if deprived of its greatest literary exemplar, embraces quite enough available instances for Hawthorne's purpose, and Mr. Stein's.

The present study shows better than any previous work the thematic unity of Hawthorne's fiction. Here surely, if anywhere, is the general intention of his books, the string the pearls were strung on, the figure in the carpet. Out of the maze of diabolic collusion which looms so large in Hawthorne's fiction (how large only the reader of Mr. Stein's book can know), the author effectively extracts Hawthorne's usable truth, a truth which is patiently expounded throughout this study, and which is summed up in the final chapter, and particularly in these last pregnant sentences: "Man must meet the challenge of the devil by recognizing his existence. He must accept the myth of the devil as one of the hidden structures of psychic reality. Only then will he apprehend the truth."

Present trends of human experience seem well calculated to impress upon us Hawthorne's worth anew.

Comments and Questions

1. Randall Stewart's response to Richard Harter Fogle's book is entirely favorable; the review, in fact, contains some very high praise. Why, then, does the reviewer employ a light, humorous touch in the second paragraph, where he places Fogle among the new critics? (Notice the humorous image suggested by the metaphor, "Mr. Fogle goes after Hawthorne a piece at a time"; the tongue-in-cheek use of Latin in the *nulla salus extra opus* phrase; the wit residing in the reviewer's mention of "the farthest reach of Mr. Fogle's apostasy.") Does the humor here detract from the work of the new critics? Or does it add to your confidence in the reviewer, and to your belief in the validity of his favorable response to Fogle's book?

2. Richard Harter Fogle's and William Bysshe Stein's books are both reviewed by Professor Randall Stewart, a noted authority on Hawthorne. While the reviewer places both writers in the camp of the new critics, he points out that Stein, unlike some new critics, "objects to the procedure . . . of treating each of Hawthorne's stories as a separate entity." You will note that an examination of Hawthorne's works as separate entities is precisely what Fogle does in his book. Yet the reviewer praises both books almost equally. Far from being an inconsistency, as might at first appear to be the case, this ability to give deserved praise to books which approach the same subject from somewhat different points of view shows, on the part of the reviewer, the admirable ability to meet a book on its own terms, to evaluate it in the light of what the author has attempted. The reviewer does not quarrel with Fogle for not writing a book like Stein's, or with Stein for not writing a book like Fogle's. Notice in this connection the last sentence of the second paragraph in the review of Fogle's book, where the reviewer indicates the aim of the book, preparatory to evaluating it in the light of how well it fulfills this aim. The understanding of the reviewer is here broad enough to see that Hawthorne is a figure complex enough to lend himself to more than one approach, and has avoided a pitfall into which some reviewers fall—namely, that of quarreling with the author for not writing a different book from the one he intended to write.

3. The review of Stein's book is particularly noteworthy for its artistic fusion of information, historical setting, and evaluation. Notice,

for instance, how the first sentence of the second paragraph gives information about what we may expect to find in the book, yet also places Stein in relation to other recent critics; how the first sentence of the third paragraph, while structurally given to information about the book, is at the same time evaluative by the inclusion of "incisive" and "immensely rewarding." Make a careful study of this review to see how the reviewer has blended the various elements demanded by a review into a satisfying whole.

CARL BODE

a review of Henry Beetle Hough's

THOREAU OF WALDEN: THE MAN AND HIS EVENTFUL LIFE

It is a dry season for Thoreau when reviewers are persuaded to praise Mr. Hough's book. Its appeal is supposedly to the "ordinary reader," the man "shut out and left behind" by "detailed critical studies and exhaustive interpretations." With him in mind Mr. Hough takes the story of Thoreau's life, simplifies it, spices it with anecdotes, adds some flavor of his own, and then serves it up. Perhaps the general reader should feel satisfied but I doubt even that.

For *Thoreau of Walden* is distinguished by a rich variety of errors. Walter Harding has collected many of them in the Spring 1956 issue of the *Thoreau Society Bulletin*. There are errors of simple fact—for instance, Henry's brother John dies a month too late. There are errors in the handling of groups of facts—for instance, Mr. Hough overlooks some of the contributions of modern scholarship to the picture of Thoreau's days at Harvard. There are errors of interpretation—for instance, Mr. Hough's idea that Thoreau went to Walden at least partly to engage "in forwarding runaway slaves."

Yet the errors in the book could be discounted if the author had anything new about Thoreau to offer. He does not. The main contribution he makes is that of his own personality. It finds its way into a good many pages which are pleasant enough reading. It should be added that certain apparent similarities exist between him and his subject: most notably love of nature, independence of spirit, and love of writing. Because he has these things in common with Thoreau, Mr. Hough's sympathy for his subject is increased, and a warmer biography is the result. Nevertheless, Thoreau deserves a better book than this.

Comments and Questions

1. Note Carl Bode's use of metaphor in paragraph one: the brief metaphor of the "dry season," and the more extended metaphor residing in his description of how Henry Beetle Hough "takes the story of Thoreau's life, simplifies it, spices it with anecdotes, adds some flavor of his own, and then serves it up." Study in particular this latter metaphor, contemplate what mental images it conjures up in your mind, and decide in what way it contributes to the reviewer's evaluation of the book.

2. In the first paragraph the reviewer includes some direct quotations whose context suggests that they come from the preface to Hough's book. In his writing, Hough was apparently addressing his reader as "ordinary," and casting aspersions on the practice of writing "detailed critical studies and exhaustive interpretations." In Hough's context, then, the word "ordinary" assumes a favorable connotation. How does the word strike you in the context that the reviewer gives it? Do you look on yourself, after reading the review, as an "ordinary" reader?

3. What is the effect of the reviewer's use of parallel structure in paragraph two: "There are errors. . . . There are errors. . . . There are errors. . . ."

4. Although the reviewer manages, in his concluding paragraph, to come up with something he can commend, the review is predominantly unfavorable. Does the reviewer convince you that the book is really as disappointing as he says it is? If so, how has he succeeded? If not, how has he failed? Examine in this connection the relative brevity of the review. Does the examiner need more space than he allows himself to prove his point? Or does the brevity help condemn the book?

NORMAN HOLMES PEARSON

a review of Robert E. Spiller's

THE CYCLE OF AMERICAN LITERATURE: AN ESSAY IN HISTORICAL CRITICISM

No short history of American literature is likely to satisfy every taste or every need. The average reader, however, exists in multiform plenty as well as ubiquity, and Professor Spiller's new literary history is well-balanced in its efforts to satisfy a wide range of average interests and concerns. Whether the critical problems of writing a brief literary history are greater or less than those of a monumental one it is difficult to say. There is too much in the one for structure, and too little in the other for demonstration. Professor Spiller's experience is likely to prove as good an example as any. He has now, at a sufficient interval of time, followed up his editorship of the three-volume *Literary History of the United States* with a compact guide and introduction which he calls *The Cycle of American Literature* and subtitles "An Essay in Historical Criticism."

Following more or less the utilitarian pattern of the *Literary History,* but always as his own master, Professor Spiller writes informative syntheses of historical stages of cultural, intellectual, and political backgrounds, and then follows these with extended individual discussions of the biographies and writings of selected authors. The chief writers are all to be found, as well as a surprising number of lesser figures, especially in the earlier periods, whom Professor Spiller has contrived to summarize with admirable skill. His proportions for the book are excellent, all difficulties considered, and his opinions reflect not only his own broad experience and research but also a close knowledge of relevant scholarship and criticism. What will seem perhaps freshest in emphasis is his expanded consideration of criticism as a genre, especially in the twentieth century. The twentieth century, Spiller describes as "the period of . . . greatest achievement." What is lacking is the space to prove this true as it is true in terms of the extraordinary contemporary wealth of fine minor writers. Viewed simply in terms of giants, the nineteenth century will not suffer in comparison.

As though to bring to his own book a coherent critical principle which the larger *Literary History* lacked, no doubt because it was ultimately the product of so many individual pens, Professor Spiller emphasizes in his Preface his adherence to an organic principle of history, the sense of the life cycle which gives his book its title. This is a familiar evolutionary concept, especially appealing in the description of the literature of a nation which has so often been called "youthful" and occasionally "mature." He finds not only a single over-all and satisfying organic movement, "but at least two secondary cycles as well." These secondary cycles he defines as

the literary movement which developed from the Eastern seaboard as a center, and culminated with the great romantic writers of the mid-nineteenth century; and that which grew out of the conquest of the continent and is now rounding its full cycle in the twentieth century. When applied to the individual work, the same theory supplies a formula for measuring the aesthetic distance of a poem or play or novel from its origins in some phase of American experience.

A prime difficulty in applying a cyclical scheme which will be valid at the same time both for experience and for art is to keep them separated.

The measurement of aesthetic distance becomes confused with the calculation of organic congruence or tension; one is never sure whether it is experience or art that is being described. It becomes difficult also not to introduce other lines of relationship and the life-spans of forms which lie outside the basic cyclical scheme, or if relevant to it need more substantiation (what William James would have called "cash") than the limits of so brief a history allow.

Professor Spiller can write: "With his next poems Whitman launched boldly into the outermost rim of cosmic consciousness." Or he can say of Jonathan Edwards's doctrine:

It is the philosophical system with which the history of American philosophy starts; but it is also the house of tragedy, in which the sense of guilt and agony survives, the release into the peace of submission fails. It is the structure of tragic realization which was repeated in the work of Poe, Hawthorne, and Melville; O'Neill, Eliot, and Faulkner.

Such statements read more fluently than lend themselves to any close analysis in reference to the distanced expression of American experience or the establishment of any predictable relationship between experience and art within the flow of the cyclical theory. Provocative and stimulating, however, such statements become; and one looks forward elsewhere to Professor Spiller's expansion of his critical cues. It is as a guide that *The Cycle of American Literature* will, however, be most useful in itself, rather than as a demonstration of what is not so much a critical theory as a claim.

Comments and Questions

1. Note that Norman Holmes Pearson's review speaks, as does Carl Bode's, of the ordinary or general reader (Pearson's term is "average"). Does the reviewer compliment *The Cycle of American Literature* by saying that this "new literary history is well-balanced in its efforts to satisfy a wide range of average interests and concerns"?

2. This review is, technically at any rate, a mixed review, in that the reviewer pays the book a number of compliments (particularly in the second paragraph) and also suggests that the book suffers from several organic weaknesses. Does the reviewer eventually indicate that his response to the book is more, or less, favorable than otherwise? Does he imply that the book is valuable despite its deficiencies, or that the deficiencies overcome any redeeming features the book may have?

3. Contrast the length of this review with Carl Bode's review of *Thoreau of Walden*. Why is this review so much longer? Notice also

the difference in tone between the two reviews. Does this difference in tone have anything to do with the difference in length between the two reviews?

꙰꙰꙰꙰꙰꙰꙰꙰

Suggestions for an Essay

Write a book review of a critical study or critical biography you have read. Keep in mind the triple purpose: to describe the book, to place it in some sort of setting, and—most importantly—to evaluate it.

THE STUDY OF A WRITER'S REPUTATION

Introduction

Scholars who have made a wide study of the body of criticism that has grown up around a literary figure sometimes write articles concerning this writer's reputation. Regardless of whether the writer lived in the past, or whether he is still producing, such an essay may concern itself with whether the writer's reputation has steadily increased, steadily decreased, fluctuated, or remained fairly constant between the time he began to write and the present.

In part, an essay on the reputation of a writer must be factual, since it is obviously necessary to give the gist of what first one and then other critics have had to say. But as in all critical writing, there is room for evaluation and interpretation. Following is Alfred Kazin's article, "Theodore Dreiser and His Critics," in which Kazin uses what Dreiser's critics have said about Dreiser to throw into bolder relief his own high estimate of the writer.

ALFRED KAZIN

Theodore Dreiser and His Critics

At a time when the one quality which so many American writers have in common is their utter harmlessness, Dreiser makes painful reading. The others you can take up without being involved in the least. They are "literature"—beautiful, stylish literature. You are left free to think not of the book you are reading but of the author, and not even of the whole man behind the author, but just of his cleverness, his sensibility, his style. Dreiser gets under your skin and you can't wait to get him out again: he stupefies with reality:

Carrie looked about her, very much disturbed and quite sure that she did not want to work here. Aside from making her uncomfortable by sidelong glances, no one paid her the least attention. She waited until the whole department was aware of her presence. Then some word was sent around, and a foreman, in an apron and shirt sleeves, the latter rolled up to his shoulders, approached.
"Do you want to see me?" he asked.
"Do you need any help?" said Carrie, already learning directness of address.
"Do you know how to stitch caps?" he returned.
"No, sir," she replied.
"Have you had any experience at this kind of work?" he inquired.
She answered that she had not.
"Well," said the foreman, scratching his ear meditatively, "we do need a stitcher. We like experienced help, though. We've hardly got time to break people in." He paused and looked away out of the window. "We might, though, put you at finishing," he concluded reflectively.
"How much do you pay a week?" ventured Carrie, emboldened by a certain softness in the man's manner and his simplicity of address.
"Three and a half," he answered.
"Oh," she was about to exclaim, but she checked herself and allowed her thoughts to die without expression.
"We're not exactly in need of anybody," he went on vaguely, looking her over as one would a package.

The city had laid miles and miles of streets and sewers through regions where, perhaps, one solitary house stood out alone—a pioneer of the populous ways to be. There were regions open to the sweeping winds and rain, which were as yet lighted throughout the night with long, blinking lines of gas-lamps, fluttering in the wind. Narrow board walks extended out, passing here a house, and there a store, at far intervals, eventually ending on the open prairie.

"He said that if you married me you would only get ten thousand a year. That if you didn't and still lived with me you would get nothing at all. If you would leave me, or if I would leave you, you would get all of a million and a half. Don't you think you had better leave me now?"

These are isolated passages—the first two from *Sister Carrie,* the third from *Jennie Gerhardt*—and normally it would be as unkind to pick passages from Dreiser as it would be to quote for themselves those frustrated mental exchanges that Henry James's characters hold with each other. For Dreiser works in such detail that you never really feel the force of any [phrase?] until you see the whole structure, while James is preoccupied with an inner meditation that his own characters always seem to be interrupting. But even in these bits from Dreiser there is an overwhelming impression that puzzles and troubles us because we cannot trace it to its source. "One doesn't see how it's made," a French critic once complained about some book he was reviewing. That is the trouble we always have with Dreiser. Carrie measuring herself against the immensity of Chicago, that wonderful night scene in which we see a generation just off the farms and out of the small towns confronting the modern city for the first time; the scene in which Hurstwood comes on Carrie sitting in the dark; Jennie Gerhardt's growing solitude even after the birth of her child; Clyde Griffiths and Roberta Alden walking around the haunted lakes when he is searching for one where he can kill her—one doesn't see the man writing this. We are too absorbed. Something is happening that tastes of fear, of the bottom loneliness of human existence, that just barely breaks into speech from the depths of our souls; the planet itself seems to creak under our feet, and there are long lines of people bitterly walking to work in the morning dark, thinking only of how they can break through the iron circle of their frustration. Every line hurts. It hurts because you never get free enough of anything to ask what a character or a situation "really" means; it hurts because Dreiser is not trying to prove anything by it or to change what he sees; it hurts even when you are trying to tell yourself that all this happened in another time, that we are cleverer about life than Dreiser was. It hurts because it is all too much like reality to be "art."

It is because we have all identified Dreiser's work with reality that, for more than half a century now, he has been for us not a writer like other writers, but a whole chapter of American life. From the very beginning, as one can see in reading over the reviews of *Sister Carrie*, Dreiser was accepted as a whole new class, a tendency, a disturbing movement in American life, an eruption from below. The very words he used, the dreaminess of his prose, the stilted but grim matter-of-fact of his method, which betrayed all the envy and wonder with which he looked at the great world outside—all this seemed to say that it was not art he worked with but *knowledge,* some new and secret knowledge. It was this that the reviewers instantly felt, that shocked the Doubledays so deeply, that explains the extraordinary bitterness toward Dreiser from the first—and that excited Frank Norris, the publisher's reader (Dreiser looked amazingly like the new, "primitive" types that Norris was getting into his own fiction). Dreiser was the man from outside, the man from below, who wrote with the terrible literalness of a child. It is this that is so clearly expressed in Frank Doubleday's efforts to kill the book, in the fact that most literary and general magazines in the country did not review the book at all, that even some newspapers reviewed the book a year late, and that the tone of these early reviews is plainly that of people trying to accustom themselves to an unpleasant shock.

Sister Carrie did not have a bad press; it had a frightened press, with many of the reviewers plainly impressed, but startled by the concentrated truthfulness of the book. The St. Louis *Mirror* complained that "the author writes with a startling directness. At times this directness seems to be the frankness of a vast unsophistication. The scenes of the book are laid always among a sort of people that is numerous but seldom treated in a serious novel." The general reaction was that of the Newark *Sunday News*, almost a year after the book had been published. "Told with an unsparing realism and detail, it has all the interest of fact. . . . The possibility of it all is horrible: an appalling arraignment of human society. And there is here no word of preachment; there are scarcely any philosophic reflections or deductions expressed. The impression is simply one of truth, and therein lies at once the strength and the horror of it."

This was the new note of the book, the unrelieved seriousness of it—but a seriousness so native, so unself-conscious, that Dreiser undoubtedly saw nothing odd about his vaguely "poetic" and questioning chapter titles, which were his efforts to frame his own knowledge, to fit it into a traditional system of thought, though he could not question any of his knowledge itself. Writing *Sister Carrie*, David Brion Davis comments, "was something like translating the Golden Plates." For Carrie was Dreiser's own sister, and he wrote without any desire to shock, without any knowledge that he could. Compare this with so "naturalistic" a book as Hardy's *Tess of the D'Urbervilles*, where the style is itself constantly commenting on the characters, and where the very old-fashioned turn of the prose, in all its complex urbanity, is an effort to interpret the story, to accommodate it to the author's own tradition of thought. Dreiser *could* not comment; so deeply had he identified himself with the story that there was no place left in it for him to comment *from*. And such efforts as he made to comment, in the oddly invertebrate chapter titles, were like gasps in the face of a reality from which he could not turn away. The book was exactly like a dream that Dreiser had lived through and which, in fact, after the failure of *Sister Carrie*, he was to live again, up to the very brink of Hurstwood's suicide.

It was this knowledge, this exclusive knowledge, this *kann nicht anders*, this absence of alternatives, that led people to resent Dreiser, and at the same time stunned the young writers of the period into instant recognition of his symbolic value to them. We never know how much has been missing from our lives until a true writer comes along. Everything which had been waiting for them in the gap between the generations, everything which Henry James said would belong to an "American Balzac"—that world of industrial capitalism which, James confessed, had been a "closed book" to him from his youth—everything free of "literature" and so free to become literature, now became identified with this "clumsy" and "stupid" ex-newspaperman whose book moved the new writers all the more deeply because they could not see where Dreiser's genius came from. To the young writers of the early twentieth century, Dreiser became, in Mencken's phrase, the Hindenburg of the novel—the great beast who pushed American life forward for them, who went on, blindly, unchangeably, trampling down the lies of gentility and Victorianism, of Puritanism and academicism. Dreiser was the primitive, the man from the abyss, the stranger who had grown up outside the Anglo-Saxon middle-class Protestant morality and so had no need to accept its sanctions. In Sherwood Anderson's phrase, he could be honored with "an apology for crudity"; and in fact the legend that *Sister Carrie* had been suppressed by the publisher's wife was now so dear to the hearts of the rising generation that Mrs. Doubleday became a classic character, the Carrie Nation of the American liberal epos, her axe forever lifted against "the truth of American life." So even writers like Van Wyck Brooks, who had not shared in the bitterness of Dreiser's early years, and who as socialists disapproved of his despair, now defended him as a matter of course—he cleared the way; in the phrase that was to be repeated with increasing meaninglessness through the years, he "liberated the American novel."

Dreiser now embodied the whole struggle of the new American literature. The "elderly virgins of the newspapers," as Mencken called them, never ceased to point out his deficiencies; the conservative academicians and New Humanists, the old fogeys and the young fogeys—all found in Dreiser everything new, brutal and alien they feared in American life. Gertrude Atherton was to say during the first World War that Dreiser represented the "Alpine School of Literature"—"Not a real American could be found among them with a magnifying glass"; Mary Austin was to notice that "our Baltic and Slavic stock will have another way than the English of experiencing love, and possibly a more limited way. . . . All of Theodore Dreiser's people love like the peasants in a novel by Bojer or Knut Hamsun. His women have a cowlike complaisance such as can be found only in people who have lived for generations close to the soil"; Stuart Sherman, in his famous article of 1915 on "The Barbaric Naturalism of Theodore Dreiser," made it clear that Dreiser, "coming from that 'ethnic' element of our mixed population," was thus unable to understand the higher beauty of the American spirit.

So Dreiser stood in no-man's-land, pushed ahead like a dumb ox by one camp, attacked by the other. Everything about him made him a polemical figure; his scandals, miseries, and confusions were as well-known as his books. The "liberals," the "modernists," defended books like *The "Genius"* because "it told the truth"—and how delighted they must have been when John S. Sumner tried to get the book banned in 1915 and anybody who *was* anybody (including Ezra Pound, John Reed and David Belasco) rushed to its defense. To the English novelists of the period (and *Sister Carrie* owed its sudden fame to the edition Heinemann brought out in London) he was like a powerhouse they envied amid the Georgian doldrums of literary London. How much of that fighting period comes back to you now when you discover Arnold Bennett on his feverish trips to America identifying all the raw, rich, teeming opportunities of American life with Dreiser, or listen to Ford Madox Ford—"Damn it all,

it *is* fun to see that poor old language, that vehicle for conveying moder-
ated thoughts, having the guts kicked out of it, like a deflated football,
over all the fields of the boundless Middle West." While Mencken, in
Dreiser's name, slew William Lyon Phelps in his thousands, the young
English discovered that Dreiser was the friend of art. Each side in the
controversy used Dreiser, and each, in its own way, was embarrassed.
How many times did the young Turks have to swallow Dreiser's bad
books, to explain away his faults, and how clear it is from reading Paul
Elmer More (who was a deeper critic than his opponents and would have
been almost a great one if he had not always tried to arm himself against
American life) that he was always more moved by Dreiser's cosmic
doubts than he could confess. More settled the problem, as he settled
every writer he feared, by studying the man's "philosophy"—where he
could show up Dreiser to his heart's content, and, in a prose that could
not have been more removed from the actualities of the subject, prove
that he had disposed forever of this intellectual upstart.

This pattern remained to the end—Dreiser was the great personifier.
When he went to Russia, even the title of the book he wrote had to
begin with Dreiser rather than with Russia; when Sinclair Lewis praised
Dreiser in his Nobel Prize speech, he did so with all the enthusiasm of a
Congressman trying for the farm vote; when Dreiser delivered himself
of some remarks about Jews, the *Nation* was not so much indignant as
bewildered that this son of the common people could express such illiberal
sentiments; when he spoke against England at the beginning of the
Second World War, there was a similar outcry that Dreiser was letting
the masses down. It is typical of Dreiser's symbolic importance that a
writer now so isolated as James T. Farrell has been able to find support
for his own work only in Dreiser's example; that the word *plebeian* has
always been used either to blacken Dreiser or to favor him; that Eisen-
stein suffered so long to make a film of *An American Tragedy* that would
be the ultimate exposure of American capitalism. When Dreiser joined
the Communists, his act was greeted as everything but what it really was
—the lonely and confused effort of an individual to identify himself with
a group that had taken him up in his decline; when he died in 1945,
in the heyday of American-Soviet friendship, one left-wing poet announced that Dreiser's faults had always been those of America anyway,
that he was simply America writ large—"Much as we wish he had been
surer, wiser, we cannot change the fact. The man was great in a way
Americans uniquely understand who know the uneven contours of their
land, its storms, its droughts, its huge and turbulent Mississippi, where
his youth was spent." Even Dreiser's sad posthumous novels, *The Bulwark* and *The Stoic,* each of which centers around a dying old man,
were written about with forced enthusiasm, as if the people attacking
them were afraid of being called reactionary, while those who honestly
liked them reported that they were *surprisingly* good. And how F. O.

Matthiessen suffered all through the last year of his life to do justice
to Dreiser as if that would fulfill an *obligation* to the cause of "progres-
sivism" in America.

But soon after the war all this changed—Dreiser was now simply
an embarrassment. The reaction against him was only partly literary,
for much of it was founded on an understandable horror of the fraudu-
lent "radicals" who had been exploiting Dreiser before his death. And
thanks not a little to the cozy prosperity of a permanent war economy,
America, it seemed, no longer required the spirit of protest with which
Dreiser had been identified. The writers were now in the universities, and
they all wrote about writing. No longer hoary sons of toil, a whole intel-
ligentsia, post-Communist, post-Marxist, which could not look at Alger
Hiss in the dock without shuddering at how near they had come to his
fate, now tended to find their new ideology in the good old middle-class
virtues. A new genteel tradition had come in. Writing in America had
suddenly become very conscious that literature is made with words, and
that these words should look nice on the page. It became a period when
fine writing was everything, when every anonymous smoothie on *Time*
could write cleaner prose about God's alliance with America than poor
old Dreiser could find for anything, when even the *Senior Scholastic,*
a magazine intended for high-school students, complained of Dreiser that
"some of the writing would shock an English class." It is of this period,
in which we live, that Saul Bellow has noted in his tribute to Dreiser: "I
think that the insistence on neatness and correctness is one of the signs
of a modern nervousness and irritability. When has clumsiness in composition been felt as so annoying, so enraging? The 'good' writing of the
New Yorker is such that one experiences a furious anxiety, in reading it,
about errors and lapses from taste; finally what emerges is a terrible
hunger for conformity and uniformity. The smoothness of the surface
and its high polish must not be marred. One has a similar anxiety in
reading a novelist like Hemingway and comes to feel that in the end
Hemingway wants to be praised for the offenses he does not commit. He
is dependable; he never names certain emotions or ideas, and he takes
pride in that—it is a form of honor. In it, really, there is submissiveness,
acceptance of restriction."

The most important expression of the reaction against Dreiser is Lionel
Trilling's "Reality in America." This essay expresses for a great many
people in America just now their impatience with the insurgency that
dominated our famously realistic fiction up to the war, and not since
Paul Elmer More's essay of 1920 has anyone with so much critical insight made out so brilliant a case against Dreiser; not since William Dean
Howells supported Stephen Crane's *Maggie* and not *Sister Carrie* has
anyone contrasted so sharply those notorious faults of style and slovenly
habits of thought which our liberal criticism has always treated as
"essentially social and political virtues" with the wonderful play of mind

and fertility of resource one finds in Henry James. Never has the case against the persistent identification of Dreiser with "reality" in America —coarse, heavy, external reality—been put with so much intellectual passion. For Mr. Trilling is writing against the decay of a liberal movement ruined largely by its flirtation with totalitarianism, by its disregard of human complexity and its fear of intellect. No one who has followed the extent to which our liberal critics have always acknowledged that Dreiser *is* a bad thinker—and have excused it on the grounds that the poor man at least "told the truth about American life"—can help but share Mr. Trilling's impatience with what has recently passed in this country for liberal "imagination."

But may it not be suggested that Henry James as a cultural hero serves us as badly as Dreiser once did? What happens whenever we convert a writer into a symbol is that we lose the writer himself in all his indefeasible singularity, his particular inimitable genius. A literature that modeled itself on Dreiser would be unbearable; a literature that saw all its virtues of literature in Henry James would be preposterous. If one thing is clear about our addiction to Henry James just now, it is that most of our new writing has nothing in common with James whatever. For James's essential quality is his intellectual appetite—"all life belongs to you"—his unending inner meditation, and not the air of detachment which so misleads us whenever we encounter it on the surface of the society James wrote about—the only society he knew, and one he despaired of precisely because it was never what it seemed. Just now, however, a certain genteel uninvolvement is dear to us, while Dreiser's bread lines and street-car strikes, his suffering inarticulate characters, his Chicago, his "commonness"—are that bad dream from which we have all awakened. As Dreiser's faults were once acclaimed as the virtues of the common man, so now we are ashamed of him because he brings up everything we should like to leave behind us.

There is no "common man"—though behind the stereotype (how *this* executioner waits!) stand those who may yet prepare all too common a fate for us all. Literary people, as a class, can get so far away from the experience of other classes that they tend to see them only symbolically. Dreiser as "common man" once served a purpose; now he serves another. The basic mistake of all the liberal critics was to think that he could ever see this world as something to be ameliorated. They misjudged the source of Dreiser's strength. This is the point that David Brion Davis documents so well in his study of what Dreiser and the early naturalists really believed. For as Mr. Davis shows, these writers and painters were "naturalists" only in the stark sense that the world had suddenly come down to them divested of its supernatural sanctions. They were actually obsessed with the transcendental possibilities of this "real" world; like Whitman, they gloried in the beauty of the iron city. In their contemplative acceptance of this world, in their indifference to social reform, in their awe before life itself, they were actually not in the tradition of political "liberalism" but in that deeper American strain of metaphysical wonder which leads from the early pietists through Whitman to the first painters of the modern city.

This gift of contemplativeness, of wonder, of reverence, even, is at the center of Dreiser's world—who can forget the image of the rocking chair in *Sister Carrie*, where from *this* cradle endlessly rocking man stares forever at a world he is not too weak but too bemused to change? And it is this lack of smartness, this puzzled lovingness for the substance of all our mystery, that explains why we do not know what to *do* with Dreiser today. For Dreiser is in a very old, a very difficult, a very lonely American tradition. It is no longer "transcendentalist," but always it seeks to transcend. This does not mean that Dreiser's philosophy is valuable in itself, or that his excursions into philosophy and science—fields for which he was certainly not well equipped—have to be excused. It does mean that the vision is always in Dreiser's work, and makes it possible. Just as the strength of his work is that he got into it those large rhythms of wonder, of curiosity, of amazement before the power of the universe that give such largeness to his characters and such unconscious majesty to life itself, so the weakness and instability of his work is that he could become almost too passive before the great thing he saw out there, always larger than man himself. The truth is, as Eliseo Vivas says in his essay, that Dreiser is "not only an American novelist but a universal novelist, in the very literal sense of the word. The mystery of the universe, the puzzle of destiny, haunts him; and he, more than any other of his contemporaries, has responded to the need to relate the haunting sense of puzzlement and mystery to the human drama. No other American novelist of his generation has so persistently endeavored to look at men under the aspect of eternity. It is no . . . paradox, therefore, that . . . while Dreiser tries to demonstrate that man's efforts are vain and empty, by responding to the need to face the problem of destiny, he draws our attention to dimensions of human existence, awareness of which is not encouraged by current philosophical fashions. . . ." To understand how this gets into Dreiser's work one must look not back of it but into it for that sense of "reality" which he thirsted for—that whole reality, up to the very shores of light, that made him cry out in *Jennie Gerhardt:* "We turn our faces away from the creation of life as if that were the last thing that man should dare to interest himself in, openly."

This is what makes Dreiser so painful—in his "atheism," his cosmology; this is what dismays us in our sensible culture, just as it bothered a generation that could never understand Dreiser's special bitterness against orthodox religion, against the churches; this is what drove Dreiser to look for God in the laboratories, to write essays on "My Creator." He may have been a "naturalist," but he was certainly not a materialist. What sticks in our throats is that Dreiser is outside the agreed boundaries of our concern, that he does not accept our "society" as the whole of reality, that he may crave after its fleshpots, but does not believe that getting along is the ultimate reach of man's effort. For we live in a time when traditionalists and "progressives" and ex-progressives alike are agreed that the man not to be trusted is the man who does not fit in, who has no "position," who dares to be distracted—when this great going machine, this prig's paradise in which we live just now, is the best of all possible worlds.

Dreiser committed the one sin that a writer can commit in our society —he would not accept this society itself as wholly real. And it is here, I think, that we can get perspective on his famous awkwardness. For what counts most with a writer is that his reach should be felt as well as his grasp, that words should be his means, not his ends. It is this that Malcolm Cowley noticed when he wrote that "there are moments when Dreiser's awkwardness in handling words contributes to the force of his novels, since he seems to be groping in them for something on a deeper level than language." This is what finally disturbs us about Dreiser in a period when fine writing is like a mirror that gives back our superficiality. Dreiser hurts because he is always looking to the source; to that which broke off into the mysterious halves of man's existence; to that which is behind language and sustains it; to that which is not ourselves but gives life to our words.

Comments and Questions

1. Notice that Alfred Kazin's essay not only indicates the nature of criticism about Dreiser during the half century since the publication of *Sister Carrie* in 1900, but also represents the writer's own estimate of Dreiser. Study how Kazin fuses these two purposes by alternately presenting a certain response which critics have had to Dreiser's works, and then himself suggesting the shortcomings of the response.

2. Throughout his essay, Kazin makes considerable use of the word "truth," claiming that truth was pre-eminently what Dreiser captured in his novels, and that truth was precisely what the America of 1900 was not ready to accept. How does Kazin define this abstract concept of truth as it relates to Dreiser and his critics? What was "untruthful" about American letters in 1900?

3. The essay suggests that Dreiser's defenders have rendered him a disservice, that they have misrepresented the nature of his achievement. What, as Kazin defines it, is the nature of this misrepresentation?

4. Kazin writes: "We never know how much has been missing from our lives until a true writer comes along." For Kazin, obviously,

Dreiser represents one such "true" writer. And Dreiser, quite obviously again, did not write books for children. Compare Kazin's argument here with Clifton Fadiman's in "My Life Is an Open Book" (see Chapter 1), where Fadiman suggests that the really "true" books are those we first appreciated as children.

5. Dreiser's reputation, we are told, has changed repeatedly as a result of the constantly changing temper and philosophical climate of America during the first half of the twentieth century. What do you think about interpreting a writer's work in the light of conditions that prevail subsequent to the time he writes? Is this good? Bad? Evitable? Inevitable? What seems to be Kazin's attitude toward these questions?

6. In the closing paragraphs of his essay, Kazin contrasts his reading of Dreiser with what he takes to be shortcomings in our contemporary attitudes. Thus he gives his essay something of a philosophical cast. Does Kazin's conclusion represent a logical, and effective, outgrowth of what has preceded it?

Suggestions for an Essay

Write an essay in which you trace the course of a writer's reputation by analyzing the criticisms you have read of his works. Try, by agreeing or disagreeing with various of your sources, to suggest your own attitude toward the writer you are studying, as Alfred Kazin suggests his attitude toward Theodore Dreiser by evaluating Dreiser's critics

9

THE WRITING OF SELF-EVALUATIONS

Introduction

Scarcely less demanding than the task of writing about the work of others (as in a book review) is the task of writing about one's own work. This latter task finds expression in a variety of forms. Many writers, in writing autobiographical reminiscences, describe phases of their work. In his *Autobiography*, for example, Mark Twain indicates some of the real-life prototypes for some of the characters in *Tom Sawyer* and the modifications he made when he transferred these prototypes to his book. Other writers, in discussing their work, produce formal pieces of literary criticism. Well known are essays such as Edgar Allan Poe's "The Philosophy of Composition," in which Poe indicates how he wrote "The Raven," and Allan Tate's discussion of his "Ode to the Confederate Dead." Many full-length books contain prefatory remarks, called Prefaces, Forewords, or Introductions, which comment on various aspects of the work which is to follow. These are particularly prevalent in works of nonfiction (such as books of literary criticism, history, philosophy, and the like), although novelists, poets, and playwrights occasionally preface their works with essays of one kind or another.

It is not surprising that writers, regardless of the nature of their writing, should choose to write about their own productions. At a personal level, the close relationship existing between a writer and his work frequently prompts him to commentary. When Charles Dickens wrote, "Like many fond parents, I have in my heart of hearts a favourite child—and his name is *David Copperfield*," he was suggesting a by no means uncommon relationship between author and book.

But most literary self-evaluation functions on a considerably higher plane than that suggested by the parent-child analogy. The serious writer, inevitably, is interested in aesthetics, in literary theory, in exploring the infinitely complex forces that operate to produce a literary work. Hence much literary self-evaluation, far from being merely chatty, addresses itself to various problems connected with the processes of artistic creation.

Since the processes of artistic creation are diverse, it is difficult to predict the nature of what a writer will say when he comments on his work. Obviously, what he says will depend on the nature of his work and on his relationship to his reader. Interest in the process of literary creation prompts some writers to indulge in self-criticism. Henry James, for example, in the prefaces to the New York edition of his works, explains in great detail the objectives of his writing, the problems deriving from these objectives, and the ways in which he attempted to meet these problems. As a part of his self-criticism James gives such pieces of information as which of his works he regards as his best (*The Ambassadors*), and which parts of specific works he regards as most satisfying artistically.

Some writers (James again figures pre-eminently among this number) seek to re-create the experience of writing, to indicate how their work came into being, and the changes it underwent.

Again, some self-evaluations seem written mainly to suggest the literary theories of the writer. Poe's "The Philosophy of Composition" has this objective so prominent as to cause some readers to doubt that "The Raven" was actually written as Poe suggests.

Another objective in self-criticism is sometimes that of justifying the work being discussed. E. B. White, in the Foreword to *One Man's Meat,* indicates why he considers it important, in a time of national emergency, to bring out a volume of personal essays.

Often self-criticism reveals something of the philosophy of the writer, something of the nature of his response to the human condition. Often this philosophical cast is, as one might suppose, indicative of the work in question. Henry Adams, for example, in his disillusioned and humorously cynical Introduction to *Mont-Saint-Michel and Chartres,* suggests by implication the deleterious effects of the multiplicity which he sees as characteristic of his own time.

If the piece of writing undergoing scrutiny is a scholarly book (such as George Santayana's *Character and Opinion in the United States*), the writer may feel a need to give the reader information that is essential for him to know if he is to read the book intelligently; he may wish to forestall adverse criticism by explaining the plan of the work and its self-imposed limitations; he will almost certainly, by one means or another, seek to establish his reader's confidence in him as a writer.

Obviously, these objectives of self-criticism are seldom found in isolation. For example, E. B. White's Foreword to *One Man's Meat,* in addition to justifying his work, reflects White's philosophy: respect for individuality is infinitely preferable to Hitlerian concepts of totalitarianism.

One objective, found in all self-evaluations, remains to be mentioned. In form and tone, almost all self-criticism approximates the informal essay. The first person singular pronoun is usually quite in evidence (as contrasted with the more impersonal approach of most critical and scholarly writing). In a word, the writer, in writing about himself, is concerned with revealing himself as a unique personality. In this respect a piece of self-criticism may almost be said to have a relevance of its own, without reference to the work it comments on. (E. B. White's Foreword, for instance, makes entertaining reading, and White emerges from it as a distinct personality.)

Below are a number of essays in which writers comment on their own writing.

GEORGE SANTAYANA

preface to

CHARACTER AND OPINION IN THE UNITED STATES

*T*he major part of this book is composed of lectures originally addressed to British audiences. I have added a good deal, but I make no apology, now that the whole may fall under American eyes, for preserving the tone and attitude of a detached observer. Not at all on the ground that "to see ourselves as others see us" would be to see ourselves truly; on the contrary, I agree with Spinoza where he says that other people's idea of a man is apt to be a better expression of their nature than of his. I accept this principle in the present instance, and am willing it should be applied to the judgements contained in this book, in which the reader may see chiefly expressions of my own feelings and hints of my own opinions. Only an American—and I am not one except by long association[1]—can speak for the heart of America. I try to understand it, as a family friend who has a different temperament; but it is only my own mind that I speak for at bottom, or wish to speak for. Certainly my sentiments are of little importance compared with the volume and destiny of the things I discuss here: yet the critic and artist too have their rights, and to take as calm and as long a view as

---

[1] Perhaps I should add that I have not been in the United States since January 1912. My observations stretched, with some intervals, through the forty years preceding that date.

possible seems to be but another name for the love of truth. Moreover, I suspect that my feelings are secretly shared by many people in America, natives and foreigners, who may not have the courage or the occasion to express them frankly. After all, it has been acquaintance with America and American philosophers that has chiefly contributed to clear and to settle my own mind. I have no axe to grind, only my thoughts to burnish, in the hope that some part of the truth of things may be reflected there; and I am confident of not giving serious offence to the judicious, because they will feel that it is affection for the American people that makes me wish that what is best and most beautiful should not be absent from their lives.

Civilization is perhaps approaching one of those long winters that overtake it from time to time. A flood of barbarism from below may soon level all the fair works of our Christian ancestors, as another flood two thousand years ago levelled those of the ancients. Romantic Christendom—picturesque, passionate, unhappy episode—may be coming to an end. Such a catastrophe would be no reason for despair. Nothing lasts for ever; but the elasticity of life is wonderful, and even if the world lost its memory it could not lose its youth. Under the deluge, and watered by it, seeds of all sorts would survive against the time to come, even if what might eventually spring from them, under the new circumstances, should wear a strange aspect. In a certain measure, and unintentionally, both this destruction and this restoration have already occurred in America. There is much forgetfulness, much callow disrespect for what is past or alien; but there is a fund of vigour, goodness, and hope such as no nation ever possessed before. In what sometimes looks like American greediness and jostling for the front place, all is love of achievement, nothing is unkindness; it is a fearless people, and free from malice, as you might see in their eyes and gestures, even if their conduct did not prove it. This soil is propitious to every seed, and tares must needs grow in it; but why should it not also breed clear thinking, honest judgement, and rational happiness? These things are indeed not necessary to existence, and without them America might long remain rich and populous like many a barbarous land in the past; but in that case its existence would be hounded, like theirs, by falsity and remorse. May Heaven avert the omen, and make the new world a better world than the old! In the classical and romantic tradition of Europe, love, of which there was very little, was supposed to be kindled by beauty, of which there was a great deal: perhaps moral chemistry may be able to reverse this operation, and in the future and in America it may breed beauty out of love.

Comments and Questions

1. Note how, in the first paragraph, George Santayana apparently depreciates himself: he cannot speak for America, since he has been absent from it for so long; he feels his "sentiments are of little importance" compared with what he discusses; he is deeply indebted to American philosophers for their role in clearing and settling his own mind. Why does Santayana picture himself in this humble light?

2. Notice the sentence in the first paragraph which reads: "Moreover, I suspect that my feelings are secretly shared by many people in America, natives and foreigners, who may not have the courage or the occasion to express them frankly." What function does this sentence perform?

3. Santayana writes: ". . . and I am confident of not giving serious offence to the judicious. . . ." Do you consider yourself judicious or injudicious? In what way has Santayana here attempted to get the reader on his side?

4. The Preface is rich in uncomplimentary implications clothed in a sort of reverse rhetoric. Take, for instance, the last sentence in the first paragraph, where Santayana says that judicious readers will realize "that it is affection for the American people that makes me wish that what is best and most beautiful should not be absent from their lives." This sentence unmistakably indicates that, at the time Santayana is writing, what is best and most beautiful is very definitely absent from the lives of the American people. Search throughout the Preface for other examples of Santayana's technique of criticizing America by implication and indirection.

5. In the second paragraph, what is the "flood two thousand years ago" to which Santayana refers?

6. Study the second paragraph closely in the light of the aims of self-evaluation suggested in the Introduction to this chapter. What does Santayana hope to accomplish by writing this Preface?

W. SOMERSET MAUGHAM

from

THE SUMMING UP

1

𝒯his is not an autobiography nor is it a book of recollections. In one way and another I have used in my writings whatever has happened to me in the course of my life. Sometimes an experience I have had has served as a theme and I have invented a series of incidents to illustrate it; more often I have taken persons with whom I have been slightly or intimately acquainted and used them as the foundation for characters of my invention. Fact and fiction are so intermingled in my work that now, looking back on it, I can hardly distinguish one from the other. It would not interest me to record the facts, even if I could remember them, of which I have already made a better use. They would seem, moreover, very tame. I have had a varied, and often an interesting, life, but not an adventurous one. I have a poor memory. I can never remember a good story till I hear it again and then I forget it before I have had a chance to tell it to somebody else. I have never been able to remember even my own jokes, so that I have been forced to go on making new ones. This disability, I am aware, has made my company less agreeable than it might otherwise have been.

I have never kept a diary. I wish now that during the year that followed my first success as a dramatist I had done so, for I met then many persons of consequence and it might have proved an interesting document. At that period the confidence of the people in the aristocracy and the landed gentry had been shattered by the muddle they had made of things in South Africa, but the aristocracy and the landed gentry had not realized this and they preserved their old self-confidence. At certain political houses I frequented they still talked as though to run the British Empire were their private business. It gave me a peculiar sensation to hear it discussed, when a general election was in the air, whether Tom should have the Home Office and whether Dick would be satisfied with Ireland. I do not suppose that anyone today reads the novels of Mrs. Humphry Ward, but dull though they may be, my recollection is that some of them give a very good picture of what the life of the ruling class was then. Novelists were still much concerned with it and even writers who had never known a lord thought it necessary to write largely about persons of rank. It would astonish anyone now who looked at the playbills of the day to see how many of the characters were titled. Managers thought that they attracted the public, and actors liked to portray them. But as the political importance of the aristocracy dwindled the public took less interest in it. Playgoers began to be ready to observe the actions of people of their own class, the well-to-do merchants and professional men who were then conducting the affairs of the country; and the rule, though never formulated, prevailed that the writer should not introduce persons of title unless they were essential to his theme. It was still impossible to interest the public in the lower classes. Novels and plays that dealt with them were generally considered sordid. It will be curious to see if now that these classes have acquired political power the public at large will take the same interest in their lives that for so long it took in the lives of the titled, and for a while in those of the opulent bourgeoisie.

During this period I met persons who by their rank, fame or position might very well have thought themselves destined to become historical figures. I did not find them as brilliant as my fancy had painted them. The English are a political nation and I was often asked to houses where politics were the ruling interest. I could not discover in the eminent statesmen I met there any marked capacity. I concluded, perhaps rashly, that no great degree of intelligence was needed to rule a nation. Since then I have known in various countries a good many politicians who have attained high office. I have continued to be puzzled by what seemed to me the mediocrity of their minds. I have found them ill-informed upon the ordinary affairs of life and I have not often discovered in them either subtlety of intellect or liveliness of imagination. At one time I was inclined to think that they owed their illustrious position only to their gift of speech, for it must be next door to impossible to rise to power in a democratic community unless you can catch the ears of the public; and the gift of speech, as we know, is not often accompanied by the power of thought. But since I have seen statesmen who did not seem to me very clever conduct public affairs with reasonable success I cannot but think I was wrong: it must be that to govern a nation you need a specific talent and that this may very well exist without general ability. In the same way I have known men of affairs who have made great fortunes and brought vast enterprises to prosperity, but in everything unconcerned with their business appear to be devoid even of common sense.

Nor was the conversation that I heard then as clever as I had expected. It seldom gave you much to think about. It was easy, though not always; gay, amiable and superficial. Serious topics were not dealt with, for there was a feeling that to discuss them in general company was embarrassing, and the fear of "shop" seemed to prevent people from speaking of the subjects in which they were most interested. So far as I could judge conversation consisted in little more than a decorous badinage; but it was not often that you heard a witticism worth repeating. One might have thought that the only use of culture was to enable one to talk nonsense with distinction. On the whole I think the most

interesting and consistently amusing talker I ever knew was Edmund
Gosse. He had read a great deal, though not very carefully, it appears,
and his conversation was extremely intelligent. He had a prodigious
memory, a keen sense of humour, and malice. He had known Swinburne intimately and could talk about him in an entrancing fashion,
but he could also talk of Shelley, whom after all he could not possibly
have known, as if he had been a bosom friend. For many years he had
been acquainted with eminent persons. I think he was a vain man and
he had observed their absurdities with satisfaction. I am sure he made
them much more amusing than they really were.

2

I have always wondered at the passion many people have to meet
the celebrated. The prestige you acquire by being able to tell your
friends that you know famous men proves only that you are yourself of
small account. The celebrated develop a technique to deal with the
persons they come across. They show the world a mask, often an impressive one, but take care to conceal their real selves. They play the
part that is expected from them and with practice learn to play it very
well, but you are stupid if you think that this public performance of
theirs corresponds with the man within.

I have been attached, deeply attached, to a few people; but I have been
interested in men in general not for their own sakes, but for the sake of
my work. I have not, as Kant enjoined, regarded each man as an end in
himself, but as material that might be useful to me as a writer. I have
been more concerned with the obscure than with the famous. They are
more often themselves. They have had no need to create a figure to
protect themselves from the world or to impress it. Their idiosyncrasies
have had more chance to develop in the limited circle of their activity,
and since they have never been in the public eye it has never occurred
to them that they have anything to conceal. They display their oddities
because it has never struck them that they are odd. And after all it is
with the common run of men that we writers have to deal; kings, dic-
tators, commercial magnates are from our point of view very unsatisfactory. To write about them is a venture that has often tempted writers, but
the failure that has attended their efforts shows that such beings are too
exceptional to form a proper ground for a work of art. They cannot be
made real. The ordinary is the writer's richer field. Its unexpectedness,
its singularity, its infinite variety afford unending material. The great
man is too often all of a piece; it is the little man that is a bundle of
contradictory elements. He is inexhaustible. You never come to the end
of the surprises he has in store for you. For my part I would much sooner
spend a month on a desert island with a veterinary surgeon than with a
prime minister.

3

In this book I am going to try to sort out my thoughts on the subjects that have chiefly interested me during the course of my life. But such conclusions as I have come to have drifted about my mind like the wreckage of a foundered ship on a restless sea. It has seemed to me that if I set them down in some sort of order I should see for myself more distinctly what they really were and so might get some kind of coherence into them. I have long thought I should like to make such an attempt and more than once, when starting on a journey that was to last for several months, have determined to set about it. The opportunity seemed ideal. But I have always found that I was assailed by so many impressions, I saw so many strange things and met so many people who excited my fancy, that I had no time to reflect. The experience of the moment was so vivid that I could not attune my mind to introspection.

I have been held back also by the irksomeness of setting down my thoughts in my own person. For though I have written a good deal from this standpoint I have written as a novelist and so in a manner have been able to regard myself as a character in the story. Long habit has made it more comfortable for me to speak through the creatures of my invention. I can decide what they would think more readily than I can decide what I think myself. The one has always been a pleasure to me; the other has been a labour that I have willingly put off. But now I can afford to put it off no longer. In youth the years stretch before one so long that it is hard to realize that they will ever pass, and even in middle age, with the ordinary expectation of life in these days, it is easy to find excuses for delaying what one would like to do but does not want to; but at last a time comes when death must be considered. Here and there one's contemporaries drop off. We know that all men are mortal (Socrates was a man; therefore—and so forth), but it remains for us little more than a logical premiss till we are forced to recognize that in the ordinary course of things our end can no longer be remote. An occasional glance at the obituary column of *The Times* has suggested to me that the sixties are very unhealthy; I have long thought that it would exasperate me to die before I had written this book and so it seemed to me that I had better set about it at once. When I have finished it I can face the future with serenity, for I shall have rounded off my life's work. I can no longer persuade myself that I am not ready to write it, since if I have not by now made up my mind about the things that seem of importance to me there is small likelihood that I shall ever do so. I am glad at last to collect all these thoughts that for so long have floated at haphazard on the various levels of my consciousness. When they are written down I shall have finished with them and my mind will be free to occupy itself with other things. For I hope that this will not be the last book I shall write. One does not die immediately one has made one's will; one makes one's will as a precaution. To have settled one's affairs is a very good preparation to leading the rest of one's life without concern for the future. When I have finished this book I shall know where I stand. I can afford then to do what I choose with the years that remain to me.

4

It is inevitable that in it I should say many things that I have said before; that is why I have called it *The Summing Up*. When a judge sums up a case he recapitulates the facts that have been put before the jury and comments on the speeches of counsel. He does not offer new evidence. And since I have put the whole of my life into my books much of what I have to say will naturally have found a place in them. There are few subjects within the compass of my interests that I have not lightly or seriously touched upon. All I can attempt to do now is to give a coherent picture of my feelings and opinions; and here and there, maybe, to state with greater elaboration some idea which the limitations I have thought fit to accept in fiction and in the drama have only allowed me to hint at.

This book must be egotistic. It is about certain subjects that are important to me and it is about myself because I can only treat of these subjects as they have affected me. But it is not about my doings. I have no desire to lay bare my heart, and I put limits to the intimacy that I wish the reader to enter upon with me. There are matters on which I am content to maintain my privacy. No one can tell the whole truth about himself. It is not only vanity that has prevented those who have tried to reveal themselves to the world from telling the whole truth; it is direction of interest; their disappointment with themselves, their surprise that they can do things that seem to them so abnormal, make them place too great an emphasis on occurrences that are more common than they suppose. Rousseau in the course of his *Confessions* narrates incidents that have profoundly shocked the sensibility of mankind. By describing them so frankly he falsified his values and so gave them in his book a greater importance than they had in his life. There were events among a multitude of others, virtuous or at least neutral, that he omitted because they were too ordinary to seem worth recording. There is a sort of man who pays no attention to his good actions, but is tormented by his bad ones. This is the type that most often writes about himself. He leaves out his redeeming qualities and so appears only weak, unprincipled and vicious.

5

I write this book to disembarrass my soul of certain notions that have hovered about in it too long for my comfort. I do not speak to persuade anybody. I am devoid of the pedagogic instinct and when I know a thing never feel in myself the desire to impart it to others. I do not much care if people agree with me. Of course I think I am right, otherwise I should not think as I do, and they are wrong, but it does not offend me that they should be wrong. Nor does it greatly disturb me to discover that my judgment is at variance with that of the majority. I have a certain confidence in my instinct.

I must write as though I were a person of importance; and indeed, I am—to myself. To myself I am the most important person in the world; though I do not forget that, not even taking into consideration so grand a conception as the Absolute, but from the standpoint of common sense, I am of no consequence whatever. It would have made small difference to the universe if I had never existed. Though I may seem to write as though significance must necessarily be attached to certain of my works, I mean only that they are of moment to me for the purpose of any discussion during which I may have occasion to mention them. I think few serious writers, by which I do not only mean writers of serious things, can be entirely indifferent to the fate that will befall their works after their death. It is pleasant to think, not that one may achieve immortality (immortality for literary productions lasts in any case but a few hundred years and then is seldom more than the immortality of the schoolroom) but that one may be read with interest by a few generations and find a place, however small, in the history of one's country's literature. But so far as I am concerned, I look upon this modest possibility with scepticism. Even in my life I have seen writers who made much more stir in the world of letters than ever I have, sink into oblivion. When I was young George Meredith and Thomas Hardy seemed certain of survival. They have ceased to mean very much to the youth of today. From time to time they will doubtless find a critic in search of a subject to write an article about them, which may cause readers here and there to get out one or other of their books from a library; but I think it is clear that neither of them wrote anything that will be read as *Gulliver's Travels*, *Tristram Shandy* or *Tom Jones* is read.

If in the following pages I seem to express myself dogmatically, it is only because I find it very boring to qualify every phrase with an "I think" or "to my mind." Everything I say is merely an opinion of my own. The reader can take it or leave it. If he has the patience to read what follows he will see that there is only one thing about which I am certain, and this is that there is very little about which one can be certain.

Comments and Questions

1. In chapter 1, W. Somerset Maugham sharply criticizes the various inadequacies of politicians. Do you react favorably or unfavorably toward this criticism? Has Maugham used any devices to get a reader on his side in his quarrel with the politicians? Compare Maugham's strictures against the politicians with George Santayana's indictment of the United States in his Preface to *Character and Opinion in the United States*. Which writer handles adverse criticism better?

2. Maugham begins chapter 1 with the statement: "This is not an autobiography nor is it a book of recollections." Yet most of this chapter is filled with recollections. Study Maugham's technique in bridging the gap between his opening comment and the contents of most of the chapter.

3. In chapter 2 Maugham indicates that "it is with the common run of men that we writers have to deal." This manual contains discussions of a considerable number of writers, their books, and their fictional characters. Survey the characters mentioned in these articles, seeing to what extent they represent "the common run of men."

4. Do the first five chapters of *The Summing Up* create interest in reading the rest of the book? That is to say, has Maugham created any appetites in you as a reader? If he has, define with as great a precision as possible the nature of these appetites.

5. In chapter 4 Maugham writes: "This book must be egotistic"; in chapter 5 he writes: "It would have made small difference to the universe if I had never existed." Comment on the surface paradox here, and what these two statements, looked at in conjunction with one another, mean.

6. Review the various aims listed for writers of self-evaluations in the Introduction to this chapter. How many of these aims are discernable in Maugham's opening chapters? Use your answer to the question to arrive at a conclusion concerning the relative richness of these opening chapters.

E. B. WHITE

foreword to

ONE MAN'S MEAT

*O*ne thing about the war, it gives a man a feeling of guilt every time he finds himself doing some habitual or comfortable thing, like eating a good meal or getting out a book in springtime. He feels he ought to be discovered, if at all, in some more pertinent attitude—establishing a beachhead or applying a tourniquet to a general's thigh. A book concerned with the routine pleasures and troubles of a peaceable life is almost embarrassing. To publish it seems a bit of effrontery, or unawareness. The author feels that the blurb on the jacket should say: "There isn't time to read this book. Put it in your pocket, and when the moment arrives, throw it straight and hard."

I see that my publishers are announcing that this particular book is in the first person singular, a fact I had hoped to conceal from them by starting a few sentences with another word than I. But since it is in the open, I won't make any bones about it. The first person singular is the only grammatical implement I am able to use without cutting myself. As a matter of fact, this quality in the book is a thing which perhaps gives it some relation to the war. It is a book of, for, and by an individual. In this respect it is anathema to our enemies, who find in individualism the signs of national decay. It is the "I" in a man which Hitler has set out to destroy. I don't know what he proposes to substitute for it and I don't think *he* does. Individualism and the first person singular are closely related to freedom, and are what the fight is about. I've always believed that the individual was the thing, not men in the mass. Reformers and planners so often go wrong on this point. A tyrant, on the other hand, knows instinctively that he will get nowhere with his schemes unless he can persuade people to think not as individuals but as a group, or, better yet, not think at all.

I have yet to meet the common man, although I have heard his name mentioned in many circles. The fellow at my elbow in the subway is the uncommonest person imaginable. "Ordinary" is the word much used to describe him, but I find him wholly miraculous and I am sure he finds himself so. On this account I have never had any sympathy for what is called the "class struggle." So defined, and so prosecuted, it is a libel on Man the Animal, and is a poor presentation of a very important case, now being tried in the highest court and with order almost impossible to restore in the courtroom. To call the restlessness of men, and their unhappiness, and their yearnings, and their victimization, a "class struggle" is merely to intensify and dignify what one professes to abhor.

A man is no cinch, nor is he anything like the next man. (Ask any barber.) In their eagerness to improve his diet, the leaders of class warfare ignore Man's glandular life. Yet I know, as surely as I know anything, that it is not alone to the urgencies of his stomach that a man answers; the active thyroid, the importunate testes, the groping and adoring soul—all these compel and direct and betray. If a man were standard, if he were a tenth part as simple an organism as Hitler implies by the nature of his program, some antique tyrant would long since have solved the world's problems and given society some practical and effective form.

Here then is a book in a time of swords, a thought or two in a time of deeds, a celebration of life in a period of violent death. Here is a record of an individual pursuing the sort of peaceable and indulgent existence which may not soon again be ours in the same measure. I offer "One Man's Meat" not with any idea that it is meaty but with the sure knowledge that it is one man—one individual unlimited, with the hope of liberty and justice for all.

Quite a good deal has happened since the last entry in the book. The storm windows are down and the screens are up. The ice has left the pond and the frogs have begun their song of songs, deep in the heart of wetness. Sugaring is over with and the trees plugged. Eel traps have been set and have been entered by eels. The field behind the barn has been top-dressed and the upper piece across the road sowed to grass. Each afternoon three patrol planes go over and are mistaken for hawks by the young chickens. The blueberry piece has been burned. Smelts are running in the brooks, martins are nesting in their house on the pole, and the dogs have killed a skunk under the old shed behind the icehouse.

In February I registered in the third draft and from now on will do as I am told, cheerfully I trust. Lambs came in March and also a new electric brooder stove, the latter by express. Tails have been docked, bushes pruned, flower borders uncovered, bank boughs taken away; and peas and radishes and spinach and carrots are in. Rhubarb is beginning to show. Mayflowers have been reported fifteen miles away in the mayflower country. Blackout curtains are up at the kitchen windows, wild cucumber up at the kitchen door. Two spring pigs, a sow and a barrow, are working the dressing in the barn cellar. Both geese have laid and set, and all twenty-two eggs have been proved infertile. The gander's face is bright orange. He is on the skids.

Sugar rationing begins next week. Hen wire is hard to get, egg cases harder. Production in the hen pens is up, and prices of other things will soon be stabilized but not the price of eggs, which, like the hens themselves, will remain flighty. Spring recess is over and measles are almost over. I have built sideboards and a headboard for the truck, and in a day or two I will receive a siren to be mounted on the truck for notifying people on my stretch of road about air raids. The scow has been painted and launched. Counterweights have been rigged on the windows of the cold frame, for easier operation and smooth effortless control. The junkheap in the alders has been ransacked and the metal put back into circulation. Newspapers, magazines, and cardboard have been dispatched to the war. Apple trees have been sprayed and the north field has been limed.

The last jar of 1941 peas was broached yesterday at lunch, and the preserve closet in the cellar begins to look bare. A new fielder's glove has arrived from Sears and with it the early morning sound of a ball rolling off the barn roof and landing back up there again with a sharp plunk. This week we have had two visits from a great blue heron and one from the superintendent of schools. It has been an early spring and an eerie one. Already we have had evenings which have seemed more like July than April, as though summer were born prematurely and needed special care. Tonight is such a night. The warmth of afternoon held over through suppertime, and now the air has grown still. In the barnyard, among the wisps of dry straw which make a pattern on the brown earth, the sheep lie motionless and as yet unshorn, their great ruffs giving them a regal appearance, their placidity seemingly induced by the steady crying of the frogs. The unseasonable warmth invests the night with a quality of mystery and magnitude. And in the east beyond the lilac and beyond the barn and beyond the bay and behind the deepening hills, in slow and splendid surprise, rises the bomber's moon.

Comments and Questions

1. The structure of E. B. White's essay will repay study. Note particularly the questions he raises in his reader's mind when, in his opening paragraph, he ostensibly deprecates the very thing he is doing: bringing out a nonutilitarian book in a time of national emergency. A reader knows that White, in what follows, will justify the activity. What methods does White use to do this?

2. How would you characterize the tone of White's opening paragraph? How has he achieved it? Does it carry throughout the Foreword? Is there any connection between this tone and the theme of the Foreword? That is, does this tone help White say what he wants to say?

3. Halfway through his essay White remarks: "I offer 'One Man's Meat' not with any idea that it is meaty but with the sure knowledge that it is one man—one individual unlimited, with the hope of liberty and justice for all." White, in a word, promises his reader that the writing in the book will reflect a unique personality—that it will not be like the writing of anyone else. Examine your reaction to the Foreword in the light of this promise. What in the Foreword differentiates

White's writing from that of other essayists with which you are familiar? From the other essayists represented in this chapter?

4. Among other techniques, make a study of White's use of metaphors. How do they contribute to what the writer is saying, and to your concept of him as a unique individual?

5. At the beginning of his fifth paragraph White indulges in a series of paradoxes: "Here then is a book in a time of swords, a thought or two in a time of deeds, a celebration of life in a period of violent death." How central is paradox to White's Foreword as a whole, and what does the paradoxical content show about the personality of the writer?

6. The sixth paragraph represents, on the surface, something of a break in the Foreword. Whereas the first five paragraphs have been philosophical, the rest of the Foreword pictures the sights and sounds which surround the writer in his daily existence. Study this second half of White's essay carefully. Is there, beneath the surface difference, anything that relates the close of the Foreword to the opening? Re-examine the opening sentence of the fifth paragraph. To what extent, and in what way, does the close of White's Foreword exemplify this abstract, philosophical statement?

7. In the Introduction to this chapter the suggestion was made that White's Foreword attempts to justify the work, to advance a philosophy of life, and to reveal the writer as a unique personality. Decide to what extent you agree with this suggestion. If you agree that White achieves these multiple aims, decide how he does so. Does he fluctuate in his writing between satisfying first one aim and then another, or are these aims simultaneously met by the texture of the writing? Do you feel that the Foreword satisfies some of the other aims listed in the Introduction to this chapter?

Suggestions for an Essay

1. Select, at any point in the course, an essay which you have especially enjoyed writing. Write an essay concerning it. Decide which of the objectives mentioned in the Introduction to this chapter should be included in the essay. Keep in mind the dual task which this sort of writing assignment involves: *a.* the essay should throw whatever light necessary on the work with which it is concerned; *b.* the essay should make interesting reading in its own right, and reveal something of the personality of the writer.

2. After you have written your final research paper, write an essay concerning it, keeping in mind the instructions suggested in writing assignment 1, above.

3. At or near the close of the term, write an essay concerning your total writing experience during the term. Although this assignment will be concerned with more than one work, keep in mind the instructions suggested in writing assignment 1, above.

4. If you wish additional practice in the technique of comparison, write an essay comparing the personalities of any two of the essayists represented in this chapter, as these personalities find reflection in the essays. (See Chapter 3 for instructions concerning the writing of comparisons.)

TECHNIQUES OF RESEARCH AND CRITICAL WRITING

Note-Taking

As soon as a researcher has tentatively decided upon a subject, the need to take notes, to be used as the raw material for the research paper, presents itself. It is a truism among researchers that a scholarly paper can be no better than the notes which go into the making of it. Hence the necessity for good, complete, and adequate notes.

Although it is necessary to have plenty of notes on hand when one begins to write a research paper, it is ordinarily better to take notes somewhat slowly in the beginning stages of research, in order to avoid taking too many notes which will ultimately be of no use. Some preliminary groping, so far as note-taking is concerned, is of course an inescapable part of research. As a subject begins to define itself, the exact direction which the research will take seldom presents itself. One may initially become interested in "Conflicts in the Novels of Willa Cather," but decide later to narrow this subject to "Violence in the Novels of Willa Cather." Making this change still leaves unanswered the question of what to say about violence in Willa Cather, and hence what notes may most profitably be taken. The quality of note-taking, therefore, will improve as research progresses. In fact, it is frequently beneficial, during the latter stages of research, to do some re-reading in order to take additional notes whose value could not have been foreseen at the time of the preliminary reading.

For convenience in arranging them in orderly fashion when it comes time to write the paper, notes should be taken on note cards or rectangular pieces of paper. A 4 by 6 card is ordinarily of sufficient size, since only one idea should be written on each card. The practical reason for this lies in the use to which note cards will ultimately be put. When it is time to write the paper, the notes should be arranged in the order in which they will be used in the paper. Since there is no way of knowing, at the time notes are being taken, in what order they will be used, there is no way of knowing whether or not two notes, which may initially seem closely connected, will ultimately be used together. Hence, if a note card contains two ideas, they may very well have to be recopied onto separate cards later.

Beginning researchers frequently think of note-taking solely in terms of jotting down information found in source material. However, as this source material finds its way into the research paper, frequent occasion will arise for *interpreting,* in one way or another, its significance. If some specific idea occurs to the researcher in connection with a note he is taking, therefore, he should write his own comment on the note card for possible future use. Brackets ([   ]) should enclose this material in order to distinguish it from the notes themselves.

As research progresses, ideas will occasionally come to one at odd times concerning how some of the work being done can ultimately be used. Do not hesitate to jot down these flashes of inspiration onto note cards, for future reference.

The page or pages in source material from which information comes, as well as the source itself, should be written on each card. This latter necessity can be greatly expedited by giving a number to each book and article in a working bibliography. Then, on each note card, simply write the number which corresponds to the number of the source being used.

Although it may seem painstaking at the time, in the long run writing correct, complete sentences on note cards, rather than relying on fragments, phrases, and the like, will save time. These latter will be intelligible at the time they are written, but may not be later when it comes time to use them in writing a paper.

The question of whether to take down an idea in one's own words or verbatim in the words of the source inevitably presents itself. While no clear-cut rule, obviously, can be given, there is something to be said in favor of copying a source verbatim, unless the quote happens to be unusually long. It is often impossible for a researcher to tell, when he is taking a note, whether or not he will want to quote his source directly. If he takes down the quote verbatim, he can decide when it comes time to write the paper whether to quote directly, or whether to incorporate the idea into the essay using his own words. But if he has put down the idea on a note card in his own words, and later decides to quote directly, he will need to track down the source once more.

In paraphrasing information, as is at least occasionally necessary, here is a word of caution. Beginning researchers sometimes feel that they are taking down information in their own words, when they may actually be borrowing the exact phraseology of their source, perhaps only changing a word here and there, or omitting portions of the material. This type of pseudo-paraphrase should be studiously and rigorously avoided. Many sentences and passages which go onto note cards ultimately find their way into a researcher's final paper. If the phraseology and style of a source have found their way onto the note cards, this phraseology and style will almost inevitably turn up in the paper, where they will draw attention to themselves because of their difference from the writer's own style. A reader cannot be blamed for using this difference in phraseology and style to accuse a writer of plagiarism. Once a reader has made this accusation, the writer has lost him. So be very certain, in taking down notes in your own words, that the notes *really are in your own words*. If you find yourself copying phrases and parts of sentences out of source material, *enclose them in quotation marks.*

The Use of Quotations

In scholarly writing, the need to use direct quotations to document critical observations frequently presents itself. Since using quotations successfully is one of the more difficult expository techniques, it demands some special consideration.

Below is an article making use of a number of quotations, some short, some longer. Following the comments and questions about the article, the author has included a short explication of each quotation, telling why he used it.

Since most of the quotations in the article come from Chapter XXII of Mark Twain's *Huckleberry Finn,* this chapter from Twain's novel is reprinted in order to make available for study the source of the quotations.

MARION LEE [1]

Irony in Chapter XXII of HUCKLEBERRY FINN

*I*n the epidemic of recent articles on *Huckleberry Finn,* critics have demonstrated anew the literary truism that it is impossible ever to say the ultimate word about a literary masterpiece. Having apparently

---

[1] The given name of the author of this manual, who wrote the article for the March, 1958, issue of *Quivera,* a literary magazine published by the English Department of the Kansas State Teachers College of Emporia. Although I

become tired of commenting on the same old text, critics have begun the amusing and, I presume, harmless game of feuding among themselves with something approaching Grangerford-Shepherdson ferocity.

Most comments about *Huckleberry Finn* include some sort of consideration of the extent of Huck's moral development and powers of discernment. Much as critics are divided over such an issue as why Huck and Jim did not flee to Illinois for freedom—the Fugitive Slave Law of 1793 has recently been invoked to help answer this pressing question—there appears to be general agreement that Huck is a rather remarkably acute observer of Man, his stupidity, and his depravity. Although entering the feud can only be interpreted as compounding a folly, I wish to suggest that Huck has frequently been interpreted as a more discerning individual than the text of *Huckleberry Finn* itself indicates.

Two elements in the novel have contributed to the mistaken emphasis. One is the number of pious comments Huck utters throughout the book. Huck is fond of such observations as that "you can't pray a lie," [1] and that "human beings *can* be awful cruel to one another." [2] What needs emphasis is the platitudinous, conventional quality of these moral observations. Huck, whenever he feels called upon to offer moral comment, inevitably echoes the conventional platitudes of the society from which many critics have him fleeing. Some commentators have clothed the famous scene, in which Huck cannot bring himself to turn Jim over to the authorities, with all the import of the decision of the thief on the cross. Yet perhaps nowhere in the novel is the conventional nature of Huck's thinking more apparent. Huck will help Jim to freedom but, in so doing, is certain he will go to Hell, because he has violated the conventional standards of society.

Another reason some readers feel that Huck possesses remarkable moral sensitivity stems from the fact that the story is told from Huck's point of view, and from the fact that Huck witnesses scenes of human stupidity and depravity throughout the novel. Since the use of Huck as narrator tends to make the reader identify himself with Huck, there has apparently been a feeling on the part of many readers that Huck must surely have reacted as deeply to such scenes as the reader himself reacts. The irony of this interpretation is that the reader reacts as deeply as he does to the scenes of stupidity and depravity precisely because Huck does *not* react deeply. Twain relies heavily on Huck's relative lack of perception to accentuate the impact of evil within the book. A consideration of Chapter XXII will illustrate this.

---

would rather have used the work of someone else, I felt it would be valuable to the student to have an author tell why he used quotations in an article; that this would constitute taking the student behind the scenes, so to speak, in a way which could not be accomplished by comment on the work of another.

The numbers in brackets identify the quotations, as those quotations are listed in the commentary on their use.

The chapter falls logically into three distinct divisions. In the first, the mob goes to Colonel Sherburn's only to be cowed into submission by the Colonel's caustic words. Huck immediately goes to the circus which is in town, and his account of the circus constitutes the second part of the chapter. The third section, beginning with "Well, that night we had *our* show," [3] tells about the poor attendance the duke and king had at their show and how the duke, in an effort to increase attendance, printed handbills of the show which contained the announcement: "LADIES AND CHILDREN NOT ADMITTED." [4] The chapter closes with the duke's comment, "There, . . . if that line don't fetch them, I don't know Arkansaw!" [5]

The first and third divisions of the chapter contain some of Twain's bitterest indictment of "the damned human race." [6] Perhaps nowhere in all literature has the meanness of the mob spirit been evoked more effectively. Through Colonel Sherburn, as he faces down the mob, Twain has said as much as perhaps will ever need to be said about the true nature of mob violence. It is important to note that the bitter denunciation of the depravity, stupidity, and cowardice inherent in the mob spirit comes from Colonel Sherburn, not from Huck. Huck simply reports what the Colonel says. In this section of the chapter Huck offers next to no editorial comment; he is the detached observer, as he ordinarily is when reporting trouble. Huck offers only two subjective comments concerning the action. The first occurs at the end of the first sentence: "They swarmed up the street towards Sherburn's house, a-whooping and yelling and raging like Injuns, and everything had to clear the way or get run over and tromped to mush, and it was awful to see." [7] This sentence contains a species of irony which pervades the entire chapter. An ironic discrepancy exists between what Huck means by the phrase, "and it was awful to see," [8] and the meaning the reader attaches to it. Huck obviously means that it was awful to see the way in which those in the path of the mob were in danger of being "tromped to mush." [9] The question is not whether the onlookers actually were in danger of their lives (although I should imagine they were not). The point is that, to the adult reader, whatever danger the onlookers experienced is not what is awful to see: it is the mob spirit itself which is awful. Huck is unable to see beneath the surface. The reader does, and the impact of the mob scene is rendered all the more vivid and horrifying through being told by a youngster who cannot see its full significance.

Huck's only other subjective comment occurs when Colonel Sherburn steps out on the front porch and silences the mob. Huck remarks, "The stillness was awful creepy and uncomfortable." [10] The context and the absence of any other subjective comment concerning the mob suggest that Huck is simply experiencing a normal human reaction to sudden stillness following upon unusual confusion. Again, it is possible for a reader to see in the statement a portent of greater evil than Huck sees.

The second division of the chapter, Huck's visit to the circus, contains several elements which indicate that the mob affected Huck far less profoundly than it does the reader. The transitional paragraph between the first and second parts of the chapter itself contains a significant species of understatement. Huck tells how he gets into the circus:

> I went to the circus, and loafed around the back side till the watch-man went by, and then dived in under the tent. I had my twenty-dollar gold piece and some other money, but I reckoned I better save it, because there ain't no telling how soon you are going to need it, away from home and amongst strangers, that way. You can't be too careful. I ain't opposed to spending money on circuses, when there ain't no other way, but there ain't no use in *wasting* it on them. [11]

Huck has just witnessed humanity at its lowest ebb. What is his first comment? That you never know when you may need money when away from home and among strangers. The implication is that strangers are uncharitable. Huck feels so strongly about this that he is moved to moralize: "You can't be too careful." [12] Again, as in the first sentence of the chapter, irony exists in the discrepancy between Huck's warning the reader about needing money among strangers, and the impression of humanity that the reader brings from the mob scene. The reader would have far more serious warnings to issue about strangers than never to be caught among them without change.

Huck's ironical understatement throughout the paragraph, and throughout the entire chapter, is unconscious. Huck is not Swift, delib-erately using ironical understatement to emphasize a point. Huck is earnest in his advice, in what he says to the reader. The emphasis is all the more vivid because the irony is unconscious. If any proof is needed for a point which seems so obvious, it should be found in Huck's almost complete naïveté at the circus. Someone who can be fooled as Huck is fooled by the circus performers is not the sophisticated individ-ual we associate with the conscious use of ironical statement.

Another indication of Huck's lack of moral sensitivity is the extreme rapidity with which he goes to the circus from the mob scene. This constitutes another discrepancy between Huck's reaction to the mob, and the reaction of the reader. The description of the mob scene scarcely leaves the adult reader in a circus mood. What is Huck's attitude? "It was a real bully circus." [13]

Huck's description of the circus contains a notable difference in tone from his description of the mob. In the mob scene Huck is reportorial. In his description of the circus he is poetical, one might almost say rhapsodical:

> It was a real bully circus. It was the splendidest sight that ever was, when they all come riding in, two and two, a gentleman and lady, side by side, the men just in their drawers and under-shirts, and no shoes nor stirrups, and resting their hands on their thighs, easy and comfortable— there must a' been twenty of them—and every lady with a lovely com-

plexion, and perfectly beautiful, and looking just like a gang of real sure-enough queens, and dressed in clothes that cost millions of dollars, and just littered with diamonds. It was a powerful fine sight; I never see anything so lovely. And then one by one they got up and stood, and went a-weaving around the ring so gentle and wavy and graceful, the men looking ever so tall and airy and straight, with their heads bobbing and skimming along, away up there under the tent-roof, and every lady's rose-leafy dress flapping soft and silky around her hips, and she looking like the most loveliest parasol. [14]

This middle section of the book generates irony within irony. First there is the obvious discrepancy between what the reader knows the circus performers to be, and Huck's impression of them. The performers, to Huck, are ladies and gentlemen. Their clothes are covered with diamonds, and must have cost millions of dollars. This is one level of irony; another exists in the discrepancy between Huck's eulogy of mankind in the persons of the circus performers, and the impression of mankind the reader takes with him from the mob scene. This deeper level of irony makes what on the surface appears a chapter lacking unity one of the most artistic things Twain ever wrote. As Huck commends the circus performers, who are, by virtue of their profession, only make-believe people, the reader is forced to juxtapose Huck's commendation of them against the only too real people who have just confronted Colonel Sherburn.

In the third section of the chapter Huck again, as in the first section, returns to his role of reporter. The duke, by printing "LADIES AND CHILDREN NOT ADMITTED" [15] on his handbill, displays a mature knowledge of human psychology, its interest in the risqué, the obscene. In this section Huck, in contrast to the second part, offers no commentary. It is the duke, not Huck, who says, "There, . . . if that line don't fetch them, I don't know Arkansaw!" [16]

Chapter XXII presents various unpleasant aspects of the human condition in the American scene as observed through the eyes of a youngster who obviously does not discern their full import. They are all the more terrifying because viewed from this unbiased view. Had some adult, some moral reformer, told the incidents in Chapter XXII, and offered, as he surely would have felt obliged to offer, some moral comment, we might accuse him of being prejudiced, and of having given a biased interpretation of the facts. Huck is not prejudiced. Therefore, the facts as he gives them stand out in all their naked, unadorned ugliness.

Other scenes throughout the novel could be cited in which Huck does not see the deeper significance behind appearances. One of *Huckleberry Finn*'s several important levels of meaning is the picture it affords throughout of human depravity and stupidity. This picture, behind the veil of appearance, is rendered all the more powerful through being told us by a boy who does not himself realize the full enormity of much that he reports. Huck's voyage down the Mississippi has been called a spiritual odyssey. And so it is. But it is not Huck's. It is our own.

Comments and Questions

1. Every direct quotation should be smoothly introduced, so that the reader may effortlessly make the transition from the essay itself to the quotation. Are the quotations in this essay properly introduced?

2. Every direct quotation, after it has been quoted, should be explicated in any way which the quotation, and the context, demand. In other words, a writer needs to tell his reader *why* he included the quotation, and what it means to him. (Proper explication of direct quotations is frequently left undone by writers who, erroneously, assume that because *they* know why they included the quotations, readers will automatically know why also.) Are the quotations in this essay properly explicated?

3. Although most critical writing makes use of direct quotations, these direct quotations inevitably constitute something of an interruption of what the writer is saying. They should therefore be used *only* when they are necessary to make the essay stronger than it would otherwise be. Study the quotations in this essay from this point of view. Are specific reasons evident for the inclusion of each direct quotation, or could some of them have been omitted?

4. Whenever a writer mentions a source, he has to make a choice between quoting the source directly or paraphrasing it. Make a study of the places in this essay which simply allude to *Huckleberry Finn,* but do not quote directly from it. Should some of these allusions and paraphrases have been direct quotations?

5. Since any direct quotation constitutes an interruption of the essay, it follows that the longer the quotation, the greater the interruption. Notice that direct quotations 11 and 14, although not exceedingly long, are somewhat extended in comparison with the other quotations. Do their contexts, and the purposes they serve, justify their length?

6. Notice that direct quotations 8, 9, 12, 15, and 16 *repeat* material which has previously been quoted. Is this a flaw in the essay, or is this repetition justified?

7. Although any direct quotation constitutes an interruption, this interruption can be minimized if what immediately precedes the direct quotation seems naturally to lead into it, and what immediately succeeds it seems naturally to follow. In other words, even though a direct quotation and what surrounds it constitute the work of two writers, the essay as a whole should read as smoothly as though everything in it had been written by a single writer. How nearly does this essay approach this ideal?

Commentary on the Use of Quotations

Quotations 1 and 2. Huck's exact phraseology helps accentuate what the article calls the "platitudinous, conventional quality" of Huck's moralizing.

Quotation 3. This quotation acts as a signpost, showing the reader exactly where, according to the article, the break between the second and third parts of the chapter occurs.

Quotations 4 and 5. These two quotations, representing the duke's point of view, contribute toward a definition of the article's central thesis, which is the contrast between Huck's relative ingenuousness, as a youngster, and the disingenuousness of adults. Used here, the quotations act as a forecast of quotations 15 and 16, where they are reiterated and explicated.

Quotation 6. This favorite expression of Twain's, which he employed to characterize Mankind, finds a place in the article because it fits the context so exactly.

Quotation 7. This quotation enters the enemy camp. In building up a picture of Huck as incapable of seeing fully beneath appearance, the article relies heavily on the almost—but not quite—entire lack of subjective comment on Huck's part during the mob scene. This being the case, it was particularly necessary to bring into the open whatever subjective comment Huck *does* make, in order to avoid the appearance of slanting the argument.

Quotation 8. Reiterating the phrase, "and it was awful to see," proved easier than attempting to paraphrase it. Allowing a reader to hear the phrase repeated from quotation 7 serves, as well, to tie together quotation 7 and the explication of it.

Quotation 9. The reasons for quoting directly in this instance are identical to those given for quotation 8. In addition, readiness to repeat Huck's pungent phraseology exhibits a willingness to bring into the open what on the surface might seem to contravert the article at this point.

Quotation 10. This quotation represents the only other subjective comment Huck offers concerning the mob scene. The reasons for quoting directly are the same as those given for quotation 7.

Quotation 11. Allowing a reader actually to *hear* Huck as he moves effortlessly from the mob scene to the circus reinforces the picture of Huck as ingenuous.

Quotation 12. This quotation sets the stage for the contrast drawn between Huck's moralizing about mankind and what an adult reader coming from the mob scene might have said.

Quotation 13. As in the case of quotation 12, this quotation helps underscore the difference between Huck's reaction to the circus and the reaction an adult reader, fresh from a scene of mob violence, might well have experienced.

Quotation 14. Huck's own words at this point define what the article means when it speaks of Huck's "poetical" and "rhapsodical" reaction to the circus. Since this passage is explicated at some length, putting the quotation before a reader constitutes, as well, a service to him.

Quotations 15 and 16. These quotations, which were previously quoted (quotations 4 and 5) by way of forecast, render more vivid the contrast made throughout the article between Huck's reaction to the human condition and the reaction of an adult. Letting a reader hear the duke's exact phraseology defines more forcefully what the article calls his "mature knowledge of human psychology, its interest in the risqué, the obscene," than any amount of commentary could have done.

MARK TWAIN

chapter XXII of

HUCKLEBERRY FINN

[In the part of the novel immediately preceding this chapter, Huck's journey down the Mississippi River, accompanied by Nigger Jim and the rascally king and duke, has been interrupted by a stop at a small village near the river. Here Huck, fresh from the Shepherdson-Grangerford feud, witnesses a murder. Colonel Sherburn, exasperated at the crudity of "old Boggs," a local drunk, shoots and kills him. After satisfying their morbid curiosity by a close scrutiny of the corpse, Colonel Sherburn's townsmen decide that conditions are right for a lynching, and move toward the Colonel's house. Huck, who is Twain's narrator throughout the book, continues his story.]

They swarmed up the street towards Sherburn's house, a-whooping and yelling and raging like Injuns, and everything had to clear the way or get run over and tromped to mush, and it was awful to see. Children was heeling it ahead of the mob, screaming and trying to get out of the way; and every window along the road was full of women's heads, and there was nigger boys in every tree, and bucks and wenches looking over every fence; and as soon as the mob would get nearly to them they would break and skaddle back out of reach. Lots of the women and girls was crying and taking on, scared most to death.

They swarmed up in front of Sherburn's palings as thick as they could jam together, and you couldn't hear yourself think for the noise. It was a little twenty-foot yard. Some sung out "Tear down the fence! tear down the fence!" Then there was a racket of ripping and tearing and smashing, and down she goes, and the front wall of the crowd begins to roll in like a wave.

Just then Sherburn steps out on to the roof of his little front porch, with a double-barrel gun in his hand, and takes his stand, perfectly ca'm and deliberate, not saying a word. The racket stopped, and the wave sucked back.

Sherburn never said a word—just stood there, looking down. The still-ness was awful creepy and uncomfortable. Sherburn run his eye slow along the crowd; and wherever it struck, the people tried a little to outgaze him, but they couldn't; they dropped their eyes and looked sneaky. Then pretty soon Sherburn sort of laughed; not the pleasant kind, but the kind that makes you feel like when you are eating bread that's got sand in it.

Then he says, slow and scornful:

"The idea of *you* lynching anybody! It's amusing. The idea of you thinking you had pluck enough to lynch a *man!* Because you're brave enough to tar and feather poor friendless cast-out women that come along here, did that make you think you had grit enough to lay your hands on a *man?* Why, a *man's* safe in the hands of ten thousand of your kind —as long as it's day-time and you're not behind him.

"Do I know you? I know you clear through. I was born and raised in the South, and I've lived in the North; so I know the average all around. The average man's a coward. In the North he lets anybody walk over him that wants to, and goes home and prays for a humble spirit to bear it. In the South one man, all by himself, has stopped a stage full of men, in the day-time, and robbed the lot. Your newspapers call you a brave people so much that you think you *are* braver than any other people—whereas you're just *as* brave, and no braver. Why don't your juries hang murderers? Because they're afraid the man's friends will shoot them in the back, in the dark—and it's just what they *would* do.

"So they always acquit; and then a *man* goes in the night, with a hundred masked cowards at his back, and lynches the rascal. Your mis-take is, that you didn't bring a man with you; that's one mistake, and the other is that you didn't come in the dark, and fetch your masks. You brought *part* of a man—Buck Harkness, there—and if you hadn't had him to start you, you'd a taken it out in blowing.

"You didn't want to come. The average man don't like trouble and danger. *You* don't like trouble and danger. But if only *half* a man—like Buck Harkness, there—shouts 'Lynch him, lynch him!' you're afraid to back down—afraid you'll be found out to be what you are—*cowards*—

and so you raise a yell, and hang yourselves onto that half-a-man's coat tail, and come raging up here, swearing what big things you're going to do. The pitifulest thing out is a mob; that's what an army is—a mob; they don't fight with courage that's born in them, but with courage that's borrowed from their mass, and from their officers. But a mob without any *man* at the head of it, is *beneath* pitifulness. Now the thing for *you* to do, is to droop your tails and go home and crawl in a hole. If any real lynching's going to be done, it will be done in the dark, Southern fashion; and when they come they'll bring their masks, and fetch a *man* along. Now *leave*—and take your half-a-man with you"—tossing his gun up across his left arm and cocking it, when he says this.

The crowd washed back sudden, and then broke all apart and went tearing off every which way, and Buck Harkness he heeled it after them, looking tolerable cheap. I could a staid, if I'd a wanted to, but I didn't want to.

I went to the circus, and loafed around the back side till the watchman went by, and then dived in under the tent. I had my twenty-dollar gold piece and some other money, but I reckoned I better save it, because there ain't no telling how soon you are going to need it, away from home and amongst strangers, that way. You can't be too careful. I ain't opposed to spending money on circuses, when there ain't no other way, but there ain't no use in *wasting* it on them.

It was a real bully circus. It was the splendidest sight that ever was, when they all come riding in, two and two, a gentleman and lady, side by side, the men just in their drawers and under-shirts, and no shoes nor stirrups, and resting their hands on their thighs, easy and comfortable —there must a' been twenty of them—and every lady with a lovely complexion, and perfectly beautiful, and looking just like a gang of real sure-enough queens, and dressed in clothes that cost millions of dollars, and just littered with diamonds. It was a powerful fine sight; I never see anything so lovely. And then one by one they got up and stood, and went a-weaving around the ring so gentle and wavy and graceful, the men looking ever so tall and airy and straight, with their heads bobbing and skimming along, away up there under the tent-roof, and every lady's rose-leafy dress flapping soft and silky around her hips, and she looking like the most loveliest parasol.

And then faster and faster they went, all of them dancing, first one foot stuck out in the air and then the other, the horses leaning more and more, and the ring-master going round and round the centre-pole, cracking his whip and shouting "hi!—hi!" and the clown cracking jokes behind him; and by-and-by all hands dropped the reins, and every lady put her knuckles on her hips and every gentleman folded his arms, and then how the horses did lean over and hump themselves! And so, one after the other they all skipped off into the ring, and made the sweetest bow I ever see, and then scampered out, and everybody clapped their hands and went just about wild.

Well, all through the circus they done the most astonishing things; and all the time that clown carried on so it most killed the people. The ring-master couldn't ever say a word to him but he was back at him quick as a wink with the funniest things a body ever said; and how he ever *could* think of so many of them, and so sudden and so pat, was what I couldn't noway understand. Why, I couldn't a thought of them in a year. And by-and-by a drunk man tried to get into the ring—said he wanted to ride; said he could ride as well as anybody that ever was. They argued and tried to keep him out, but he wouldn't listen, and the whole show come to a standstill. Then the people begun to holler at him and make fun of him, and that made him mad, and he begun to rip and tear; so that stirred up the people, and a lot of men begun to pile down off of the benches and swarm towards the ring, saying, "Knock him down! throw him out!" and one or two women begun to scream. So, then, the ring-master he made a little speech, and said he hoped there wouldn't be no disturbance, and if the man would promise he wouldn't make no more trouble, he would let him ride, if he thought he could stay on the horse. So everybody laughed and said all right, and the man got on. The minute he was on, the horse begun to rip and tear and jump and cavort around, with two circus men hanging onto his bridle trying to hold him, and the drunk man hanging onto his neck, and his heels flying in the air every jump, and the whole crowd of people standing up shouting and laughing till the tears rolled down. And at last, sure enough, all the circus men could do, the horse broke loose, and away he went like the very nation, round and round the ring, with that sot laying down on him and hanging to his neck, with first one leg hanging most to the ground on one side, and then t'other one on t'other side, and the people just crazy. It warn't funny to me, though; I was all of a tremble to see his danger. But pretty soon he struggled up astraddle and grabbed the bridle, a-reeling this way and that; and the next minute he sprung up and dropped the bridle and stood! and the horse agoing like a house afire too. He just stood up there, a-sailing around as easy and comfortable as if he warn't ever drunk in his life—and then he begun to pull off his clothes and sling them. He shed them so thick they kind of clogged up the air, and altogether he shed seventeen suits. And then, there he was, slim and handsome, and dressed the gaudiest and prettiest you ever saw, and he lit into that horse with his whip and made him fairly hum—and finally skipped off, and made his bow and danced off to the dressing-room, and everybody just a-howling with pleasure and astonishment.

Then the ring-master he see how he had been fooled, and he *was* the sickest ring-master you ever see, I reckon. Why, it was one of his own men! He had got up that joke all out of his own head, and never let on to nobody. Well, I felt sheepish enough, to be took in so, but I wouldn't a been in that ring-master's place, not for a thousand dollars. I don't know; there may be bullier circuses than what that one was, but

I never struck them yet. Anyways it was plenty good enough for *me;* and wherever I run across it, it can have all of *my* custom, every time.

Well, that night we had *our* show; but there warn't only about twelve people there; just enough to pay expenses. And they laughed all the time, and that made the duke mad; and everybody left, anyway, before the show was over, but one boy which was asleep. So the duke said these Arkansaw lunkheads couldn't come up to Shakspeare; what they wanted was low comedy—and may be something ruther worse than low comedy, he reckoned. He said he could size their style. So next morning he got some big sheets of wrapping-paper and some black paint, and drawed off some handbills and stuck them up all over the village. The bills said:

AT THE COURT HOUSE!
FOR 3 NIGHTS ONLY!
The World-Renowned Tragedians
DAVID GARRICK THE YOUNGER!
AND
EDMUND KEAN THE ELDER!
*Of the London and Continental
Theatres,*
In their Thrilling Tragedy of
THE KING'S CAMELOPARD,
OR
THE ROYAL NONESUCH!!!
Admission 50 cents.

Then at the bottom was the biggest line of all—which said:

LADIES AND CHILDREN NOT ADMITTED.

"There," says he, "if that line don't fetch them, I don't know Arkansaw!"

The Uses and Abuses of Secondary Sources in Research Writing

No scholar cares to publish his findings on any subject without first making himself aware of what other writers have had to say. In the first place, a researcher needs to avoid the danger of announcing to the world an idea which, while it may be new to him, may actually be—if not as old as the hills—ten or twenty years old, which is just as bad. Assume, for example, that a research scholar or critic, reading Willa Cather's *The Professor's House* in 1960, happens to be struck by the way in which Willa Cather's death theme finds symbolic expression in terms of houses, and by the way in which this symbolic expression gives coherence to a book which, on the surface, appears lacking in unity. Should this researcher write an article putting forth this idea, and should the article find its way past an unwary editor and into print (which, mercifully, would be extremely unlikely), our researcher would find himself in the embarrassing position of having announced to the world the same idea which E. K. Brown had announced seven years earlier in his critical biography of Willa Cather (see Chapter 4). Reading what other writers have said about one's subject, then, becomes a simple matter of self-protection. Our hypothetical researcher might have read every work concerning Willa Cather *except* Brown's book, and still be unaware of Brown's interpretation of *The Professor's House*—hence the need, ideally, to read everything that has been written about one's subject. While a student, during a limited period devoted to research, will ordinarily not be able to approximate this ideal, it will be possible, and highly desirable, to read widely enough in secondary sources to get the feel of what has been written. If the press of time makes it necessary to choose from among secondary sources, it may be helpful to choose recent books, since writers—often in their prefaces— not uncommonly give a résumé of previous scholarship concerning their subject.

A second, and allied, reason for being familiar with what previous researchers have written is that such familiarity allows one authoritatively to indicate the exact nature of the original contribution he is making. The originality of this contribution may lie in one of three categories:

1. A writer may strike out in a new direction altogether. (See Professor Randall Stewart's critical review of R. H. Fogle's *Hawthorne's Fiction: The Light and the Dark,* reprinted in Chapter 7, where the reviewer indicates that Fogle's work owes nothing specifically to previous scholarship.) In such a case, obviously, it is essential for a scholar to know all that has been written about his subject, in order to have assurance that his contribution *is* unique.

2. A writer may disagree with another's findings, or with a more or less established critical position. (See E. K. Brown's essay on Willa Cather's *The Professor's House,* reprinted in Chapter 4, where, by way of justifying his essay, he remarks that, in his opinion, Porterfield has been guilty of misreading the book.)

3. A writer may develop fully an idea which a previous scholar has merely touched in passing.

But reading the work of other scholars frequently carries broader benefits than the opportunity of noting specific instances of agreement or disagreement. An intelligent and literate research scholar or critic who has spent a great amount of time studying a given subject will quite likely make some observations about that subject which would not have occurred to another student, who may be equally intelligent and literate. The work of another scholar not infrequently has the ability to act as a catalytic agent for another's thoughts and impressions.

A word should be said about the use of secondary sources for the purpose of reinforcing one's own opinions. This practice should be indulged in very sparingly. Any scholarly paper, after all, should represent some contribution, however modest, to the sum of human knowledge. If this is the case, the paper will of course not only be able to stand alone, without support from previous researchers, but will, to the extent that its contribution *is* original, be *obliged* to stand alone. It is occasionally permissible, and perhaps even desirable, to cite another writer in establishing the validity of some tangential point. But if an essay is punctuated with "As Professor Blank has so aptly put it . . ." a reader will very shortly assume that the writer has nothing new to contribute, that he is merely paraphrasing Professor Blank, and that it might be better to read Professor Blank in the original.

Above all, a writer should keep *his* ideas uppermost in his writing, never allowing secondary sources to overshadow his own thinking. Student researchers sometimes assume that, because of their relative inexperience, they cannot contribute anything original. Nothing could be farther from the truth. The province of research is wide. The last word has not yet been said. The writer's own ideas, not the ideas of those laboring in the same or in a neighboring vineyard, must be kept central.

Footnoting

The footnoting of a scholarly work constitutes the garb in which the writer presents his thoughts. In one sense this outward apparel is not nearly so important as what it clothes. In another sense it is equally as important. Whether one should make the analogy from "clothes make the man" to "proper footnoting makes the scholarly paper" is more than doubtful. But the converse, that "improper footnoting unmakes the scholarly paper," is most certainly true. Proper footnoting, after all, is a rather mechanical matter and consists largely in following the scholarly fashions of the day. The relative simplicity with which proper footnoting can be accomplished augments the danger of doing it improperly. For if something is done improperly which, after all, is not difficult, such a failure will reflect a sloppy, undisciplined mind, one which is averse to, or incapable of, following directions.

Reprinted below is a scholarly article containing a considerable number of footnotes. Following the article is an analysis and interpretation of these footnotes. Studying the footnotes, together with the commentary concerning them, should give a beginning researcher all, or almost all, of the information he needs to document a research paper correctly.

VIRGINIA OGDEN BIRDSALL

Hawthorne's Fair-Haired Maidens: The Fading Light

*P*robably no reader of Hawthorne's four major novels can have failed to notice the similarities which exist among certain of the participating heroines. It would seem that if a lady had handled her first assignment well, Hawthorne could nearly always manage to find a place for her in his next production. Hence, not only did Hester of *The Scarlet Letter* turn up again as Zenobia in *The Blithedale Romance* and as Miriam in *The Marble Faun,* but, even more obviously, Phoebe of *The House of the Seven Gables* later found parts as Priscilla in *Blithedale* and Hilda in *The Marble Faun.*

Yet various critics of these romances have suggested that Hawthorne may well have felt himself to be haunted rather than actually won over by such ladies as Phoebe, Priscilla, and Hilda, and that his attitude toward them remained always ambivalent. Subconsciously, they point out, he seems to have felt attracted to the dark ladies and to have thought the fair maidens a little dull and wishy-washy, even though on the conscious level of plot spinning he insisted that the dark ladies be either punished or killed off and that the fair maidens be allowed to carry the day.[1] It is interesting, in this connection, to ask oneself just what Hawthorne did require of these fair-haired, gentle creatures of his own imagination—his rays of sunshine in a gloomy world, his kindlers and maintainers of the reassuring household fire. And in seeking the answer, one fact becomes startlingly clear: that these bright redeemers are not, after all, mere representatives of a static type. On the contrary, Hawthorne's attitude toward them and the roles he gives them to play change significantly and sometimes even drastically from book to book.

There can be little question, of course, that Hawthorne saw this

---

[1] See Frederic I. Carpenter, "Puritans Preferred Blondes," *NEQ,* IX (June 1936), 253–272, and Philip Rahv, "The Dark Lady of Salem," *PR,* VIII (September-October 1941), 362–381. Rahv calls Hawthorne's blondes "the sexually anesthetic females to whom he officially paid homage" and his dark woman "a dream-image of sexual bliss" (p. 369).

type of woman as functioning in a specific way with reference to the world around her. In her he envisioned a purity which existed nowhere else except in children. Through the medium of her soul the world might be seen and comprehended more clearly. Through her love, a man might find his place in the chain of humanity. Ideally, she was, like Phoebe, "a religion in herself, warm, simple, true, with a substance that could walk on earth, and a spirit that was capable of heaven." [2] Or, in a nutshell, she was the village uncle's Susan:

A slender maiden, though the child of rugged parents, she had the slimmest of all waists, brown hair curling on her neck, and a complexion rather pale, except when the sea-breeze flushed it. A few freckles became beauty-spots beneath her eyelids. How was it, Susan, that you talked and acted so carelessly, yet always for the best. . . . And whence had you that happiest gift of brightening every topic with an unsought gayety, quiet but irresistible, so that even gloomy spirits felt your sunshine, and did not shrink from it? Nature wrought the charm. She made you a frank, simple, kind-hearted, sensible, and mirthful girl. Obeying nature, you did free things without indelicacy, displayed a maiden's thoughts to every eye, and proved yourself as innocent as naked Eve.
It was beautiful to observe how her simple and happy nature mingled itself with mine. She kindled a domestic fire within my heart, and took up her dwelling there, even in that chill and lonesome cavern, hung round with glittering icicles of fancy. She gave me warmth of feeling, while the influence of my mind made her contemplative.[3]

The description would do just as well for Phoebe, but in spite of the curling brown hair, the sunshine, and the New England background, it is significant to note that it will not quite do for Priscilla and even less will it altogether suffice for Hilda. For Priscilla, as well as Hilda, another description from one of Hawthorne's sketches perhaps comes closer: "Here was the pure, modest, sensitive, and shrinking woman of America,—shrinking when no evil is intended, and sensitive like diseased flesh, that thrills if you but point at it; and strangely modest, without confidence in the modesty of other people; and admirably pure, with such a quick apprehension of all impurity." [4] Apparently, Hawthorne's ambivalent attitude toward his symbol of innocence and purity pre-dated even the first of his major novels. Nor would the ambivalence appear to have been only sex-motivated. On the moral level also, Hawthorne saw that self-conscious purity could lead to preciousness.

---

[2] *The Novels and Tales of Nathaniel Hawthorne,* ed. Norman Holmes Pearson (New York, 1937), p. 343. References to this volume will hereafter be indicated by parentheses in the text.
[3] Nathaniel Hawthorne, "The Village Uncle," *Twice-Told Tales II* (Boston and New York, 1900), pp. 109-110.
[4] Nathaniel Hawthorne, "Sketches from Memory," *Mosses from an Old Manse* (Boston, 1883), p. 490. Since this description, in context, is included as part of a satirical comment on English travellers in America, it reflects a point of view with which Hawthorne probably did not agree. The fact remains, however, that such ideas were present in his mind.

Yet between Phoebe and Priscilla, Priscilla and Hilda the meaningful differences lie not so much in their varying degrees of self-consciousness as in their varying degrees of effectiveness in their given roles as mediums, conservers, and redeemers. In short, does what they stand for really matter? Is purity and innocence the really important thing, and in fact, can such qualities exist at all in the real world? In the *Seven Gables,* Hawthorne would seem to answer these questions with a vigorous affirmative. But in *Blithedale* there is uncertainty in his affirmation, and in *The Marble Faun* of several years later the uncertainty has become a genuine doubt.

One of the most apparent evidences of this shifting attitude lies in the decreasingly important part which Hawthorne allows his brown-haired maiden to play. In many ways Phoebe is the central figure in the *Seven Gables.* Not only does she have the largest number of lines to speak, but her sunny cheerfulness shines pervasively on each of the other characters, on the garden, and on the house itself. No one and nothing that matters remains untouched by her genial influence. But what of Priscilla and Hilda? It is true that in *The Blithedale Romance* each of the major characters is, to some extent, damned or saved in accordance with his relationship to Priscilla. Yet she has faded into the background as a character, and the colorful figures of Zenobia and Hollingsworth have virtually blotted her out. And in *The Marble Faun,* Miriam has become the figure whose influence is significant,[5] and Hilda is left to be little more than an onlooker, except in the circumscribed sphere in which she and Kenyon move.

The question as to Phoebe's, Priscilla's, and Hilda's relative effectiveness can, then, be put more specifically. As Hawthorne's vision broadened from the narrow confines of a house and garden to the expanded environs of a Utopian community[6] and finally to the "perplexed and troubled world" of Rome, did he, either consciously or unconsciously, find the answers his brown-haired maiden could supply inadequate? Or the question might perhaps be phrased another way. As Hawthorne came to know more of the evils and complexities of life, did he find human innocence less believable and less influential? It would be only a modest overstatement to say that in the *Seven Gables* the guilty are raised up by the innocent, while in *The Marble Faun* the innocent are pulled down by the guilty.

This is not to imply, of course, that in the *Seven Gables* Hawthorne

---

[5] For a convincing statement of this somewhat controversial position, see Darrel Abel, "A Masque of Love and Death," *UTQ,* XXIII (October 1953), 9–25. "Through their association with Miriam, all the other characters enact their roles. That is, we see what happens when worldly experience enters the lives of nature and instinct, of egotism and the conviction of sin, of innocence and Puritan orthodoxy and of art" (p. 21).

[6] Philip Rahv suggests that the relationship between Coverdale and Zenobia is "intrinsically the relationship between New England and the world" ("The Dark Lady of Salem," p. 378).

was an easy optimist. The new Eden to which Phoebe and Holgrave set out in the final chapter seems an unconvincing, fairy-tale contrivance and promises to become little more than a new beginning of the same old cycle. But the cheerfulness and the possibilities for redemption which Phoebe brings into the old house *are* convincing; and if she seems somewhat sentimentalized in the manner of Richardson's Pamela,[7] still Hawthorne believed in her and loved her, and so can we, with only minor reservations. The critic who suggests, however, that with Hester, Hawthorne had renounced experience once and for all and that thereafter the "victory of the blonde principle of purity" [8] is assured, has not bothered to look below the superficial level of plot in the two later novels. Hester has been left out of account altogether in the *Seven Gables*, but in *Blithedale* and *The Marble Faun* she is back again, and the "principle of purity" seems to pale into insignificance before her regal advance.

At this juncture, a line from Hawthorne's *English Notebooks*, which describes the smoke-blackened walls of St. Paul's, does not seem hopelessly beside the point. "It is much better than staring white," he observed, "the edifice would not be nearly so grand without this drapery of black." [9] Priscilla and Hilda may live happily ever after and Zenobia and Miriam may be duly punished for their wickedness, but Zenobia's life has had more richness in it than Priscilla's sterile existence could achieve if she lived to be a hundred; and Miriam displays a depth of human warmth and complexity beside which Hilda's white purity seems a spiritual dead end. In a sense, then, experience can be said to have triumphed in these later romances simply by virtue of the superior fullness and human reality of its representatives.

Nor do Priscilla and Hilda come off much better as spokesmen for the New England moral tradition. Like Phoebe, both of them are to some extent conservatives and hence defenders of the status quo. But while Phoebe, "a part of whose essence it was to keep within the limits of law" (p. 294), triumphs over Holgrave's radicalism,[10] Priscilla's lawfulness amounts to little more than a feeble, instinctive protest against an unorthodox idea, and Hilda, finding that in Rome her beliefs are challenged wherever she turns, seems painfully unsure of her answers. "Can the faith in which I was born and bred be perfect," she asks, "if it leave a weak girl like me to wander, desolate, with this great trouble crushing

---

[7] Morton Cronin, "Hawthorne on Romantic Love and the Status of Women," *PMLA*, LXIX (March 1954), 97.

[8] Carpenter, "Puritans Preferred Blondes," p. 262.

[9] Nathaniel Hawthorne, "Up the Thames," *Our Old Home* (Boston and New York, 1900), p. 370n.

[10] "The happy man," says Holgrave to Phoebe, "inevitably confines himself within ancient limits. I have a presentiment that, hereafter, it will be my lot to set out trees, to make fences,—perhaps, even, in due time, to build a house for another generation,—in a word, to conform myself to laws, and the peaceful practice of society. Your poise will be more powerful than any oscillating tendency of mine" (p. 428).

me down" (p. 794)? Often she even refuses to face the evil realities which confront her—as when she sees Miriam kneel before the model on the steps of the fountain; and it is apparent that she feels a desperate need to find a mother, whether it be in the Virgin whose shrine she tends or in the Mother Church. Although, in the end, she persists in firmly rejecting Kenyon's heterodox thoughts, still she remains confused; and when Kenyon cries "O Hilda, guide me home!" she can only answer with an equally anguished cry, "We are both lonely; both far from home! . . . I am a poor, weak girl, and have no such wisdom as you fancy in me" (p. 855). There seems no solution for her or for Kenyon but to return to "that native homeliness, those familiar sights, those faces which she had known always, those days that never brought any strange event; that life of sober week-days, and a solemn sabbath at the close" (p. 787).

But if Hilda can no longer supply any easy intellectual answers, still her spiritual role remains to be considered. Most Hawthorne readers have agreed that the omnipresent brown-haired girl of his novels represents for him the redeeming power of love, and in support of this belief, they point to his often-quoted letter to Sophia: "Indeed, we are but shadows; we are not endowed with real life, all that seems most real about us is but the thinnest substance of a dream,—till the heart be touched. That touch creates us,—then we begin to be—thereby we are beings of reality, and inheritors of eternity. . . ." [11] Perhaps this conviction explains Hawthorne's almost compulsive need to include a pure New England girl in every novel. Even in his last abortive phase pale heroines keep cropping up, whether the plot requires them or not. But after Phoebe, even their powers of love begin to fade. In Phoebe, Hawthorne envisaged his ideal: "Holding her hand, you felt something; a tender something; a substance, and a warm one: and so long as you should feel its grasp, soft as it was, you might be certain that your place was good in the whole sympathetic chain of human nature. The world was no longer a delusion" (p. 327).

By comparison, Priscilla's love for Hollingsworth seems totally uncreative. Hawthorne undoubtedly intended to suggest that love for her could be redeeming. Zenobia speaks specifically to Hollingsworth of "this girl, whom, if God ever visibly showed a purpose, He put into your charge, and through whom He was striving to redeem you" (p. 568). And presumably Coverdale's failure to assert his love for Priscilla dooms him always to look on life from the outside.[12] In Priscilla, however, Hawthorne has created not a reality but a theory—"a leaf floating on the

---

[11] Quoted in F. O. Matthiessen, *American Renaissance* (New York, 1951), p. 255.

[12] At the end of *Blithedale*, Coverdale speaks of his love for Priscilla as "one foolish little secret, which possibly may have had something to do with these inactive years of meridian manhood, with my bachelorship, with the unsatisfied retrospect that I fling back on life" (p. 585).

dark current of events" (p. 538); and by the time he gets to Hilda, even the theory is almost gone. "It seemed to Kenyon," writes Hawthorne, ". . . that all modes of crime were crowded into the close intricacy of Roman streets, and that there was no redeeming element" (p. 827). Hilda lives so far above the world that she can have virtually no function at all with regard to the rest of humanity, and in her relationship with Miriam, it is Hilda who needs humanizing by contact with experience and not Miriam who can hope to find redemption by association with innocence. "You need a sin to soften you" (p. 710), Miriam tells her, and earlier she has exclaimed, "O Hilda, your innocence is like a sharp steel sword" (p. 627). Even Kenyon, the man of marble, seems to have more of a heart than does Hilda, however earnestly Hawthorne may protest the contrary to be true. Her actions speak louder than his words.[13]

With Hawthorne, such a steady loss of faith in the redemptive qualities of his New England girl could only result in a steadily deepening pessimism, and hence it is hardly surprising to find that his mood is far darker in *Blithedale* than in the comparatively sunshiny *Seven Gables* and darker still in *The Marble Faun*. In Priscilla's purity and innocence, Hawthorne may still have envisoned the possibility of redemption for men wise enough to seize upon it; but Hilda, in spite of her detachment and her spirituality, proves to be as mortal and as subject to sin as the rest of humanity. For Phoebe and Priscilla, purity was its own sufficient shield—protecting Phoebe from Holgrave's mesmerism and Priscilla from contamination by Westervelt and violation by Zenobia. But Hilda's consciousness of her own purity actually causes her to sin against Miriam: "your very look," says Miriam, "seems to put me beyond the limits of human kind" (p. 709).[14]

Perhaps what Hawthorne had seen of terrible human suffering in England and in Italy had made him doubt his own conception of innocent womanhood. "How superficial are the niceties of such as pretend to keep aloof!" he exclaimed in *Our Old Home*. "Let the whole world be cleansed, or not a man or woman of us all can be clean." [15] Hilda suggests something of the same attitude when she says: "While there is a single guilty person in the universe, each innocent one must feel his innocence tortured by that guilt" (p. 712). Hilda is, indeed, "tortured by that guilt" or at least by the burden of concealing it, and later she is tortured again by "a painful doubt whether a wrong had not been com-

---

[13] As Carlos Kling points out in his article on "Hawthorne's View of Sin" (*Personalist*, XIII [April 1932], 119–130), "Purity and innocence in Hilda and Kenyon are shown to be hard and rigid and unforgiving; and virtue should be warm and human and bending, not a marble whiteness" (p. 128).

[14] Whether intentionally or not, Hawthorne seems here to suggest that Hilda was guilty of much the same thing as the Puritans in *The Scarlet Letter*. Guided by a rigid moral code, she has forced a human being to live outside the circle of humanity.

[15] Hawthorne, "English Poverty," *Our Old Home*, p. 440.

mitted . . . towards the friend once so beloved" (p. 812). Such consciousness of guilt and sin is a long step from Phoebe's rather self-congratulatory innocence. It is true that worldly experience has a maturing effect on Phoebe in the course of the novel and that, like Hilda, she emerges with a deeper understanding of human life; but she does not suffer agonies in the process, and she herself does not sin.

Another equally clear indication of Hawthorne's changing attitude is to be found in the transformation of the active Phoebe into a passive Priscilla and later into a withdrawn Hilda—a transformation which would seem to tie in with the religious role always assigned to the fair-haired maiden. In Phoebe this religious association is already coming out strongly: "In her aspect there was a familiar gladness, and a holiness that you could play with, and yet reverence it as much as ever. She was like a prayer, offered up in the homeliest beauty of one's mother-tongue" (p. 343). Phoebe, however, is not explicitly called upon to fill the formal religious requirement that Hawthorne later postulates for womanhood [16]—a requirement which would tend to emphasize not the reality of a woman but her ethereality and other-worldliness. At one point Coverdale thinks of Priscilla as "diaphanous with spiritual light" (p. 515), and earlier he has confessed to Zenobia:

I have never found it possible to suffer a bearded priest so near my heart and conscience as to do me any spiritual good. I blush at the very thought! Oh, in the better order of things, Heaven grant that the ministry of souls may be left in charge of women! . . . The task belongs to woman. God meant it for her. He has endowed her with the religious sentiment in its utmost depth and purity, refined from that gross, intellectual alloy with which every masculine theologist—save only One . . . has been prone to mingle it. I have always envied the Catholics their faith in that sweet, sacred Virgin Mother, who stands between them and the Deity, intercepting somewhat of his awful splendor, but permitting his love to stream upon the worshipper more intelligibly to human comprehension through the medium of a woman's tenderness. (pp. 510, 511)

Similarly, Kenyon says to Miriam: "between man and man there is always an insuperable gulf. They can never quite grasp each other's hands; and therefore man never derives any intimate help, any heart sustenance, from his brother man, but from woman—his mother, his sister, or his wife" (pp. 754, 755). For his own heart sustenance, Kenyon turns to a vestal virgin whom he can worship.

Possibly, indeed, one of the main troubles with Hilda is traceable to Hawthorne's having asked too much of her. He asks her to play two parts at once, and as a result, she falls apart as a character. In creating her he has clung to his view of woman as a pure and virginal spirit even

---

[16] Hawthorne, says Morton Cronin ("Hawthorne on Romantic Love," pp. 95, 96), would "extend woman's historic role as the spiritual fortifier of man to include the professional ministry of souls."

while insisting that not even the most innocent can be immune from some experience of sin. He is trying to hold together in one creation the dark vision of the burden of suffering and the bright vision of redeeming love; and because he fails, the dove and the sinner remain two different people, neither of whom can be very effective in her human relationships. Even at the end, when the spiritual Hilda comes down to earth from her tower, she comes "to be herself enshrined and worshipped as a household saint" (p. 855). The virginal spirit and the earthly girl remain unreconciled. What Hawthorne seems to have looked for and failed to find is much the same thing that Hilda herself seeks in an ideal figure of the Virgin Mother: "a face of celestial beauty, but human as well as heavenly, and with the shadow of past grief upon it" (p. 790). If he never succeeds in making Hilda's humanity convincing, it may be simply because the ideal he had set up was impossible of human attainment. He needed a figure who could cope adequately with the complexities of evil in Rome and still remain herself essentially unstained—hardly an easy task for any woman of flesh and blood.

Because Hawthorne has asked too much of both Hilda and Priscilla at the spiritual level, neither of them even approaches Phoebe's remarkable blend of spirituality and earthiness. Phoebe, with her "activity of body, intellect, and heart," finds herself completely in control of the situations she encounters. She may be variously described as an angel on "the wings of the morning" and a "purifying influence" but she is also a "little country-girl" and "a verse of household poetry" and she possesses an "innate fitness" for household tasks whereby she can create a warm home anywhere. Priscilla, on the other hand, achieves no such perfect balance. In fact Hawthorne goes out of his way to point out her unfitness for the practical side of life at Blithedale: "she let the poultry into the garden; she generally spoilt whatever part of the dinner she took in charge; she broke crockery . . . [and] was as unserviceable a member of society as any young lady in the land" (p. 482). Hawthorne seems to have intended that Priscilla's spirituality should supply the overintellectual and egotistical inhabitants of Blithedale with a necessary balance and that Blithedale in turn should provide Priscilla with a "decided place among creatures of flesh and blood." But because she seems to be more of a theory than a reality for Hawthorne, she never achieves flesh and blood and in fact comes close to evaporating into a mere symbol. Hilda's failure either to give or achieve a balance is, of course, even more drastic. As an angel, a vestal virgin, the epitome of purity and innocence, Hilda never behaves like the kind of person to whom Miriam should say: "you, for all you dwell so high above the world, have certain little housewifely ways of accuracy and order" (p. 628). There is no housewifely earthiness about her at all.

It is interesting to notice, too, that the farther Hawthorne pushes his New England girls into disembodied spirituality, the more frequently he tends to present them in terms of symbols. Although Phoebe, with her singing and her flitting, sunshiny nature, is occasionally compared to a bird, the identification is more sentimental than seriously symbolic. But the dove in *Blithedale* who "kept her desolate perch on the peak of the attic-window" and the whole flock of doves who frequent Hilda's tower seem to have definite symbolic implications. Of another dove, which appears in an earlier Hawthorne sketch, the narrator inquires: "Can this be the very dove . . . that brought the message of peace and hope to the tempest-beaten passengers of the ark?" [17] Such a question would imply that Hawthorne saw the dove as bringing spiritual solace to a disturbed world, and his emphasis on the dove-like qualities of Priscilla and Hilda lends an additional degree of abstraction to their already shadowy existences.

There is, moreover, still another of Hawthorne's symbols—or it might more accurately be called one of a cluster of symbols—which receives subtle but persistent emphasis in the later romances and which lifts both Hilda and Priscilla even higher into the realm of abstraction and unreality. At the lowest level of this symbolic cluster, it is fairly obvious that all three fair-haired maidens function in relation to the rest of the characters as mediums. Of Phoebe, Hawthorne remarks: "Her physical organization . . . being at once delicate and healthy, gave her a perception, operating with almost the effect of a spiritual medium" (p. 301). And later: "Her eyes looked larger, and darker, and deeper; so deep, at some silent moments, that they seemed like Artesian wells, down, down, into the infinite" (p. 348). Priscilla, of course, is explicitly cast in the role of a medium and at one point is described as a being so insubstantial that "the sun, at mid-day, would shine through her" (p. 549). The same symbolism is employed, somewhat less persistently, with reference to Hilda. She is a consummate copyist because, through her eyes and soul, art works are seen as "through a perfectly transparent medium" (p. 815), and she looks at all matters "through the clear crystal medium of her own integrity" (p. 811).

At the second level of the symbolic cluster, the New England maidens become not only mediums but rays of sunshine as well, thus combining transparency with warmth. "There is," exclaims Holgrave, "a wonderful insight in Heaven's broad and simple sunshine" (p. 298).[18] Undoubtedly Hawthorne's constant comparisons of his fair-haired maidens to rays of sunshine were meant to suggest this quality of clear vision as well as the qualities of warmth and cheerfulness, and in fact, he thought clear vision

---

[17] Hawthorne, "A Virtuoso's Collection," *Mosses from an Old Manse*, p. 541.

[18] In Hawthorne's "The Hall of Fantasy" (*Mosses from an Old Manse*, p. 204), sunshine is specifically referred to as a medium: " 'the fantasies of one day are the deepest realities of a future one.' . . . 'The white sunshine of actual life is necessary in order to test them. I am rather apt to doubt both men and their reasonings till I meet them in that truthful medium'."

impossible without the warmth of love.[19] But Hawthorne's ultimate symbol for such warmth, transparency, and cheerfulness is not sunshine. It is wine. This final symbol is first introduced rather unobtrusively in *Blithedale* and seems simply intended to suggest the presence of certain potentialities in Priscilla. In *The Marble Faun*, however, the symbol is in danger of getting out of hand and seems almost to be pursued not as a *symbol* of Hilda's redeeming qualities but as a *substitute* for them. The element of human love is disappearing.

The use of the wine symbol with reference to Priscilla is far from being immediately evident but it is certainly present. The first suggestion comes when Zenobia remarks: "She has never before known what it is to live in the free air, and so it intoxicates her as if she were sipping wine" (p. 473). Later she is called "the gentle parasite" (p. 512), thus establishing an association with the parasitic grape vine of Coverdale's retreat, and still later Westervelt describes her silvery veil as "imbued . . . with the fluid medium of spirits" (p. 558). Finally, in drawing a moral from the story he has been relating, Coverdale reverts once again to the wine symbol:

The moral which presents itself to my reflections . . . is simply this,— that, admitting what is called philanthropy, when adopted as a profession, to be often useful by its energetic impulse to society at large, it is perilous to the individual whose ruling passion, in one exclusive channel, it thus becomes. It ruins, or is fearfully apt to ruin, the heart, the rich juices of which God never meant should be pressed violently out, and distilled into alcoholic liquor, by an unnatural process, but should render life sweet, bland, and gently beneficent, and insensibly influence other hearts and other lives to the same blessed end. (p. 583)

Hilda is linked to the wine symbol somewhat more explicitly when Hawthorne says of her: "Her heart seemed so full, that it spilt its new gush of happiness, as it were, like rich and sunny wine out of an over-brimming goblet" (p. 800). Actually, however, the significant fact in *The Marble Faun* is the prominence with which the rich and sunny wine itself figures in the novel. This is not just any wine. It is the "Sunshine" of Monte Beni, and its descriptive resemblance to Hilda is notable—particularly since it seems to have special value for Kenyon. Upon tasting it, he remarks that it "is like the airy sweetness of youthful hopes, that no realities will ever satisfy! . . . I feel myself a better man for that ethereal potation . . . This is surely the wine of the Golden Age . . . As I understand you, it is a sort of consecrated juice, and symbolizes the holy virtues of hospitality and social kindness" (pp. 717, 718). To these remarks, the Monte Beni butler replies: "The wine, Signore, is so

---

[19] In his *American Notebooks,* Hawthorne speaks of love, "the divine, the life-giving touch," as having made him "A man with the right perception of things—a feeling within him of what is true and what is false." *The American Notebooks of Nathaniel Hawthorne,* ed. Randall Stewart (New Haven, 1932), pp. 89, 90.

fond of its native home, that a transportation of even a few miles turns it quite sour. And yet it is a wine that keeps well in the cellar . . . and gathers fragrance, flavor, and brightness, in its dark dungeon.[20] That very flask of Sunshine, now, has kept itself for you, sir guest (as a maid reserves her sweetness till her lover come for it) . . ." (pp. 718, 719). And Hawthorne himself expands upon its rare qualities: "to drink it was really more a moral than a physical enjoyment . . . as it stood in Kenyon's glass, a little circle of light glowed on the table round about it, as if it were really so much golden sunshine" (p. 718). Much later, when Hilda has disappeared and Kenyon is seeking consolation, Hawthorne writes: "In a case like this, it is doubtful whether Kenyon could have done a much better thing than he actually did, by going to dine at the Café Nuovo, and drinking a flask of Montefiascone; longing, the while, for a beaker or two of Donatello's Sunshine. It would have been just the wine to cure a lover's melancholy, by illuminating his heart with tender light and warmth, and suggestions of undefined hopes" (pp. 817, 818). When happy, hopeful Hilda isn't available, Hawthorne seems to feel that Sunshine will do very nearly as well in supplying the requisite happiness and hope.

If such a substitution can even be suggested, a question immediately comes to mind. What has happened to Hawthorne's faith in the redemptive quality of human relationships? It may possibly be enlightening, in this connection, to look at certain passages in *Septimius Felton*. There the fair-haired maiden, Rose Garfield, has become totally ineffectual and, in fact, has no vestige of a significant saving relationship with the erring Septimius. The elixir of life has become all in all: "Never was there anything as bright as this . . . and never was there such a hue as the sunlight took in falling through it and resting on his floor. And strange and beautiful it was, too, to look through this medium at the outer world, and see how it was glorified and made anew. . . ." [21] Here Hawthorne seems to have wholly abandoned his belief in the redemptive quality of his fair-haired maiden, and isolation—withdrawal "from the common bond and destiny" [22]—has triumphed.

Certainly Hawthorne has not yet reached so extreme a position as this in *The Marble Faun*. Hilda has not been altogether rejected, and she even enjoys a feeble sort of victory on the narrative level. Yet when she is compared first to Priscilla and then to Phoebe, the signs of Hawthorne's growing doubt seem unmistakable, and at least one conclusion can be safely drawn. For Hawthorne, women like Phoebe, Priscilla, and

---

[20] It does not seem mere coincidence that Hilda is later described as having acquired "a deeper look into the heart of things; such as those necessarily acquire who have passed from picture galleries into dungeon gloom and thence come back to the picture gallery again" (p. 806).

[21] Nathaniel Hawthorne, *The Dolliver Romance, Fanshawe, and Septimius Felton* (Boston, 1883), pp. 400, 401.

[22] Ibid., p. 382.

Hilda represented far more than simply a type of innocuous female symbolic of his own repressed sexual instincts. They were invariably called
upon to play key parts in his portrayal of human relationships, and they
became increasingly involved in his whole comprehensive view of human
nature and of good and evil. Consequently, if Hawthorne felt compelled
to question their fitness to live in the real world and to play their accustomed roles, the questions he asked could only have had the broadest
implications. With the changes from Phoebe to Priscilla and from Priscilla to Hilda, the optimistic light shed by Hawthorne's faith in redeeming human love has begun perceptibly to fade.

Commentary on the Use of Footnotes

Footnote 1. Frequently beginning researchers think of footnotes
too exclusively as a means of acknowledging the source of material
quoted in the text. This footnote makes use of an equally important function of footnoting: giving the reader information which the writer feels
is important for him to know, but which would be out of place in the
text itself. In this instance the author evidently felt that it would have
thrown the article out of balance to mention specifically Carpenter's and
Rahv's contributions to Hawthorne scholarship, even though their contributions form the basis for what the author says in her second paragraph.

Since the author, in mentioning the attitude of various critics toward
Hawthorne's heroines, does not quote directly from either Carpenter
or Rahv in the article itself, she had an option of referring or not referring to them in a footnote. No rule can possibly be laid down for
how much or how little to footnote in situations of this kind. A writer
must simply ask himself where a reader logically might wish a footnote.
In this case the author evidently decided that a reader might be sufficiently interested in knowing some of the sources of information concerning critical attitudes toward Hawthorne's heroines to warrant a
footnote.

The references to Carpenter and Rahv represent primary (i.e., first)
references to magazine articles. Notice that full bibliographical information is given (name of author, title of article, name of magazine, volume
number, month and year of issue, and page number). Since these footnotes simply refer the reader to the articles in question, the inclusive
page numbers for the articles are given, rather than specific page
numbers, as would have been the case had the footnotes referred to
material quoted in the text.

Footnote 2. A writer should always tell a reader the exact source of a direct quotation. Essentially, this obligation represents a service to a reader. If a reader is interested enough to read a book or article, he may very conceivably wish to read for himself some of the sources which were used in making it. This footnote fulfills this obligation and represents a primary reference to an edited book. Note, as in the case of a primary reference to a magazine article, that full bibliographical information is given (name of book, name of editor, place and date of publication, and page number on which the quotation occurs).

The last sentence suggests a good way of handling repeated quotations from a given source. Every footnote reference in a text constitutes an interruption of the thought, since the author is in effect asking his reader to leave off reading the text and make his eyes travel to the bottom of the page to read something else. Therefore, footnote references in a book or article should be kept at a minimum. The author, throughout her article, quotes repeatedly from *The Novels and Tales of Nathaniel Hawthorne*. Knowing that it would give her article a terribly cut-up appearance to footnote every quotation from Hawthorne, the author simply tells a reader once and for all what edition of Hawthorne she has used, and then includes page numbers in parentheses directly after each quotation.

Notice that it is conventional to use (p.), an abbreviation for "page," (or pp., for "pages," as in footnote 3) when referring to a book; whereas these abbreviations are omitted when the reference is to a magazine article.

Footnote 3. This footnote represents a primary reference to a story which is itself a part of a book. Note that, as always with primary references, full bibliographical information is given.

Footnote 4. This footnote represents another primary reference to a story taken from a book. Notice that the author uses this footnote to visit with the reader.

Footnote 5. As in footnote 1, the author refers to a work in which a reader may find a more elaborate treatment of a critical point briefly touched upon in the article, and she quotes a key sentence from the work to which reference is made.

Footnote 6. Additional documentation is given.

Footnote 7. This is a primary reference to a magazine article.

Footnote 8. This footnote constitutes what is known as a "secondary reference" (i.e., every reference to a work subsequent to the initial, or "primary," reference). Carpenter's article has already been mentioned in footnote 1, where full bibliographical information was given. It would be superfluous to repeat full bibliographical information every time a writer's work is mentioned in a footnote (this may happen dozens of times in very long or detailed articles, or in books); hence only Carpenter's last name, and the name of the article, suffice at this point. Since no other work by Carpenter finds mention in the article, the footnote would not have been incorrect had only Carpenter's last name been used, and the title omitted.

Footnote 9. The (n.) following the page number in this footnote is an abbreviation for "note," and signifies that the information in Hawthorne to which this footnote refers was itself found in a footnote in Hawthorne's work.

Footnote 10. Notice that the information given in this footnote (as is the case in footnotes 12, 13, 16, 18, 19, and 20) constitutes additional documentation, the author apparently feeling that to have included this additional documentation in the text would throw the article out of balance, but that making it available to her reader in a footnote will help reinforce the argument. Some discretion, obviously, needs to be exercised in using footnotes to give information and additional documentation. If a writer makes repeated and protracted use of this device (which the author here does not), a reader may get the feeling that the real article he is reading is the one contained in the footnotes, or that, at best (or worst), he is reading two articles simultaneously. Whenever a writer is moved to make use of footnotes for additional information and documentation, he should be certain that the material really does not belong somewhere in the body of the essay.

Footnote 11. This footnote indicates that the writer did not take the quotation from its original source (which in this case would be a letter), but has copied it from another secondary source. Manuscript and other hard to obtain material is frequently handled in this way. By citing a well-known or readily available source which reproduces the document being quoted, a writer can perform a service to a reader who may wish to refer to the document as a whole. In this instance, however, Matthiessen quotes very little more of Hawthorne's letter than does the writer of the article.

Footnotes 12 and 13. Additional documentation is given.

Footnote 14. The author uses this footnote to visit further with her reader concerning a particular point.

Footnote 15. This is a secondary reference to Hawthorne's *Our Old Home,* first mentioned in footnote 9.

Footnote 16. Additional documentation is given.

Footnote 17. This is a secondary reference to Hawthorne's *Mosses from an Old Manse,* first mentioned in footnote 4.

Footnotes 18, 19, and 20. Additional documentation is given.

Footnote 21. This is a primary reference to a book.

Footnote 22. The "Ibid." in this footnote is an abbreviation for the Latin *ibidem,* meaning "in the same place." This widely used device indicates that a footnote refers to the same work as the one immediately preceding it. Traditionally, the "Ibid." has been italicized, since it is an abbreviation of a Latin word. Its wide currency as a convention in footnoting has, however, caused some writers to abandon the use of the italics.

Divergence over a question such as whether or not to italicize "Ibid." points up a principle sometimes lost sight of: that footnoting is after all a convention, and that like all conventions it has undergone changes. (A number of years ago, for example, nearly all scholars, when footnoting a book, indicated the name of the publisher, along with the place and date of publication. Today omission of the name of the publisher is becoming more and more common in some fields.)

Although no one form of footnoting can be said to be exclusively correct, some footnoting practices are so universally followed as, practically, to constitute—for the time being at least—rules. So far as form in footnoting is concerned, of utmost importance is the adoption of *one* accepted form of documentation and its consistent use. Inconsistency in footnoting, while not a capital crime, certainly indicates lazy mental habits on the part of a writer, and will hence prejudice a reader unfavorably against him.

Prefaces

A preface (sometimes called a foreword, or introduction) is an essay, written by the author, which precedes the work it accompanies, and which the author hopes his reader will read before turning to the work itself. What the preface writer says to his reader will depend on the nature of his work, and on his relationship to his prospective reader. Quite obviously, he wants to make his reader like him, or, what amounts to the same thing in scholarly work, have enough confidence in him to want to read his work. The preface writer accordingly will often seek to present himself in a favorable light through the tone he uses, as well as to present his academic credentials, to exhibit his fitness for the task he has undertaken. Often, as well, a writer will use a preface to explain the plan of his work, the method of organization, the self-imposed limits he has set himself, and the like, so that a reader will not be able to quarrel with him for not writing a different work from the one he wrote. The preface may also be used to give the reader any instruction or information which the author feels he must know before he can read the work intelligently.

Although almost anything can be found in some preface if one looks at enough of them, the bulk of most prefaces consists of attempts to fulfill three aims:

1. To win the reader's regard and confidence.

2. To forestall adverse criticism by explaining the plan for the work.

3. To give the reader information which it is essential for him to know if he is to read the work intelligently.

Tables of Contents

The book which contains no table of contents is a rarity. A table of contents, which precedes the main body of the work, simply indicates the main divisions of the work (usually chapters) and the page numbers on which these divisions begin. Not infrequently, in the case of scholarly works and textbooks, the various chapters themselves contain divisions, which can be indicated in the table of contents, so that a specific part of a chapter may be found more quickly and easily. (See the Table of Contents to this manual for an example.)

Appendixes

Occasionally, for one reason or another, writers need to supply readers with material which would be out of place in a work itself. (This is more frequently the case with book-length works than with works of article length.) Such material ordinarily follows the close of the work, in a section called an appendix. Here are some of the major categories of information which may follow a scholarly work:

1. Important documents relating to the work itself may be printed, so that they may be referred to by the reader. F. R. Leavis, for example, at the end of his book, *The Great Tradition*, reprints Henry James's essay, "*Daniel Deronda*: A Conversation." Leavis, in discussing George Eliot and Henry James, has compared Isabel Archer (James's heroine in *The Portrait of a Lady*) and Gwendolen Harleth (the heroine in George Eliot's *Daniel Deronda*) in considerable detail. He consequently feels that a reader may wish to read James's own comments on George Eliot's book.

2. Chronological tables sometimes accompany works that utilize an historical approach. Anthologies of literature, for example, frequently contain such tables, so that a student may, at a glance, see

something of the time relationships existing among the works he is studying.

3. Tables of statistics and financial information may be supplied, should they bear a relationship to the work.

Glossaries

A glossary is a list of terms which the writer uses in a work, and which he feels he needs to define for his reader. Such terms commonly fall into one of two categories:

1. There may be common terms or phrases which, in the work in which they are used, have specialized or unusual meanings. Such terms are to be found in textbooks of literary criticism, for example, or in works relating to some field of specialized knowledge, where technical terms, borrowed from the common storehouse of language, have taken on meanings different from the common meanings. (In literary criticism the word "conceit" provides an example. Used in connection with the discussion of poetry, the term signifies an extended and elaborate comparison, a meaning very different from its common one.)

2. There may be words—either common or unusual—which have archaic meanings. Any student of Chaucer is familiar with the inevitable glossary accompanying his works, giving modern English equivalents for those of Chaucer's words which have dropped out of the language, or which, although still used, have substantially changed in meaning.

Bibliographies

Although ordinarily considered apart from the appendix, the bibliography is related to it, since both follow the work with which they are connected, and both supply information. A bibliography lists works relating to a given subject. There are several kinds:

1. Complete bibliographies list every known source on a given subject and are customarily printed as books in themselves.

2. Select bibliographies are what the term indicates: they make no claim to completeness, but rather represent a selection on the part of the compiler. Customarily, the inclusion of a work in a

select bibliography suggests that it has special relevance or merit. Hence it is a recommendation to a work to include it in a select bibliography.

3. Some bibliographies are annotated. That is, following each entry the bibliographer supplies a brief (sometimes only a one- or two-sentence) description of the work, usually carrying a value judgment. Annotated bibliographies are ordinarily select.

4. A particular kind of select bibliography is that which may accompany a scholarly article or research paper. Such a bibliography customarily includes only the sources, primary and secondary, which actually contributed to the paper.

5. Of interest and of use only to the researcher, during the period of research, is what is sometimes called a working bibliography. This is simply a listing of works, or references to works, which the researcher has come across, and which he thinks may be pertinent to the research he is doing. Studying card catalogues and indexes, reading generally in one's field of interest, browsing in the stacks of a library—all of these activities potentially provide items for the researcher's working bibliography. If the research is to be at all extensive, it is helpful to copy each entry in the working bibliography onto a separate sheet of paper, so that notations concerning the nature of each work may subsequently be made when the work is studied.

Bibliography entries are alphabetized according to the last name of the author. With the exception of the inversion of the author's name, the bibliography entry corresponds to the form used in primary references in footnoting. For example, F. O. Matthiessen's *American Renaissance*, mentioned in footnote 11 of Virginia Ogden Birdsall's article, "Hawthorne's Fair-Haired Maidens: The Fading Light" (see Chapter 10), would appear thus in a bibliography:

Matthiessen, F. O., *American Renaissance* (New York, 1951).

The only other respect in which bibliographical entries differ from footnote entries lies in the case of page references. Whereas a footnote entry to a magazine article, when it refers to a quotation in the text, cites the page from which the quotation is taken, the bibliographical entry indicates the inclusive pages on which the article is found. Page numbers are never given for books, unless only a portion of the book applies to the purpose of the bibliography.

Indexes

Most scholarly books, although not all, include indexes, designed to help a reader locate information which he goes to the book to obtain. The process of making an index includes these steps:

1. One must first decide on the major categories to be included in the index. For example, in a critical biography of a literary figure the writer might decide to include names of individuals mentioned in the book; names of literary works; names of magazines; names of places associated with his author; references to genres; phrases from his author's works or theory which are widely current; and subjects which his author stresses. The indexer must always ask himself the question: What items will be useful to a new reader, or to a person using the book as a reference? There is no use referring to material which readers coming to the book will not have remembered from their previous experience, because they will not know to look up such material. Remember also that it is helpful to refer to items as many times as possible by the use of main headings and subheadings. For example, our hypothetical biographer mentioned above, when inserting the name of a place associated with his author, might subdivide this entry into such divisions as "author's reaction to"; "influence on author's work"; "effect on author's work habits"; etc.

2. Once the major categories have been decided upon, making an index becomes something of a mechanical process. The indexer, armed with 3 by 5 cards, reads his work and, whenever he comes across an item included in his list of major categories, writes the item and page number on a card, using a separate card for each entry.

3. When the work has been entirely read in this manner, the cards are arranged alphabetically. All the page numbers referring to a given item are transferred to one card and arranged numerically. These cards then constitute the index.

THE CRITICAL ESSAY

Introduction

The object of all research and critical reading should be the production of a work of some sort (essay, article, book) embodying the results of that study.

Below are essays that have grown out of literary study. Actually, these essays are not very different in kind from some of the other essays in this manual, except that most of the essays in previous chapters have concerned *one* work, whereas each of the essays in this chapter reflects its author's study of a writer's work as a whole.

In addition to the essays in this chapter, Virginia Woolf's "The Novels of Thomas Hardy" (see Chapter 5), Howard W. Webb, Jr.'s "The Meaning of Ring Lardner's Fiction: A Re-evaluation" (see Chapter 5), and Virginia Ogden Birdsall's "Hawthorne's Fair-Haired Maidens: The Fading Light" (see Chapter 10) all concern themselves with the entire body, or with a substantial part, of the work of a writer, and hence afford additional examples of how literary study may result in a comprehensive essay.

BARBARA SEWARD

Elizabeth Bowen's World of Impoverished Love

*W*ith the recent publication of *A World of Love*, Elizabeth Bowen has renewed her claim on serious critical attention. Curiously, to date she has been given little such attention, although she is generally recognized as one of our foremost writers. More curiously, what attention she has received has tended to ignore the full significance of her work by overstressing her compassion for the innocent idealist trapped in the modern world. Certainly Miss Bowen is enormously sympathetic to the idealist who is desolated by a callous society; nevertheless she is equally aware that the callous society is itself made up of desolated idealists. And, more fundamentally, she perceives that the root of the trouble is in the ideals themselves, that society is in its present negative condition because too many individuals have for too long been pursuing unfulfillable romantic desires at the expense of immediate, living realities. Appalled by the tragic inability of our world to meet the demands of the innocent romantic, Miss Bowen has throughout her career been still more appalled by the romantic's inability to meet the crying demands of our world.

In all of her novels an exalted and uncompromising love breaks its wings against the wall of contemporary society. The earlier novels explore the immediate tragedy of uncorrupt, idealistic love in an age that is neither uncorrupt nor idealistic, while *A World of Love* is concerned with three women who have drowned the present in their love for a man killed in the first World War. Although the change in the latest novel from love for the living to love for the dead reflects a certain difference between pre- and post-war attitudes, this difference is not basic. The resemblance between the earlier heroine's idea of her beloved and his actual nature is at best no greater than the resemblance between a ghost and a living man. And the innocent girl lost in her dream of love is no more capable of handling the realities of her world than are the women who have ceased to wind their clocks with the death of a soldier in World War I. Miss Bowen explores a persistent theme—the tragic dangers of romantic excesses in the twentieth century—although she modifies and adapts that theme to meet the requirements of a society that has altered in superficials but continues to make the same fundamental mistake.

In the six pre-World War II novels, from *The Hotel* (1927) through *The Death of the Heart* (1939), the pattern in which her theme is presented resembles that of classical tragedy. A heroine of great stature is marred by a single flaw or weakness which brings about her downfall. The weakness, one that might normally lie dormant throughout the heroine's life, is brought out and enhanced by the warped characters among whom she finds herself. And the catastrophe that results from this combination of inner flaw and outer circumstance is disastrous not only to the heroine but also to all others involved. In classical tragedy, however, individuals are morally culpable in that they knowingly overreach themselves, whereas in Miss Bowen's work they commit their errors blindly as victims of forces they can neither recognize nor control. Her most brittle and vicious sophisticates share with her most idealistic heroines a common and terrible injustice: all have alike been irrevocably deprived of the fruitful lives they might have led.

The innocents are the more sympathetic since they have not yet lost faith, hope, and trust. We meet them on the threshold of experience, young, sensitive, not happy, but unconsciously awaiting a greater thing than happiness. Because they are still uncorrupted and emotionally unimpaired, they are inevitably strangers to their deficient family or social circles. Of necessity they exist in an inner realm of private dreams, and, like most romantic dreamers, seek to verify their ideals by giving them life in the external world. Reaching out to the remote because the near-at-hand is uncongenial, they generally manage to fall in love with men who are not accepted in their immediate social spheres. Lois's Gerald (*The Last September*), Emmeline's Markie (*To The North*), Karen's Max (*The House in Paris*), and Portia's Eddie (*The Death of the Heart*) derive at least part of their appeal from being of a divergent walk of life and so representing relief or refuge from the unsatisfying familiar. When Karen explains to Max her reasons for keeping their love tryst, she speaks of her home and family in terms that the other heroines would understand too well: "I found I was in prison—no, locked into a museum. . . . *They* keep me away from everything that has power; they would be frightened of art if I painted really well."

But while the bluebird of bliss is certainly not in their own back yards, neither is it to be found in any other place on the modern scene. The innocent girls at first fail to perceive this because, since they chiefly exist in the realm of private emotions, they tend to project these emotions onto the world, mistaking inner longing for external fact. As Miss Bowen observes: "In the first great phase of love . . . the beloved is not outside one. . . . In this dumb, exalted and exalting confusion, what actually happens plays very little part" (*The Death of the Heart*). If Sydney is blind to Mrs. Kerr's coldness (*The Hotel*), Janet to Edward's weakness (*Friends and Relations*), Emmeline to Markie's egotism, and Portia to Eddie's duplicity, it is because in every instance the introverted heroine interprets her beloved in terms of her own ideal, is in fact more in love with her private dream than with an actual human being.

Yet it is because of this that their love has so much beauty. If the heroines were not introverted idealists with little experience beyond their own personal emotions, they would probably not have attained the same totality of love. If they were not isolated from the hollow society around them, they would not have been able to bring to love uncorrupted and undiminished hearts. It is because they are alone, romantic, unaware of the prevailing tawdriness of things that they are capable of love in the grand manner, are capable of an unhesitant, uncompromising devotion that can hold back nothing and means no less than everything. One of the tragic facts about life as Miss Bowen sees it is that pure and absolute love demands for its existence at least a partial ignorance of the true nature of our world.

Far more tragic, however, are the effects of such ignorance. "It is not only our fate but our business to lose innocence," writes Miss Bowen in

"Out of a Book" (*Collected Impressions*, 1950); she shows in her novels that innocence cannot and should not last because it is a product of romantic youth having devastating results in the adult world. It is first of all devastating to the innocent themselves, as the disparity between their ideals and the truth is gradually revealed to them. Emmeline, driven literally to her death by the loss of her illusion, is perhaps the most striking example. But we are given the unmistakable impression that Janet, Karen, and even Portia have also little left to hope for from life. Had their love been less unknowing, less immoderate from the outset, it might have borne less bitter fruit.

And it is not only the innocent heroines who suffer the effects of their intemperate romanticism. All of those whom they love and many with whom they are associated come in for more than a full share of pain. The love objects in most cases undergo with the heroines a loss of illusions, but where the heroines lose illusions about their beloveds, the beloveds lose illusions about themselves. The mounting distress Markie feels with Emmeline may be taken as representative: "Her goodness had an unconscious royalty and was overbearing: under her too high idea of life and himself some part of him groaned, involuntary" (*To The North*, 1950). Certainly Mrs. Kerr's final desolation by Sydney, Edward's decade-long fear of Janet, and Eddie's increasing horror of Portia all spring from a similar source. In each instance the beloved, measured against perfection's rod, sees himself fall appallingly short, and is left in the end with as bleak a vision as that of the heroines themselves.

Even the comparatively uninvolved bystanders fall victim to the ravages of innocence. Sydney's Mr. Milton and Janet's sister Laurel are deeply and unjustly hurt because they happen to be in the path of impetuous romantic love. Equally unjust and scarcely less serious is the hurt Major Brutt receives when Portia heedlessly and permanently closes Anna's doors to him. But perhaps most terrible of all is the havoc Karen leaves behind her, ruining the life of her dearest friend, contributing directly to her mother's death, and leaving her child to be brought up by well-meaning, incompetent strangers. None of these girls ever viciously or deliberately injures others, but all remain so intent upon their grand obsessions that they are insufficiently aware of the damage they may do: "Their singleness, their ruthlessness, their one continuous wish makes them bound to be cruel and to suffer cruelty" (*The Death of the Heart*). Cut off from other people's values by their private dreams, the idealistic heroines are as great a menace to society as is society to them.

Ironically, in the last analysis their very purity is their tragic flaw. If they cannot understand other people's values, it is simply that those values are too corrupt for them; if they cannot love other people for what they are and not for what they ought to be, it is that, having encountered no guile within themselves, they have no way of recognizing guile in others. The romantic innocents are doomed to destroy themselves and those around them not because they share our failings but because as yet they largely lack them. Lacking them, they have no basis for human interaction, are bound to make mistakes and to bring about unhappiness. Their existence in a more exalted sphere than ours destines them to solitude and so to tragedy. For in their isolation they are anti-social in a world in which one cannot and must not live alone.

They are, however, more sinned against than sinning. Idealistic innocence is romantic and anti-social because present-day society falls so markedly short of perfection that uncompromising idealists can find no outlets for themselves. As Eddie protests to Portia, "How can we grow up when there's nothing left to inherit, when what we must feed on is so stale and corrupt?" But while the pure in heart are doomed by their isolation from modern life, the society that can find no place in itself for innocence is at least as desolating a spectacle as is that of innocence betrayed. To understand the full import of Elizabeth Bowen's pre-war novels, one must look beyond the central characters to the contemporary social background against which their tragedies are played out. Here, thrown into relief by the heroine's heroic standards, the decadence of our era is glaringly revealed.

The particular segments of modern society analyzed in these novels are the British upper and middle classes. Here in microcosm Miss Bowen sees operating the same forces that are destroying individuals and nations throughout our civilization today. In her view both classes are suffering, like her heroines, from what she has called "the disorientated romanticism of the age" (*Collected Impressions*); but unlike the heroines, her typical members of upper and middle classes are not dominated and broken by transcendent dreams of love. Their romantic longings, no less destructive or impossible, are a great deal less attractive. For while the heroines cannot adjust to this world because they feel too deeply for mistaken things, the people around them, equally mistaken, cannot adjust because too often they fear to feel at all.

The upper classes in particular, shaken by the present, are shown as lifelessly clinging to the dry husks of the past. Having lost the power and respect they commanded in earlier eras, they seek to ignore their loss by maintaining desperate shadows of traditions that now lack body. For example, all the habiliments of gracious living are preserved— tennis parties, dinners, servants, proper dress, and appropriate talk. But the true grace has quite gone out of them: where once there was warmth and concern for others, the desire to impress alone remains. The same conditions prevail in the narrower orbit of the home. That of the Quaynes in *The Death of the Heart* is a typical example: "In this airy vivacious house, all mirrors and polish, there was no place where shadows lodged, no point where feeling could thicken. The rooms were set for strangers' intimacy, or else for exhausted solitary retreat." Whether (as in *The Hotel*) the family homestead has been abandoned, or (as in the ensuing novels) it is elegantly maintained, the vital ingredients of family custom and family intimacy have been lost. Without these the upper-class houses, however stately and impressive, remain at best but chilly monuments of the unrecapturable past.

At worst they become the breeding grounds of cold or ruined lives. Hugo Montmorency, forever regretting the trip to Canada he lacked the vitality to make, and Karen Michaelis's Aunt Violet, passively dying of cancer to the life she never lived, symbolize the decay of a class un-adapted to present conditions. Edward Tilney, broken by the scandal of his mother Elfrida's love, is the product of a frightened society clutch-ing morality's outward forms in the absence of inner substance. Mrs. Kerr, Lady Naylor, and Anna Quayne, hardened against emotion, brittle and ruthless in human relationships, typify the defensive position of those raised in a loveless and vulnerable realm. Unwilling or unable to adjust to a new order, and afraid of caring too much for the old that is crum-bling under their feet, Miss Bowen's upper-class people remain suspended between two worlds, hopelessly engaged in making the worst of both.

These characters, even the vicious, are treated with compassion. Like everyone else in the novels, they remain as much victims as victimizers because they are weak, unaware, or blighted by their environment. But the point is inescapable: upper-class England in the twentieth century is a sterile and decadent phenomenon, frantically fleeing the demands of the present in the futile pursuit of the past. Far from being a snob, as she has astonishingly been labeled (see Elizabeth Hardwick, *PR*, 16, 1949, 1114–1121), Elizabeth Bowen is terribly aware of the dangers and weaknesses of her own class. Far from being suffused with romantic nostalgia for the golden age of the aristocracy, she is attacking that very nostalgia as a force that is blighting a whole social group.

She does not, however, view the middle class in rosier light. Whereas the upper class has lost the old values of home and social position, the middle class has never possessed them. To Miss Bowen these things are important. Having a home that is really one's own, in which one's an-cestors have lived, gives one a sense of belonging, of being a link in an unbroken chain. Having some sort of social status, being accepted as part of a definite group, gives one a sense of security and of individual worth. Lacking these stabilizing conditions, the middle class as Miss Bowen presents them are "tangles of mean motives" (*The House in Paris*), a rootless, restless lot. Unsure of themselves and afraid of others, they remain in constant competition for prizes they do not really want and strive incessantly for power they do not know how to use.

Emmeline's Markie and Portia's Eddie are products of this unfortunate class. Cut from similar cloth, each exhibits insecurity and ego-weakness, most notably in his love relationship. Markie wants and thinks he loves Emmeline because she represents to him something he cannot attain; to prove his own worth he attempts to rule her, and when he cannot, he resents her. Eddie seeks out Portia's affections because she serves as a link with Anna's upper-class world and because her devotion flatters his ego; when the ego-boosting backfires and her innocence shows him his smallness, true to type he turns against her. But if Markie and Eddie are dismal examples of Miss Bowen's middle class, they are tame beside Mme. Fisher and her fatal Paris house. For this powerful misuser of power, who finds her life's greatest fulfillment in driving Max Ebhart to suicide, dwarfs all the other middle-class characters as a symbol of the extreme to which the need for self-assertion can go.

The trouble with Mme. Fisher and her weaker counterparts is that they lack clearly defined directions in which to channel their energies. Miss Bowen has explicitly stated: "The outsize will is not necessarily an evil; it is a phenomenon. It must have its outsize outlet, its big task. If the right scope is not offered it, it must seize the wrong" (Bowen's Court, 1942). Her novels show that too often middle-class people are not offered the right scope, for they have been born to no definite status, have no real homes or connections to cultivate, no preordained niche in the social scheme. Thrown back on their own resources to rise or fall by their own worth, they are driven to prove themselves somehow, too often at each other's expense. Society, failing to provide men's egos with sufficient positive outlets, has left the ambitious to prey on each other in an animalistic void. Energetic individualism, with its worship of the striving will, is a middle-class aspect of romanticism that has worn dangerously thin.

The public predicament is then at the heart of the personal disaster. Coming upon a world in which the upper class has atrophied and the middle is tearing itself apart, innocence has small chance for survival. Since man is a social animal, he must either accept his impossible world or be annihilated by it, must either make Karen's meager compromise or suffer Emmeline's violent death. Either way he is defeated and in turn perpetuates defeat. For the thing is of course a vicious circle: the society that breaks the individual is made up of broken individuals; the cold and ruthless characters, from Mrs. Kerr to Anna, were once as uncorrupted as any of the heroines. The tragedy of an innocent girl, reflecting that of the people around her, expands beyond the individual to become the tragedy of an era and a misdirected way of life.

In the six pre-war novels no remedy is offered. The disease must get worse before it gets better; man must come to some sort of awareness of his predicament before he can set about to resolve it. Miss Bowen shows in these novels that twentieth-century society between world wars was still pursuing nineteenth-century dreams of personal glory, traditional sanctity, or superhuman love, without sufficient awareness that the dreams had turned to nightmare. She shows that the dreams had turned to nightmare not only because they were out of date but because they were egotistical, asocial or anti-social, and unrealizable in the actual world. Using each other without charity or scruple to fulfill unfulfillable personal fantasies, men were blindly destroying all social cohesion and rushing their world towards inevitable disaster.

The Heat of the Day (1949), written during the war, records this disaster. In it the same forces that were at work in her earlier novels are shown to have been carried to frightening conclusions. Where love was previously doomed because it was innocent and based on illusion, it is here doomed because the sky has fallen and there is no longer any shelter even for mature, well-founded love. Where the individual was previously doomed because he was unable to adapt himself to his society, he is here doomed because there is virtually no society left to adapt to. But the tragedy that has expanded to annihilating proportions is shown to have sprung from the same bewildered roots. "Fantasy is toxic," writes Miss Bowen in *Bowen's Court*: "the private cruelty and the world war both have their start in the heated brain." In her wartime novel she presents more graphically even than before the inseparable relationship between the diseased romanticism of individuals and the havoc of the world at large.

Robert Kelway, whose very photograph reveals "romanticism fired once too often," is the most vivid example. A member of the rootless middle class, he is meant to represent the forces within that class that can work for fascism. His home, loveless and perpetually for sale, symbolizes the sterile, transient environment Miss Bowen sees as prevalent on his social level; his romantic worship of the fascist ideal because it offers the individual a definite place in a definite order, springs from the desperate insecurity she feels is corollary to the middle-class emphasis on untrammeled individualism for its own sake. "Freedom," says Robert, "Freedom to be what?—the muddled, mediocre, damned." His treason is a tragic commentary on a society that has run the risk of losing its invaluable freedom by failing to give its members anything else. For the free also need constructive outlets for their energies, need to feel that their lives derive enduring value through contributing to an order greater than themselves.

While Robert carries to ruinous ends the misguided quest for self-realization we have seen driving earlier middle-class characters, Stella reveals the total collapse of the upper-class orientation. She has given up the last of her houses and now lives homeless in rented flats, and she has been outcast from her social group by the scandal of modern divorce. A "soul astray" in her class and her world, she has become acutely aware of the aristocracy's disintegration; her thoughts at her cousin's home, Mount Morris, make this appallingly clear: "Was it not here in this room and under this illusion that Cousin Nettie Morris—and who now knew how many more before her?—had been pressed back, hour by hour, by the hours themselves, into cloudland? Ladies had gone not quite mad, not quite even that, from in vain listening for meaning in the loudening tick of the clock." Time, gaining in the earlier novels on a class that clung to the past, has by the second world war won its devastating victory.

Unfortunately time's devastation embraces more than a single class; it embraces a whole era and that era's chance for love. Stella and Robert, their world crumbling, see their one sound and solid abode in love; but this too is doomed from the outset, for love cannot stand where all else falls: "They were not alone, nor had they been from the start, from the start of love. Their time sat in the third place at their table. They were the creatures of history. . . . The relation of people to each other is subject to the relation of each to time." Here, as in all the earlier novels, external society's corruptions close fatally in on love. But there is a difference now in degree: this time the destruction is final and there is no possible future for Stella and Robert's love or for that of the generation whose tragedy they enact.

Not all hope is lost, however. Though the older generation is shattered, there is a chance that the young may rebuild the world. Stella's son Roderick, who has the realism to adapt Mount Morris to modern times, may revive in the post-war world the enduring values of home. Louie, whose natural son is born in despite of social constrictions, may revive the values of parenthood and the undeflected heart. The hope of the future lies with these two and with the generation they represent. Here for the first time in her fiction Miss Bowen has offered a possible remedy for society's long disease, perhaps because in its greatest crisis the patient more fiercely than ever needs help.

In *A World of Love* (1955) this positive tendency becomes considerably more pronounced, carries in fact the book's principal import. The tragic world, though still present and certainly not unimportant, is no longer complete in itself but rather serves as essential background to a now affirmative foreground. Nevertheless, Miss Bowen's theme, like the society she writes of, has undergone no radical changes. The generation she presented as broken by war in *The Heat of the Day* is perceived in no happier light from the post-war point of view. The younger generation, hope of the future in the preceding work, carries the same vital role in this. And cutting across the generations, the basic warning against romantic extremism that has run through her novels from first to last is, in *A World of Love,* more distinctly than ever restressed.

The whole tragic aspect of the story is shown to have romantic roots. Antonia and Lilia, middle-aged when the book opens, are still in love with a man who was killed in their early youth. Each has repeated the usual pattern of an idealistic love, doomed by external conditions (World War I in this instance), and not to be lived up to in later life. These particular women, however, seem even worse off than usual. For where the broken-hearted in earlier novels generally managed at least a poor compromise future, these two have been unable to do anything further with life at all. It's true that one has married and the other has had a career, but emotionally they have advanced not one moment beyond Guy's death. "The living were living in his lifetime," Antonia perceives: "They were incomplete." More serious still, they are virtually ghosts casting over the present the past's fatal shadow.

For in a real sense their impassive existence is more negative than death. Not only have they ceased to acknowledge the present by ignoring calendars and clocks, allowing their home to become defunct, withdrawing from social interaction, but they have lost the vitality even of memory. The discovery of Guy's letters is for them a painful ordeal because it forces upon them emotion, reminding them of what they were and so of what they have become. And their condition is not unique: it is that of their whole generation, as the party at Lady Latterly's is intended to make clear. For with its Alice-in-Wonderland unreality, Lady Latterly's "phantasmagoric . . . circle of the displaced rich" reproduces on larger canvas a similar picture to Antonia's home. In both atmospheres alike the too-vivid recollection of Guy electrifies the dead air with an energy studiously unwelcomed for more than thirty years.

The trouble with these people is that they have endured too much too long. Having lived through two great wars, they have seen the world they were born to demolished, have suffered the betrayal of faith and love, and so turned in dread or exhaustion from the demands of an alien future. They are less to be blamed than pitied, and there is even a point or two in their favor: What is left of our age after war's devastations offers little to attract the heart. But what he and the rest of them fail to acknowledge is that each individual is responsible for rebuilding a possible world, and that in seceding from the present they are not only stultifying their own lives but imperiling the chance of the next generation to work out mankind's salvation.

Lilia's daughter Jane, for example, has grown up under her elders' shadow. As a result she has been for too many years "without emotional curiosity"; and when she does fall in love, at the start of the story, it is inevitably with the seeming ghost of Guy, the sole emotional magnet in her enervated environment. But while she appears to be a victim of the same romantic nostalgia that afflicts the adult world around her, she turns out to be the means of breaking its enchantment. For Jane, unlike the others, wants to bring her ghost alive into the here and now instead of burying it and herself with it beneath three decades' unstirred dust. By reviving through Guy's letters the immediate reality of the past, she forces Lilia and Antonia to air their long-submerged illusion and so to recognize its deficiencies in the light of present day.

The laying of Guy's ghost, symbolically expressed by Big Ben's demolishing strokes followed by refreshing rain, has a positive effect on all of those concerned. Once Antonia has accepted Guy's irrevocable death and the waste of her own life, lived as though he were immortal, she is able to confront what may be left of the future. Once Lilia has acknowledged that her ingrown worship of the dead has negated any happiness she might have found in marriage, she can begin to bridge the gulf between her husband and herself. But most positive of all is the effect on Jane. No sooner is she freed of her imaginary romance than she is ready to form a realistic attachment. Her opportune discovery of a genuine, living love presents explicitly at the novel's close what has been implicit from the beginning: that love, when it is rooted in the possible world, is, now as ever, our greatest good.

In contrast to the preceding novels, *A World of Love* is optimistic, and as such marks an alteration in Miss Bowen's outlook as a novelist. Whereas in the past her books stressed the tragedy of an age that destroys love, home, and security, her latest expresses the hope that these values can be revived. Now, when humanity hangs in the balance between salvation and annihilation, she has chosen to emphasize directly those aspects of life that make it worth saving. At the same time, the principal themes of her most recent novel are essentially what they have been from the beginning of her career. Here as before we find the same warning against our romantic afflictions: love founded on impossible fantasy, nostalgia for the past, and the basic quest for self-fulfillment in the realms of the unreal. Once again we feel her conviction that the forces that make and break the world have their source in the private individual and the use he makes of love.

Commentary

In writing her article, Barbara Seward employs a number of writing techniques which have been discussed throughout this manual. It may be instructive to examine these in turn, indicating to what degree the author has used them, and occasionally commenting on her degree of success. While such a commentary will not constitute a complete analysis of the article, it may serve to show how a writer can integrate a number of writing techniques into a unified whole.

The author does little in a formal way to indicate the reason for her interest in Elizabeth Bowen (see Chapter 1), but implies several reasons. The opening paragraph suggests that Miss Bowen is worthy of "serious critical attention," but has thus far received little; and the closing paragraph, containing a discussion of the more positive approach to the human condition noticeable in *A World of Love,* points out that "Now, when humanity hangs in the balance between salvation and annihilation, she [Miss Bowen] has chosen to emphasize directly those aspects of life that make it worth saving." The writer here feels that Elizabeth Bowen has a peculiar relevance to the problems we face at present. Such observations, together with the generally appreciative tone of the article, combine to suggest why Miss Bowen's work deserves consideration.

Although the author—wisely, it would seem—refrains from giving synopses of Miss Bowen's novels, a reader, even though unfamiliar with them, would know considerable about their contents (see Chapter 2) from reading the article. The opening paragraph tells us that "Miss Bowen is enormously sympathetic to the idealist who is desolated by a callous society; nevertheless she is equally aware that the callous society is itself made up of desolated idealists." Various examples throughout the article indicate the classes from which Miss Bowen draws her characters, the nature of her plots, their locale and time. An admirable feature of this article is the author's ability to present considerable information about Miss Bowen's novels without making it appear gratuitous.

Comparisons (see Chapter 3) figure so prominently throughout the article that it might almost be said to be built around them. A comparison between Miss Bowen's plots and classical tragedy runs throughout the article. In making various generalizations about Elizabeth Bowen's works, the author repeatedly cites instances from various novels which illustrate the generalizations. There are comparisons between the upper and middle classes as they appear in the novels, comparisons between the earlier and later works. The author, interestingly, forgoes a common critical device: the article contains no comparison or contrast between Elizabeth Bowen's novels and those of other writers. The many comparisons and contrasts drawn from among Miss Bowen's own books may have caused the author to feel that a consideration of other writers would have complicated the discussion unduly. Such a consideration might, as well, have been foreign to the author's purpose, since she seems concerned, not with Elizabeth Bowen's literary milieu, but with changes as well as continuity within the novelist's work itself.

The article contains no mention of form (see Chapter 4), the writer apparently feeling that Miss Bowen's significance lies more in the nature of her themes than in the way she has ordered her material.

Basic to the entire article is the author's conception of the evolution of her writer's thought (see Chapter 5). The second paragraph strikes a keynote by hinting at a difference between the early novels and *A World of Love*. This hint is taken up and fully developed in the last part of the essay, which deals specifically with *A World of Love* and the way in which it is optimistic, in contrast to the preceding novels. Of equal importance with this emphasis on the evolution in her writer's thought, however, is the author's insistence that "the principal themes of her [Miss Bowen's] most recent novel are essentially what they have been from the beginning of her career." In discussing changes, it is easy to ignore similarities. The ability to discern permanence in the midst of change is a mark of maturity in a critic. The author, throughout her article, demonstrates this ability to a high degree.

The author seems unconcerned with point of view (see Chapter 6) as a narrative technique. Her silence on this point would seem to argue simply that point of view is not a central consideration in her evaluation of Miss Bowen's fiction.

At the beginning of the article we are told the nature of Elizabeth Bowen's reputation (see Chapter 8). Miss Bowen, we learn, has been given little serious critical attention, "although she is generally recognized as one of our foremost writers." The ramifications of the paradox suggested here are not explored, however, and the mention of Miss Bowen's reputation seems, as much as anything, a convenient method of getting into the essay.

Direct quotations (see Chapter 10)—in every instance relatively short ones—are much in evidence. In the majority of instances, these quotations appear at places in the article where the author has interpreted her novelist's meaning or has offered a critical judgment. Using the novelist's own words at these key points in the article carries a conviction which paraphrase could scarcely hope to do.

In keeping with her silence concerning other authors with whom Elizabeth Bowen might have been compared, the author makes less use of secondary material (see Chapter 10) than do some critics. An exception occurs in the case of the several quotations from Miss Bowen's *Collected Impressions* and *Bowen's Court,* where the author indicates pronouncements Miss Bowen has made, preparatory to showing how these pronouncements find embodiment in the novels. Only one writer besides Miss Bowen is mentioned in the article: Elizabeth Hardwick's opprobrious label for Miss Bowen comes under critical fire. Since the opening paragraph suggests that "what attention she [Miss Bowen] has received has tended to ignore the full significance of her work by overstressing her compassion for the innocent idealist trapped in the modern world," the author, had she cared to, might have indicated— perhaps in a footnote—the sources of these misleading interpretations. To do this, of course, inevitably gives an article a somewhat argumentative air; and the author, possibly feeling that the best approach was a positive one, chose to present her own interpretation of Elizabeth Bowen's significance, rather than to become embroiled in quarrels with other critics.

NORMAN FOERSTER

Thoreau as Artist

I

*I*nveterate observer and recorder that he was, at heart Thoreau was assuredly not a naturalist, but rather—what? A literary artist? This answer, one of the commonest, has behind it not only the authority of his friend Channing, who said that Thoreau regarded literature as his profession, but also that of Thoreau himself, who declared, in unmistakable terms: "My work is writing." Yet it must be remembered that in his lifetime he published only two books, the *Week* and *Walden;* that the creative impulse in him was neither vehement nor persistent, most of his *Journal* being a bare record of facts; and that he wanted both the spur of fame and the desire to serve men, at least as these aims are usually conceived by writers. If writing was his work, it was his work in much the same sense in which surveying and pencil-making were his work: he was not a surveyor or manufacturer of pencils, nor was he a man of letters.

Poet, at all events, he was not, for a man can scarcely be a poet without achieving a certain bulk of successful verse, and the total bulk of Thoreau's verse, most of it unsuccessful, would fill less than an ordinary volume. That he wrote it at all is to be explained less in terms of his artistic powers, since he lived in a time of renaissance when the homespun of prose was disparaged in favor of purple singing-robes, in a time when, it has been said, one could not throw a stone in the city of Boston without hitting a poet. So Thoreau versified; his prose works abound in interjected poems or poetic fragments, many of which have the odd effect of serving, not to lift the reader aloft on the wings of sudden inspiration, but to make him halt in consternation before a veritable New England glacial boulder, shapeless and inert. There is little in him of the lyrical poet's instinct to burst into song at every provocation of nature. Although he tells us repeatedly that he is inspired, he also tells us that the mood is gone before he can versify it; the best poetry, he says broadly, is never expressed—an assertion not without its measure of truth. Indeed, it was fatally true of his own practice. Delicately perceptive of the concrete world, eagerly responsive to beauty, inwardly living the life of the poet, he was so intent on understanding and appropriating his visions that when the time came for singing them he was dumb.

THE POET'S DELAY

> In vain I see the morning rise,
>   In vain observe the western blaze,
> Who idly look to other skies,
>   Expecting life by other ways.
>
> Shall I then wait the autumn wind,
>   Compelled to seek a milder day,
> And leave no curious nest behind,
>   No woods still echoing to my lay?

In these lines is something of his Puritanical distrust of all art; "very dangerous", he says elsewhere, is the talent for composition, since "I feel as if my life had grown more outward when I can express it." With him it is always *my life,* never the glory of divine poetry:—

> "My life hath been the poem I would have writ,
>   But I could not both live and live to utter it."

In natural metrical skill he was more deficient even than Emerson. Most of his verses are benumbed, and crawl along, with an occasional spurt, like a grasshopper in the autumn. For example:—

> "Let such pure hate still underprop
> Our love, that we may be
> Each other's conscience,
> And have our sympathy
> Mainly from thence."

If Donne deserved hanging for not keeping accent, what of Thoreau? The following is a more just specimen, typical in subject, form, and mood:—

TALL AMBROSIA

> Among the signs of autumn I perceive
> The Roman wormwood (called of learned men
> *Ambrosia elatior,* food for gods,
> For by impartial science the humblest weed
> Is as well named as is the proudest flower)
> Sprinkles its yellow dust over my shoes
> As I brush through the now neglected garden.
> We trample under foot the food of gods
> And spill their nectar in each drop of dew.
> My honest shoes, fast friends that never stray
> Far from my couch, thus powdered, countrified,
> Bearing many a mile the marks of their adventure,
> At the post-house disgrace the Gallic gloss
> Of those well-dressed ones who no morning dew
> Nor Roman wormwood ever have done through,
> Who never walk, but are transported rather,
> For what old crime of theirs I do not gather.

In such lines he is a forerunner of Robert Frost; if Emerson's judgment is right, he could also be a successor and improver of Simonides, as in the best of all his poems, the Walden verses on "Smoke":—

> "Light-winged Smoke, Icarian bird,
> Melting thy pinions in thy upward flight;
> Lark without song, and messenger of dawn,
> Circling above the hamlets as thy nest;
> Or else, departing dream and shadowy form
> Of midnight vision, gathering up thy skirts;
> By night star-veiling, and by day
> Darkening the light and blotting out the sun;—
> Go thou, my incense, upward from this hearth,
> And ask the gods to pardon this clear flame."

Virtually blank verse, this delicate yet classically firm little poem suggests the possibilities of that form for lyrical use. Had Thoreau lived in the England of Elizabeth, he might well have been a builder of lofty rhyme; like Whitman, although for other reasons, he was a great poet *in posse*.

His poetic feeling, however, is worthily embalmed in his prose. Moments of inspiration, as he remarks, are not lost merely because they fail to leave a deposit in verse; the impression abides, and in due time is expressed in a form equally genuine if less ardent: when time has emphasized the essential truth in these ecstatic states,—

"in cooler moments we can use them as paint to gild and adorn our prose. . . . They are like a pot of pure ether. They lend the writer when the moment comes a certain superfluity of wealth, making his expression to overrun and float itself."

Without this superfluity of wealth, Thoreau's prose would be shorn of most of its beauty and power. If not a great poet, Thoreau is a great prose writer.

II

The first and last impression produced by Thoreau's prose is its sincerity, its unflinching truth. It is faithfully idiosyncratic, the mirror of his sincerity of character. "I would rather sit on a pumpkin and have it all to myself than be crowded on a velvet cushion"—who but Thoreau could have written that? Speaking of the art of writing, Thoreau leans upon that universally applicable maxim of the transcendentalists: "Be faithful to your genius!" This is for him the central precept.

"The one great rule of composition—and if I were a professor of rhetoric I should insist on this—is, to *speak the truth*. This first, this second, this third: pebbles in your mouth or not."

He was instinctively and somewhat bitterly suspicious of "the *belles-lettres* and the *beaux arts* and their *professors*, which we can do without." He would simply say, with Buonaparte: "Speak plain; the rest will follow," with his eye on the truth and not on the ornaments. He would not seek expressions, but thoughts to be expressed—and even this did not satisfy him, for best of all, he says somewhere, is "the theme that seeks me, not I it". He is only to report, to obey, to serve as agent, to lend himself to an utterance "free and lawless as a lamb's bleat": an account true enough of his habit if one bears in mind that he was a somewhat wolfish lamb bred in a highly civilized tradition. His distinction in this matter, however, is not in his theory of style, which is the common property of the romantic school, but in his practice, which is all but unequalled in its resoluteness. Cardinal Newman, despite his admirable statement of the twofold aspect of style, of the marriage of thought and word, and his assertion that his own aim was to express truth with no admixture of rhetoric, clearly enough was enamored of Roman eloquence. Similarly, to take an instance from Thoreau's Rome, the youthful Emerson, relishing resounding phrases and noble periods, never, in later years, quite freed himself from the seductions of adventitious beauty. The ideal of Emerson's style, says Mr. Brownell, is eloquence; that of Thoreau's, we may add in contrast, is truth. So rigorously does Thoreau follow his ideal that he demands of every sentence that it be "the result of a long probation", expressing in words what had already been expressed in action. He applies this ideal, not only to writing, but quite as much to reading. "What I began by reading," he says, "I must finish by acting." In a good book he looked first of all, perhaps, for the gadfly in it, and rejoiced in its sting, not unlike the Puritans of the old Concord who magnified their sins and lashed them with a grim joy. It may well be that the idiosyncratic quality of Thoreau's prose style springs more from the Puritan in him than from the romanticist, more from the voice of conscience than from the "lamb's bleat".

The charm of Thoreau's prose rests, then, on its complete sincerity, and his prose is to be enjoyed to the full only by readers who find his personality attractive. Yet it has definite qualities that win the approval of any discriminating reader. His sentences, for one thing, are alive. Living in his way, an intense life constantly alert to what was going on in his inner being and in nature, he could not well write a page devoid of life, like the flaccid writing of the ordinary journalist. A writer without a full experience, as he says, used "torpid words, wooden or lifeless words, such words as 'humanitary', which have a paralysis in their tails". His own diction is fresh, dewy, an early morning diction. It has the enormous advantage of unusual concreteness—to be expected of a writer whose perceptions were so highly trained, and whose aversion was metaphysics. And his store of concrete words and images he used with gusto, if not abandon, responding to his theme, seeking to penetrate, by sympathy, to its heart or essence, as in this perfect account of the nighthawk's antic swoop and boom:—

"The night-hawk circled overhead in the sunny afternoon—for I sometimes made a day of it—like a mote in the eye, or in heaven's eye, falling from time to time with a swoop and a sound as if the heavens were rent, torn at last to very rags and tatters, and yet a seamless cope remained."

That slight turn, "or in heaven's eye", with its unexpected shifting of the image, is typical of his restrained animation. Or take the following instance of his expressiveness, with its "puff-ball" figure drawn straight from nature, its fit phrasing, and its satiric *aplomb*:—

"On gala days the town fired its great guns, which echo like pop-guns in these woods, and some waifs of martial music occasionally penetrate thus far. To me, away there in my bean-field at the other end of the town, the big guns sounded as if a puff-ball had burst; and when there was a military turn-out of which I was ignorant, I have sometimes had a vague sense all the day of some sort of itching and disease in the horizon, as if some eruption would break out there soon. . . ."

Figures of speech abound in such passages, as in all his writing—his concreteness is largely a figurativeness. His acquaintance with nature is, of course, reflected in his metaphors and similes, as in that perfect comparison of the big guns with a puff-ball; or in his comparison of the weeping of Ossian's heroes with the perspiration of stone in the heat of summer; or in his comparison of the man of intellect with a barren, staminiferous flower, and of the poet with a fertile and perfect flower; or in that graphic comparison, mentioned by Channing, of the branches of Darby's oak with gray lightning stereotyped on the sky.

His love of paradox, his fondness for puns (in which he rivals his favorite poets of the great period of English literature), and the ever-present element of surprise in his style, are additional manifestations of his desire fully to rouse himself and his reader to the inner nature of his theme, whether it be nighthawks, or celebrations by the rude bridge that spanned the river, or the sense of time and space. A penetrating impression must be made, at all costs. He is never, or almost never, languid, but holds his stilus firmly, as in this sentence, which illustrates its own meaning:—

"A sentence should read as if the author, had he held a plow instead of a pen, could have drawn a furrow deep and straight to the end."

Here the emphasis falls distinctly and precisely where it should fall; so does it, to take another example, in this:—

"When the wind blows, the fine snow comes filtering down through all the aisles of the wood in a golden cloud."

A penetrating effect, again, is achieved by his conciseness. Writing of De Quincey, Thoreau remarks that a good style must have a strength in reserve, must be "concentrated and nutty". His own style, especially in the satiric and critical passages, is compact and germinal, acridly nutty, like an acorn:—

"Do not stay to be an overseer of the poor, but endeavor to become one of the worthies of the world."

"Time is but the stream I go a-fishing in."

"It takes a man to make a room silent."

"One man may well feel chagrined when he finds he can do nearly all he can conceive."

"How can we expect a harvest of thought who have not had a seedtime of character?"

He would not spread himself thin, either in his life or in his writing. Everything must be deliberate and concentrated.

"The writer must direct his sentences as carefully and leisurely as the marksman his rifle, who shoots sitting and with a rest, with patent sights and conical balls beside."

And indeed, as a stylist, Thoreau is something of a marksman; now his sentences crack close at hand, now they sound as from a remoter station, reverberating solemnly, as if nature had taken them unto herself and charged them with a meaning of her own.

Such command is invaluable in satire and wit. Humor, that "indispensable pledge of sanity", he had, but a good-natured spontaneous wit, with a trace of sharpness, was more characteristic. Says Channing:—

"There was a lurking humor in almost all that he said,—a dry wit, often expressed. He used to laugh heartily and many times in all the intercourse I had, when anything in that direction was needed. . . . No one more quickly entertained the apprehension of a jest; and his replies often came with a startling promptness."

Instances are everywhere, even in the sober *Journal,* as when he tells of a party, warm and noisy, where he suffered himself to be introduced to two young women, one of whom "was as lively and loquacious as a chickadee; had been accustomed to the society of watering-places, and therefore could get no refreshment out of such a dry fellow as I", while the other, said to be pretty, could not make herself heard, "there was such a clacking", and he sagely concludes that parties are social machinery designed for matrimonial connections, and prefers to eat crackers and cheese in the silent woods with old Joseph Hosmer. Or take the following reaction to the *ewig Weibliche:*—

"When you are once comfortably seated at a public meeting, there is something unmanly in the sitting on tiptoe and *qui vive* attitude,— involuntary rising into your throat, as if gravity had ceased to operate, —when a lady approaches, with quite godlike presumption, to elicit the miracle of a seat where none is."

Or finally this, in a milder vein, on a Puritan method of paying the clergy:—

" 'In 1662, the town agreed that a part of every whale cast on shore be appropriated for the support of the ministry.' No doubt there seemed to be some propriety in thus leaving the support of the ministers to Providence, whose servants they are, and who alone rules the storms; for, when few whales were cast up, they might suspect that their worship was not acceptable. The ministers must have sat upon the cliffs in every storm, and watched the shore with anxiety."

Much of the charm of Thoreau's best pages resides in this lurking humor, this dry wit always ready to kindle. Without them, he might have been an intolerably disagreeable social critic, though he might still have written pleasantly of nature,—a possibility not so remote when we learn that in his last years he blotted the humorous parts of his essays, saying: "I cannot bear the levity I find". He spoke like Endicott at Merry Mount.

III

With Carlyle and Ruskin and other typical writers of his century, Thoreau obviously excelled in the expressive side of art; but what of form? His sense of form has been placed with Emerson's (Emerson, to speak brusquely, having none). It is true that both Transcendentalists had the same weaknesses, even preparing their essays in the same manner by extorting them, so to say, out of their jewel-laden diaries. There is, however, a difference of degree. Thoreau's sentences and paragraphs cohere better than do Emerson's: he generally leaves the impression of continuity even when he lacks the reality, while Emerson often has the reality without leaving the impression. Thoreau, that is, writes from Parnassus, Emerson from Delphi. Thoreau again, if less noble, is more luminous—not only because his subjects are different, but also because his mode of thinking is more concrete. Although wanting a true sense of the value of architectonics in literature, he loved shapeliness, fine carving, beauty of form, "elegance", as he termed it— the informing quality that is simply the flowering of a nature well-tempered and wisely civilized, a humane nature. Much of this love of beauty he must have derived from his intimate studies in Greek and Latin literatures. "I do not know," he remarks, "but the reason why I love some Latin verses more than whole English poems is simply in the elegant terseness and conciseness of the language." His feeling for beauty is thus not unlike that of the school of Pope and Dr. Johnson, although in saying this one should remember that he all but ignored the eighteenth century and differed far from Johnson in regarding *Lycidas* as perhaps the finest example of true elegance in English. In his own work he attained in large measure his ideal of elegance, partly through revision (a facile writer, he resorted constantly to the use of the file), and partly through his realizing in his character something of the classical decorum. He believed that beauty is the final excellence, that whereas a first inspection of good writing should reveal its common-sense, a second should reveal its severe truth, and a third beauty.

He was well fitted to see beauty in external nature. Coming back to nature from the ancient classics, he perceived with added force the meaning of the third of "those celestial thrine",—Truth, Goodness, Beauty,—in the loveliness of line, and light and shade, and color. Despite his provincial ignorance of the plastic arts—an ignorance emulating Emerson's—he succeeded in some degree in acquiring the point of view of the plastic arts through training his eye for landscape. Again and again in his writings he dominates the natural scene, composing it with the craftman's sense of design, displaying a feeling for balance, repetition, emphasis, harmony, quite apart from his feeling for spiritual significance lurking behind or expressed by outer beauty. He could enjoy beauty as such. His layman's interest in aesthetic principles is indicated by his careful reading of William Gilpin on landscape, and of Ruskin's *Modern Painters*. When in the field he had a habit of now and then inclining his head to one side, or even stooping enough to reverse the picture completely in order to refresh himself with the ideal beauty suggested by the scene when thus severed from its normal associations. It is noteworthy that when the woodsmen come to desecrate his Walden pine groves he does not tremble to the foundations, but calmly remarks: "It makes some new and unexpected prospects", and while these prospects are in the making quietly enjoys the picture before him: "A pretty forest scene, seeing oxen, so patient and stationary, good for pictures, standing on the ice,—a piece of still life." One of the woodchoppers "appeared to me apparently half a mile distant, as in a picture of which the two trees were the frame". After an extended description of this picture, he observes that some scenes have an obvious pictorial quality, needing no composition, no idealization, being already pictures, ready for the recording pencil.

Such pictures he was constantly watching for, training himself to recognize them when others would have passed them by. He would be an artist as well as a naturalist. Daily, while living in town, he took occasion to view the sunset, that ever-repeated yet never-repeated masterpiece of nature: "Every day a new picture is painted and framed, held up for half an hour, in such lights as the Great Artist chooses, and then withdrawn." Everywhere he looked for new "effects" wrought by that Artist, the master *improvisatore,* in the flowing world of nature. He never tired of seeing the familiar meadows, woods, ponds, and hills of Concord varied without repetition by his shifting points of view and by the always unique caprices of the weather: he was as active in this aesthetic pursuit as in his scientific interest in names, dates, and temperatures. To-day he beholds Walden remote and eerie in the mist; tomorrow he shall thrill to the "clear, cold, Novemberish light" that glitters from downy twigs and lies vividly upon the "silver-plated river". He stands on Strawberry Hill late on a misty September afternoon: "Annursnack never looked so well as now seen from this hill. The ether gives a velvet softness to the whole landscape. The hills float in it. A blue veil is drawn over the earth." Thus day after day and year after year he studied the landscapes of Concord.

The result of all this study was the inimitable charm, the intimate mastery, of all of his descriptions of nature, whether an individual leaf or the whole of a vast prospect. That sensuous equipment that served him as an observer of natural fact, served him equally as an observer of natural beauty, giving him a high degree of truth in both spheres. What other writer of our time has perceived so subtly and expressed his vision with so delicate a truth? Ruskin, beside Thoreau, seems theatrical, melodramatic, entranced by his own powers, giving nature the stamp of his expansive personality: Thoreau's self-restraint steadies his insight, lets him penetrate closer to the heart of nature as to his own heart. His magical truth has won him many a devoted reader who finds himself indifferent to, or exasperated by, Thoreau's personal piquancy and his paradoxical satire of human society. Who that knows *Walden* can forget those glorious white pines of "Baker Farm"?—

"Sometimes I ramble to pine groves, standing like temples, or like fleets at sea, full-rigged, with wavy boughs, and rippling with light, so soft and green and shady that the Druids would have forsaken their oaks to worship in them."

One sentence could scarcely do more. Or take his reproduction of the song of the red-winged blackbird, whose liquid notes fill the meadows in early spring:—

"The strain of the red-wing on the willow spray over the water to-night is liquid, bubbling, watery, almost like a twinkling fountain, in perfect harmony with the meadow. It oozes, trickles, tinkles, bubbles from its throat,—*bob-y-lee-e-e,* and then its shrill, fine whistle."

Or take his exquisite insight into the beauty of the leaves of the tree known as the scarlet oak:—

"Stand under this tree and see how finely its leaves are cut against the sky,—as it were, only a few sharp points extending from a midrib. They look like double, treble, or quadruple crosses. They are far more ethereal than the less deeply scalloped oak leaves. They have so little leafy *terra firma* that they appear melting away in the light, and scarcely obstruct our view. . . . Lifted higher and higher, and sublimated more and more, putting off some earthiness and cultivating more intimacy with the light each year, they have at length the least possible amount of earthy matter, and the greatest spread and grasp of skyey influences. There they dance, arm in arm with the light,—tripping it on fantastic points, fit partners in those aerial halls. So intimately mingled with it are they, that, what with their slenderness and their glossy surfaces, you can hardly tell at last what in the dance is leaf and what is light. And when no zephyr stirs, they are at most but a rich tracery to the forest windows."

Or, once more, the beauty of Concord apples:—

". . . unspeakably fair,—apples not of Discord, but of Concord! . . . Painted by the frosts, some a uniform clear bright yellow, or red, or crimson, as if their spheres had regularly revolved, and enjoyed the influence of the sun on all sides alike,—some with the faintest pink blush imaginable,—some brindled with deep red streaks like a cow, or with hundreds of fine blood-red rays running regularly from the stem-dimple to the blossom end, like meridional lines, on a straw-colored ground,—some touched with a greenish rust, like a fine lichen, here and there, with crimson blotches or eyes more or less confluent and fiery when wet,—and others gnarly, and freckled or peppered all over on the stem side with fine crimson spots on a white ground, as if accidentally sprinkled from the brush of Him who paints the autumn leaves. Others, again, are sometimes red inside, perfused with a beautiful blush, fairy food, too beautiful to eat,—apple of the Hesperides, apple of the evening sky!"

Comments and Questions

1. Find the paradox in Norman Foerster's opening paragraph and determine its function in the essay.

2. Among other contrasts, Foerster sets Thoreau's poetry over against his prose. In fact, Foerster devotes the first part of his three-part essay largely to Thoreau's poetry, even though the essay as a whole concerns Thoreau's artistry as a prose writer. What relationship exists between this opening section of the article and the other two sections? Is this beginning too indirect a way to approach a discussion of Thoreau's prose, or does this section throw light on Thoreau as literary artist in prose?

3. At the opening of the second section of the essay, Foerster writes: "The first and last impression produced by Thoreau's prose is its sincerity, its unflinching truth." Exactly how does Foerster define the abstraction "truth," as it finds expression in Thoreau's prose?

4. Foerster makes wide use of allusions to other writers. Decide upon his reasons for doing this and the degree of success he achieves.

5. Throughout his discussion of Thoreau's style, Foerster quotes various of Thoreau's own pronouncements concerning literary expression. Do these quotations reinforce Foerster's thesis, and if so, how?

6. Foerster quotes a sentence from Thoreau which reads: "A sentence should read as if the author, had he held a plow instead of a pen, could have drawn a furrow deep and straight to the end." Foerster then suggests that "Here the emphasis falls distinctly and precisely where it should fall. . . ." Where, according to your reading of this sentence, *does* the emphasis fall? Do you agree with Foerster's evaluation of the sentence? Should Foerster have indicated where he thinks the emphasis in the sentence falls, or is the point he wishes to make made more emphatic by allowing the sentence to stand alone?

7. In the second part of his essay Foerster discusses Thoreau's style as that style embodies itself in the individual sentence. In the third part he discusses form. Do you find his approach the same in the two sections, or different? Is one section more successful than the other, or

are both of equal merit? For which, according to the essay, is Thoreau's work more notable: style or form?

8. Following your study of Foerster's essay, try to reconstruct the nature of Foerster's research and study which led to his writing it. Compare and contrast what seems to you to have been Foerster's preparation with the experience you have had studying your writer.

OTIS B. WHEELER

Faulkner's Wilderness

*A*lmost from the first contact with the new world of North America white men have recognized in many ways that theirs was a unique kind of experience with the wilderness. Here was a primeval land, fresh from the hand of God, except for the puny and insignificant inroads made upon it by the aboriginal red man. The newcomers were of a relatively sophisticated race, grown up where the face of the land had for centuries been altered by man's tools and according to his desires. But in the primeval wilderness it was God's will, and none of man's, that was manifest.

Faulkner's is not the first reaction in American literature to this experience. Passing over the diarists and naturalists of the colonial period, we can see it beginning about the time of our national independence with Freneau and Bryant. But this reaction is in terms almost wholly derivative from the well-established tradition of Primitivism in English literature. Specifically, wild nature is the manifestation and locus of a Divine Spirit to which man, jaded and corrupted by civilization, may turn for spiritual refreshment and instruction. This reaction is epitomized in Bryant's "Thanatopsis" and "To a Waterfowl."

Cooper's reaction is more significant and more original. For it is he who defines the terms of a paradox which Faulkner is still working at: if the wilderness is God's work, what is the meaning of man's destruction of it in the name of civilization and culture? And there is a corollary problem: if the wilderness is the locus and manifestation of Divine Spirit, where is man to turn for spiritual renewal when the wilderness is gone?

I

In Faulkner's treatment, the wilderness has two roles, apparently discrete, but eventually harmonized in a pattern that transcends human experience. First, it is the teacher of moral and spiritual truth; second, it is the victim of the Anglo-Saxon's rapacity.[1] Although Faulkner begins by approaching the two themes separately, he eventually comes to interweave them in the final versions of the Ike McCaslin stories. For instance, the separate stories "Lion" and "Delta Autumn" are primarily concerned with the theme of wilderness as victim. In contrast, "The Old People" and the brief *Saturday Evening Post* version of "The Bear" deal mainly with the theme of wilderness as teacher. But in the *Go Down, Moses* version of "The Bear" the two themes are fused, as they are also in the total effect of the stories and transitional commentaries in *Big Woods*.

The first theme is worked out on both dramatic and symbolic levels as the rites of puberty for young Ike McCaslin.[2] At one point Faulkner calls the wilderness Ike's "college," and adds, "the old male bear itself was his alma mater." [3] But more often the education is described in religious terms. Under the tutelage of Sam Fathers, his spiritual father and, in more ways than first appear, the priest of a primitive wilderness religion, Ike "entered his novitiate to the true wilderness. . . . It seemed to him that at the age of ten he was witnessing his own birth" (p. 195). In this novitiate he undergoes the tests which will mark his transition from boyhood to manhood. Or to put it in abstract terms, he comes step by step to an awareness of the spiritual and moral verities which, says Faulkner, underlie human existence. By watching the dogs who run Old Ben, but stop short of bringing him to bay, he begins to learn what fear is. But in the situation of the one dog who overcomes her fear sufficiently to get close enough to be raked by the bear's claws ("The wilderness had patted lightly once her temerity," p. 199) he begins to learn the meaning of bravery. He personally knows fear as he feels himself watched by the bear; and he learns a little more about bravery as Sam Fathers tells him, "Be scared. . . . But don't be afraid" (p. 207). After journeying alone into the wilderness without food and finally without the aid of watch or compass, stripped, so to speak, to his fundamental humanity, he is worthy to see the bear, the symbol of the essential wilderness, the apotheosis of the wilderness spirit. It is a moment of mystical unity: "They had looked at each other, they had emerged from the wilderness old as earth, synchronized to the instant by something more than the blood that moved the flesh and bones which bore them, and touched, pledged something, affirmed, something more

---

[1] Faulkner sees rapacity, in fact, as the basis of civilization. See Ursula Brumm, "Wilderness and Civilization: A Note on William Faulkner," *Partisan Review*, XXII, 340–350 (Summer, 1955).

[2] For a detailed discussion of the parallels with primitive puberty rites, see Kenneth J. LaBudde, "Cultural Primitivism in William Faulkner's 'The Bear,'" *American Quarterly*, II, 322–328 (Winter, 1950).

[3] *Go Down, Moses* (New York, 1942), p. 210. Subsequent page references to this volume appear in the text.

lasting than the frail web of bones and flesh which any accident could obliterate." [4]

But he is not yet a man. There is the test of taking life, how he conducts himself in the face of a death which he has engineered. This test is worked out in "The Old People" where Ike kills his first buck and Sam marks his forehead with the hot blood, and reports, "He done all right" (p. 165). The full meaning of the ceremony is something Ike is able to verbalize only much later. Part of it is a cleansing of futile and irrelevant emotions. He thinks to himself, Sam Fathers had "consecrated and absolved him of weakness and regret . . . —not from love and pity for all which lived and ran and then ceased to live in a second in the very midst of splendor and speed, but from weakness and regret" (p. 182). But the final meaning is best expressed by Ike as an old man, over eighty, in "Delta Autumn," as he recalls again the sacramental first buck: "I slew you; my bearing must not shame your quitting life. My conduct forever onward must become your death" (p. 351).

What altogether has the wilderness taught? It might be summed up as the code of the hunter: bravery, strength, endurance, honor, pride, dignity, humility, pity, love of life, of justice, and of liberty. These are the qualities that Sam or Ike or Cass Edmonds or the unnamed father of the boy in the short version of "The Bear" talk about at one point or another. They are the virtues that the boy learns in a more or less empirical way. These virtues are enforced by three general insights: the knowledge of death, the sense of the sublime, and the sense of mystic unity. The last of these has already been pointed out in one way in young Ike's triumphant vision of the bear; that is unity on a spiritual level. Corresponding to this spiritual unity is the idea of physical unity stated when Ike comes back to the spot in the forest where Lion and Sam Fathers are buried, along with one of Old Ben's paws. He muses, "There was no death, not Lion and not Sam: not held fast in earth but free in earth and not in earth but of earth, myriad yet undiffused of every myriad part" (p. 328). Yet all life has an equally insistent aspect of mortality, a knowledge of which makes the aspect of immortality more precious. This knowledge of death is expressed in Ike's meeting with the rattlesnake only a few minutes after he has left the graves just mentioned. Calmly he hails the huge old rattler in the Indian language of Sam Fathers: "Chief . . . , Grandfather." And through his mind runs the thought, "the old one, the ancient and accursed about the earth, fatal and solitary." The smell of the snake is for him "evocative of all knowledge and an old weariness and of pariah-hood and of death" (p. 329).

Enforcing all the lessons of the wilderness is the sense of sublimity

---

[4] Short version of "The Bear," in Raymond W. Short and Richard B. Sewell, eds., *Short Stories for Study* (3rd ed.; New York, 1956), p. 326.

which Ike feels in contact with it: "the unforgettable sense of the big woods—not a quality dangerous or particularly inimical, but profound, sentient, dynamic and brooding" (p. 175). If this is not precisely the traditional definition of the sublime, nevertheless it seems to be Faulkner's version of it, his attempt to define the emotional quality of a situation in which we traditionally find the emotion of the sublime.

The situation in which the wilderness teaches, that is, the chase, contains by implication the other role of the wilderness—the role of victim. Yet it is not a simple situation because, since the wilderness has a moral role, its destruction has a moral quality.

In order to understand the complexities of the situation we must begin by understanding that there are two kinds of people involved. Ike and Sam Fathers pre-eminently represent the initiated, though in addition Sam is, like Old Ben, a symbol of the wilderness itself. These people have learned fully what the wilderness has to teach and have thereby become in a sense priests of a wilderness religion. They may attain this status because they are free, either by birth or renunciation, of the taint which marks the other type of person—the Anglo-Saxon heritage of rapacity. Sam, the son of a Chickasaw chief and a Negro slave woman, has never had it. Ike, descended from Carothers McCaslin, one of the most rapacious men in the history of Yoknapatawpha, renounces his heritage, gives his lands to a cousin, McCaslin Edmonds, in whom the traits of Carothers McCaslin have bred truer and who in turn passes on these traits to his descendant—Carothers Edmonds of "Delta Autumn." Such men, and others of even less sophistication, are the uninitiated. They may joy in the wilderness, in "those fierce instants of heart and brain and courage and wiliness and speed," [5] but they can never become initiates in the manner of Ike and Sam. Boon Hogganbeck is the nearest thing to the pure type. He has "the mind of a child, the heart of a horse and little hard shoe-button eyes without depth or meanness or generosity or viciousness or gentleness or anything else . . ." (p. 227). But even he falls short of the generalized type which Faulkner characterizes in his introduction to *Big Woods*: "Then came the Anglo-Saxon, the pioneer, the tall man roaring with protestant scripture and boiled whiskey, . . . turbulent because of his over-revved glands . . . , innocent and gullible, without bowels for avarice or compassion or forethought either . . . turning the earth into a howling waste from which he would be the first to vanish . . . because . . . only the wilderness could feed and nourish him." [6]

Rapacity Faulkner finds a peculiarly American way. As he says in *A Fable*, horse-stealing is an American institution, illustrative of "an invincible way of life . . . , the old fine strong American tradition of rapine. . . ." [7] To fall before this rapacity, whether expressed by the

---

[5] *Ibid.*, p. 329.
[6] *Big Woods* (New York, 1955), pp. [iv–v].
[7] *A Fable* (New York, 1954), pp. 167–168.

hunter's gun, the woodsman's axe, the sawmill, or the cotton farm financed by the money-hungry bankers in Jefferson, is the first and obvious way in which the wilderness is victim.

But we must remember that it is not one of the rapacious who engineers the death of the great bear. Although Boon Hogganbeck wields the knife that finds his heart, it is Sam Fathers, the initiated, who finds and trains the dog Lion and who directs the hunt; and he is abetted in all this by his acolyte, Ike. On the face of things it would seem inconsistent, even sacrilegious, for the true believer to destroy the source of his belief. But the motive behind the act gives it a sacramental quality. This motive is the reverent desire to save the wilderness from the worse fate that awaits it at the hands of the uninitiated. As Sam says, "Somebody is going to [shoot Old Ben] some day." And Ike replies, "I know it. That's why it must be one of us. . . . When even he don't want it to last any longer" (p. 212). Thus the other way in which the wilderness falls victim is through the sacrificial act of its devotees. The sacrificial quality is even further emphasized by the fact that the act is a self-immolation for one of the devotees: Sam is so much a part of the wilderness that at the moment of Old Ben's death he too falls, to be carried home to his death bed, though he has no visible wound.

Now, are these devotees true believers if they take it upon themselves to determine the fate of the Great Mother? The answer lies in Ike's statement ". . . when even he don't want it to last any longer." They do not determine the fate; they act only as instruments to accomplish a design immanent in Nature. And who better than the true believers, the initiated, would know of this immanent design?

The allegations of such design are explicit in nearly all of the wilderness stories. The Big Woods is referred to as that "doomed wilderness." The hunters and dogs and bear are "ordered and compelled by and within the wilderness in ancient and unremitting contest according to the ancient and immitagable rules . . ." (p. 192). As they enter the last stages of the hunt for Old Ben, Ike can play his part with undivided heart and mind because "it seemed to him that there was a fatality in it. . . . It was like the last act on a set stage. It was the beginning of the end of something, he didn't know what, except that he would not grieve" (p. 226). As an old man in "Delta Autumn" he is able to verbalize what he could only feel as a boy. "[God] said, 'I will give man his chance. I will give him warning and foreknowledge, too, along with the desire to follow and the power to slay. The woods and the fields he ravages and the game he devastates will be consequence and signature of his crime and guilt, and his punishment' " (p. 349). The result of man's rapacity, thinks Uncle Ike, is the moral and social chaos of the world on the brink of World War II: "No wonder the ruined woods I used to know don't cry for retribution! he thought. The people who destroyed it will accomplish its revenge" (p. 364).

These destructors and the fate they bring upon themselves are presented in three forms in Boon, Lion, and "Roth" Edmonds. At the end of "The Bear" Ike finds Boon sitting beneath a tree full of squirrels frenziedly beating the parts of an old gun together and shouting, "Get out of here! Don't touch them! Don't touch a one of them! They're mine!" (p. 331). He has senselessly played his part in the destruction of the wilderness, has slain the great bear with only a sheath knife, and without knowing it has led himself into the pathetic and ludicrous situation of trying to patch up an old gun to shoot a squirrel.[8] And this is the last time Boon appears in any of the stories.

Lion is just a four-legged symbol of the same destructiveness. He embodies "courage and all else that went to make up the will and desire to pursue and kill, . . . endurance, the will and desire to endure beyond all imaginable limits of flesh in order to overtake and slay." And his eyes are in quality just like Boon's: "yellow eyes as depthless as Boon's, as free as Boon's of meanness or generosity or gentleness or viciousness" (pp. 237–238). His fate, of course, is to have his entrials raked out by the bear as he leaps to a death grip on the bear's throat. In a fundamental, physical sense, the end of the wilderness is the end of Boon and of Lion for, as Faulkner says, "only the wilderness could feed and nourish [them]." Moreover, neither has any spiritual dimension.

"Roth" Edmonds of "Delta Autumn" is both heir and perpetrator of this destruction on a more sophisticated level. His eclipse is moral rather than physical. Where Boon and Lion are simply amoral, Edmonds is immoral, devious, degenerate. Whereas his cousin Ike is initiated, Roth is never to be initiated because the wilderness that might have been his teacher is no longer a force in the land, is reduced to a pitiful remnant down in the bottom land where the Yazoo and Mississippi meet. The fundamental difference between Ike and Roth is on the question of whether the life of man is underlain by moral verities which make man essentially good or whether men are restrained from unlimited pursuit of anti-social aims only by external forces. Ike contends that "most men are better than their circumstances give them a chance to be" (p. 345). Roth believes that men behave only when someone with the authority and strength to punish is looking at them. So Roth carries on a secret liaison with a part-Negro girl and when she appears at the hunting camp with their child, will not face her to say he is casting her off, but leaves a bundle of money to speak, better than he realizes, his selfish devious materialism. Uncle Ike, as the bearer of the money, has hardly had time to compass entirely the moral horror of Roth's action before he learns of a corresponding enormity, perpetrated this time against the sad remnant of the wilderness: Roth has killed a doe with a shotgun. If Ike is unhappy to witness this moral chaos, Roth is even more unhappy

---

[8] This is Faulkner's own explanation of Boon's motives in this scene. See Frederick L. Gwynn and Joseph L. Blotner, eds., "Faulkner in the University," *College English*, XIX, 1–6 (Oct., 1957).

to be involved in it. Ike has at least known happiness and serenity, and he still knows the security of convictions about enduring moral values. But Roth is a violent, confused, dissatisfied man, tasting always the bitterness of his decadence, but never comprehending the roots of it.

It is not too much to say, then, that Ike is the last priest of a dying cult, both doomed and avenged by an immanent principle in its source, the wilderness. As for the question of where man is to turn for spiritual renewal when the wilderness is gone, there seems to be no solution: we are apparently to be a race of Roth Edmondses. This is a negative philosophy of history, a prophecy of decline. There is no basis in the wilderness stories for the apparently optimistic belief reflected in Faulkner's Nobel Prize speech that man will "endure" and "prevail." This prophecy of decline will be more meaningful if we return for a moment to Cooper.

II

At the outset I said that Cooper is the first American writer to formulate the problem that Faulkner is trying to answer. Cooper also offered his solution in the Leatherstocking novels, and there are some striking similarities between these and the Ike McCaslin stories. On the narrative level both use as a central character a woodsman par excellence, a man landless, wifeless, childless, avuncular, proud, humble, dignified, and courageous, a man uncomfortable in the settlements. Both writers treat both youth and old age of the character, though Cooper also treats the middle age of his hero. Both authors at moments of crisis in the chase show a kind of headlong narrative style in which violence and brutality are presented as natural adjuncts of the atavistic muscular frenzy which prevails. As Faulkner puts it, "Those fierce instants of heart and brain and courage and wiliness and speed." Because of changes in conventions of characterization and narrative method over the space of a hundred years, the differences are much more obvious; but at bottom I think more superficial. We no longer have sentimental heroes and heroines to clutter up the action, and in dialog we are spared the rhetoric of sensibility. We are also spared the infinitely repeated pattern of jeopardy and escape, not to mention the tedious auctorial intrusion. But these differences are merely functions of time and place and are far less important than the fundamental likenesses growing out of the choice of theme.

On what we may call the symbolic or philosophical level there are similarities, too, but also some important differences. For both writers the wilderness man is the locus of the most perfect morality, but where Ike's morality has been taught by the wilderness, Natty's has been only nurtured. Cooper could not blink the fact that the noble savage was a myth, that the pure wilderness product was more apt to be a vicious Magua than a noble Natty. Natty's fundamental goodness comes from his white man's "gifts," the product of his early Christian nurture; after the seeds of virtue have been thus planted the wilderness provides a refuge in which they can grow without suffering the contamination that adulthood spent in the settlements would bring. This, in short, is a basically Christian doctrine, whereas Faulkner's is pantheistic.

For Cooper, too, the wilderness is a victim of the white man's rapacity, though he doesn't use that particular term. And for Cooper the destructors are again the authors of their own punishment. In *The Prairie* Natty says, "Look around you, men; what will the Yankee choppers say, when they have cut their path from the eastern to the western waters, and find that a hand, which can lay the 'arth bare at a blow, has been here and swept the country, in the very mockery of their wickedness. They will turn on their tracks like a fox that doubles, and then the rank smell of their own footsteps will show them the madness of their waste." [9] But this is not quite the way Faulkner sees it. The difference is that Cooper does not justify the rape of the forest as part of a larger and inevitable pattern. Within the limits of the Leatherstocking tales it is judged a wilful, sinful waste of God's gifts. And the man who so judges it is unquestionably the morally dominant character of the tales—really the one great character. At the same time, the action of the tales is built around the tribulations and eventual successes of upper-class characters whose interests are necessarily identified with civilization. In the ascendancy of these minor characters, the major character must be eclipsed.[10] Within the tales, there is no satisfying explanation of this esthetically perverse arrangement, and we can only conclude that Cooper suffered from a dissociation of sensibility. His heart was with Natty, his head on the side of civilization. This is not the case with Faulkner. As a twentieth-century man, his thinking is no longer conditioned by an implicit faith in the progress of western civilization. If anything, an unconscious assumption of the decline of the west is the conditioning factor. Therefore, his heart and mind are undivided when he contemplates man against the backdrop of the wilderness; and the unity of vision is reflected in the esthetic unity of the work. For this reason, if for no other, Faulkner's treatment of the wilderness theme may have a more lasting value as art than Cooper's.

[9] Everyman edition, p. 77.
[10] See Roy Harvey Pearce, "The Leatherstocking Tales Re-examined," *South Atlantic Quarterly*, XLVI, 524–536 (Oct., 1947).

Exercises

1. Write a critique of this article, similar in nature to the one in this manual which accompanies Barbara Seward's "Elizabeth Bowen's World of Impoverished Love."

2. Write a set of study questions on this article, similar in nature to those in this manual which accompany Norman Foerster's "Thoreau as Artist" and other selections.

INDEX